create

inspiring recipes for every day of the week

PROFESSIONAL SERIES 750

NEW FREEDOM TO
create

YOUR VITAMIX PROFESSIONAL SERIES 750 will completely change your perception of what a blender can do. Its powerful performance is the perfect match for those who are passionate about the culinary arts. A chef's creations are a dynamic fusion of craft, science, artistry and improvisation; using professional tools will help ensure your success and inspire your creativity.

With incomparable versatility and power, the Vitamix Professional Series 750 can perform the tasks of several different kitchen tools. Go ahead and chop, cream, blend, heat, grind, churn, emulsify, crush, whisk, frappe, purée, powder and whip!

This collection of recipes was designed to take advantage of the unique capabilities of the Vitamix Professional Series 750, and to lead the way on your own culinary journey. Now you can achieve expert results quickly and easily.

pre-set programs for consistent results

The Vitamix Professional Series 750 features four Pre-Set Programs: Smoothies, Frozen Desserts, Soups, and Purées. All have been engineered to create your favorites with a touch of a button. A fifth Pre-Set Program, Cleaning, turns that necessary phase into an effortless final step. Recipes that include Pre-Set Program instructions are indicated with an icon.

Don't be surpised if certain recipes are processed on Pre-Set Programs you wouldn't expect—such as a fondue on the Soup Program or a smoothie on the Frozen Dessert Program. It just means that recipe is processed in a similar way as the defined Pre-Set Program.

everything is easier, every day

Create brings you hundreds of recipes for meals and snacks to enjoy every day of the week. You'll find this book is divided just like your busy week, too. *Energize Your Weekdays* is full of recipes and tips to help you prepare healthy and delicious meals for every part of the workday. *Relax and Entertain on Weekends* provides recipes and ideas for both leisurely meals and for hosting special occasions.

If it's Monday morning and you need a high-energy breakfast, look in the *Smoothies* chapter of *Energize Your Weekdays.* Want a few "wow" recipes for a Saturday night get-together? Look in the *Appetizers, Dips & Spreads,* and *Cocktails* chapters of *Relax and Entertain on Weekends.* When you suddenly find yourself pulling together an impromptu gathering, look in the *Coffees & Cocoas* chapter in *Energize Your Weekdays* for fast and memorable specialty drinks.

Create is all about maximizing the power of your Vitamix Professional Series 750 to help you save time and create great meals to enjoy with family and friends. With Vitamix, every meal is easier, healthier and more delicious!

DESSERTS

milkshakes

frozen desserts

baked desserts

dessert condiments

COCKTAILS

cocktails

energize your

weekdays

BREAKFASTS / LUNCHES / DINNERS

START YOUR DAY RIGHT with fast and healthy *Smoothies* (page 13). Full of vitamins and nutrients, smoothies are also a great way to use up leftover fruits and veggies. *Breakfast Mains* (page 35) contains recipes for muffins, scones and more, plus butters, jellies, spreads and syrups. Save time in the morning by making specialty coffees at home with the recipes in *Coffees & Cocoas* (page 57).

weekdays

breakfasts

SMOOTHIES / BREAKFAST MAINS / COFFEES & COCOAS

blackberry
pear smoothie

preparation: 5 minutes | **processing:** 1 minute
yield: 4 ¾ cups (1.1 L)

1 cup (240 g) plain yogurt

⅔ cup (160 ml) water

2 bananas, peeled

1 pear, halved, cored

2 cups (280 g) frozen blackberries

1. Place all ingredients into the Vitamix container in the order listed and secure lid.

2. Select Purée program.

3. Switch machine to Start and allow machine to complete programmed cycle.

nutritional information

per 1 cup (240 ml) serving: *Calories: 142, Total Fat: 1 g, Saturated Fat: 1 g, Protein: 4 g, Fiber: 6 g, Carbohydrates: 31 g, Sodium: 38 mg, Cholesterol: 4 mg*

for two or twenty

turn smoothies into sorbets

Smoothies make healthy and delicious breakfasts, snacks and even lunches in a pinch...but you can also turn them into sorbets for desserts that are elegant enough for any special meal.

Technically, a sorbet refers to a smooth, non-dairy frozen sweetened purée. We expand the definition here to include any smooth frozen sweetened purée. To transform your smoothie into a sorbet, purée all ingredients (adding the ice or frozen fruit last) until smooth and stiff. Once made, the frozen dessert is best served up immediately. Spoon the sorbet into chilled serving bowls and garnish with orange zest, lemon zest or mint leaves.

summer blush
smoothie ⬤

preparation: 5 minutes | **processing:** 1 minute
yield: 4 ¼ cups (1.0 L)

½ cup (120 ml) water

2 cups (300 g) grapes, red or green

2 Tablespoons (30 ml) agave
nectar or honey (optional)

2 cups (300 g) frozen
unsweetened peach slices

1 cup (150 g) frozen
unsweetened raspberries

1. Place all ingredients into the Vitamix container
   in the order listed and secure lid.

2. Select Smoothie program.

3. Switch machine to Start and allow machine
   to complete programmed cycle, using the
   tamper to press the ingredients into the blades.

nutritional information

per 1 cup (240 ml) serving: *Calories: 129, Total Fat: 0 g,
Saturated Fat: 0 g, Protein: 1 g, Fiber: 3 g, Carbohydrates: 32 g,
Sodium: 11 mg, Cholesterol: 0 mg*

farmer's market

produce at its peak

Frozen fruits and vegetables
are easy to find and ready to
use any time of the year. Fresh
produce tastes best—and has
the most nutrients—when
grown, picked and served at
its peak. You'll find the freshest
at your local farmer's market.
Growing seasons differ by
region, but here are some
seasonal highlights:

winter: citrus fruits, kale,
chard, cabbage, onions
(white, red or yellow)

spring: spinach, cucumber,
pineapple, lettuce,
strawberries, green onions

summer: melons, raspberries,
blackberries, blueberries,
fresh herbs (mint, basil,
parsley), peaches, apricots,
nectarines, bell peppers,
tomatoes, kiwi, zucchini

fall: pears, apples,
sweet potatoes, potatoes,
winter squash

all year: grapes, bananas,
carrots, celery

triple berry *smoothie* ❄

preparation: 5 minutes | ***processing:*** 45 seconds | ***yield:*** 4 ½ cups (1.0 L)

1 cup (240 ml) water

1 cup (240 g) low fat vanilla yogurt

1 cup (150 g) frozen unsweetened strawberries

1 cup (160 g) frozen unsweetened blueberries

2 cups (200 g) frozen unsweetened raspberries

1. Place all ingredients into the Vitamix container in the order listed and secure lid.

2. Select Frozen Dessert program.

3. Switch machine to Start and allow machine to complete programmed cycle.

nutritional information

per 1 cup (240 ml) serving: *Calories: 114, Total Fat: 1 g, Saturated Fat: 0 g, Protein: 3 g, Fiber: 5 g, Carbohydrates: 25 g, Sodium: 36 mg, Cholesterol: 3 mg*

frozen strawberry *grape smoothie* ⬤

preparation: 5 minutes | ***processing:*** 1 minute | ***yield:*** 2 ½ cups (600 ml)

1 cup (150 g) green grapes

1 cup (150 g) red grapes

1 cup (150 g) frozen unsweetened strawberries

½ cup (120 ml) ice cubes

1. Place all ingredients into the Vitamix container in the order listed and secure lid.

2. Select Smoothie program.

3. Switch machine to Start and allow machine to complete programmed cycle.

nutritional information

per 1 cup (240 ml) serving: *Calories: 117, Total Fat: 1 g, Saturated Fat: 0 g, Protein: 0 g, Fiber: 2 g, Carbohydrates: 30 g, Sodium: 17 mg, Cholesterol: 0 mg*

fruit salad
smoothie ⬤

preparation: 5 minutes | **processing:** 1 minute
yield: 3 cups (720 ml)

½ cup (75 g) green grapes

1 medium orange, peeled, halved, seeded

½–inch–thick (1.3 cm) slice pineapple,
core included, halved

½ cup (65 g) peeled and
chopped cucumber

1 medium carrot, halved

¼ medium apple, seeded

2 cups (480 ml) ice cubes

1. Place all ingredients into the Vitamix container
   in the order listed and secure lid.

2. Select Smoothie program.

3. Switch machine to Start and allow machine
   to complete programmed cycle.

nutritional information

per 1 cup (240 ml) serving: *Calories: 83, Total Fat: 0 g,
Saturated Fat: 0 g, Protein: 1 g, Fiber: 3 g,
Carbohydrates: 21 g, Sodium: 18 mg, Cholesterol: 0 mg*

planning ahead

breakfast
in a hurry

A little prep time on the
weekends can help make
your weekday breakfasts
all about grab-and-go.
If you have pre-washed
and pre-measured produce
waiting for you, you can just
toss ingredients right into
your Vitamix.

Simply prep the fruits
and veggies you'll need for
your favorite recipes, then
refrigerate or freeze in 1–cup
amounts in tightly sealed
bags or containers. The night
before, set out any other
ingredients that don't need
refrigeration next to your
Vitamix. A pre-chilled glass
will make your smoothie
even more of a treat. The
time you've saved by working
ahead might even earn
you one more hit of the
snooze button!

fruit combo
smoothie ⬤

preparation: 5 minutes | ***processing:*** 1 minute | ***yield:*** 2 ¼ cups (540 ml)

½ cup (60 g) fresh pineapple chunks,
core included

½ medium orange, peeled, seeded

½ ripe pear, cored

½ medium apple, cored, halved

1 cup (240 ml) ice cubes

1. Place all ingredients into the Vitamix container
   in the order listed and secure lid.

2. Select Smoothie program.

3. Switch machine to Start and allow machine
   to complete programmed cycle.

nutritional information

per 1 cup (240 ml) serving: *Calories: 78, Total Fat: 0 g, Saturated Fat: 0 g,*
Protein: 1 g, Fiber: 4 g, Carbohydrates: 20 g, Sodium: 1 mg, Cholesterol: 0 mg

mixed berry and green tea smoothie ❄

preparation: 5 minutes | **processing:** 45 seconds
yield: 3 ½ cups (840 ml)

1 ½ cups (360 ml) green tea, chilled

2 Tablespoons (30 ml) honey

½ orange, peeled, seeded

1 banana, frozen, halved

2 cups (280 g) frozen mixed berries

1. Place all ingredients into the Vitamix container in the order listed and secure lid.

2. Select Frozen Dessert program.

3. Switch machine to Start and allow machine to complete programmed cycle.

nutritional information

per 1 cup (240 ml) serving: *Calories: 161, Total Fat: 0 g, Saturated Fat: 0 g, Protein: 1 g, Fiber: 4 g, Carbohydrates: 39 g, Sodium: 5 mg, Cholesterol: 0 mg*

planning ahead

ready, set, freeze

Any time you have just a few pieces of fruit or vegetables left over, there's no need to toss them; remember their smoothie potential. Store small bags of fruit or veggies in the freezer for adding to blended treats when inspiration strikes.

All kinds of frozen produce work especially well in smoothies as the frozen texture contributes to a smoothie's thick consistency without watering it down.

Unopened frozen produce can be stored up to a year. Once opened, thawed produce can be re-frozen if it is placed in a tightly closed, heavy-duty resealable bag; exposure to air and moisture will contribute to freezer burn.

key lime kiwi
smoothie ⬤

preparation: 5 minutes | **processing:** 1 minute | **yield:** 2 ½ cups (600 ml)

¼ cup (60 ml) water

½ lime, peeled

2 ripe kiwis, peeled, halved

1 large ripe pear, halved, cored

1 Tablespoon honey

1 cup (240 ml) ice cubes

1. Place all ingredients into the Vitamix container in the order listed and secure lid.

2. Select Smoothie program.

3. Switch machine to Start and allow machine to complete programmed cycle.

nutritional information

per 1 cup (240 ml) serving: *Calories: 122, Total Fat: 0 g, Saturated Fat: 0 g, Protein: 1 g, Fiber: 5 g, Carbohydrates: 31 g, Sodium: 4 mg, Cholesterol: 0 mg*

apple pie
smoothie ⬤

preparation: 5 minutes | **processing:** 1 minute | **yield:** 2 ½ cups (600 ml)

¾ cup (180 g) vanilla yogurt

1 ½ apples, quartered, cored

½ teaspoon apple pie spice

1 Tablespoon brown sugar

1 cup (240 ml) ice cubes

1. Place all ingredients into the Vitamix container in the order listed and secure lid.

2. Select Smoothie program.

3. Switch machine to Start and allow machine to complete programmed cycle.

nutritional information

per 1 cup (240 ml) serving: *Calories: 148, Total Fat: 1 g, Saturated Fat: 1 g, Protein: 3 g, Fiber: 3 g, Carbohydrates: 34 g, Sodium: 49 mg, Cholesterol: 5 mg*

peach cobbler
smoothie ❄

preparation: 5 minutes | **processing:** 45 seconds
yield: 4 ½ cups (1.0 L)

2 cups (480 g) vanilla yogurt	2 teaspoons wheat germ
1 teaspoon vanilla extract	4 teaspoons rolled oats
1 teaspoon honey	2 cups (372 g) frozen unsweetened peach slices
½ teaspoon nutmeg	8 ice cubes

1. Place all ingredients into the Vitamix container in the order listed and secure lid.

2. Select Frozen Dessert program.

3. Switch machine to Start and allow machine to complete programmed cycle.

nutritional information

per 1 cup (240 ml) serving: *Calories: 153, Total Fat: 1 g, Saturated Fat: 1 g, Protein: 5 g, Fiber: 1 g, Carbohydrates: 30 g, Sodium: 67 mg, Cholesterol: 7 mg*

family time

fun pops for kids

By freezing smoothies, you can turn them into another kid favorite—sweet frozen treats. Pour any prepared smoothie into ice pop molds (small paper cups will do) and freeze until almost solid. Insert wooden craft sticks into each "pop" so the sticks stand straight. Return to the freezer until completely solid.

When ready to enjoy, remove pops from the molds, running warm water over the outside of the molds to loosen if necessary. Depending on smoothie ingredients, the pops can be fruity (containing fruit, juices and ice) or creamy (containing yogurt, honey or other liquid sweeteners).

You can also play with texture by adding a few fresh berries or other ingredients to each pop as it just starts to freeze.

freshen up

 Are peaches in season? Substitute 1 large ripe pitted peach for the frozen peach slices and increase ice cubes to 1 cup (240 ml).

cabbage, peach
and carrot smoothie

preparation: 5 minutes | **processing:** 1 minute
yield: 2 ½ cups (600 ml)

½ cup (120 ml) water

¾ cup (50 g) sliced green cabbage

1 cup (150 g) red grapes

1 medium carrot, halved,
about ¾ cup (100 g) chopped)

1 cup (186 g) frozen unsweetened peach slices

½ cup (120 ml) ice cubes

1. Place all ingredients into the Vitamix container in the order listed and secure lid.

2. Select Smoothie program.

3. Switch machine to Start and allow machine to complete programmed cycle.

nutritional information

per 1 cup (240 ml) serving: *Calories: 88, Total Fat: 0 g, Saturated Fat: 0 g, Protein: 1 g, Fiber: 2 g, Carbohydrates: 21 g, Sodium: 31 mg, Cholesterol: 0 mg*

spring green
smoothie ⬤

preparation: 5 minutes | **processing:** 1 minute | **yield:** 4 ¾ cups (1.1 L)

½ cup (75 g) green grapes

1 orange, peeled, halved, seeded

½ lemon, peeled, seeded

½ cucumber, cut into large chunks

½ green apple, seeded

1 cup (67 g) kale, spine removed

1 cup (50 g) romaine lettuce

1 cup (60 g) parsley leaves

1 cup (150 g) frozen pineapple chunks

2 cups (480 ml) ice cubes

1. Place all ingredients into the Vitamix container in the order listed and secure lid.

2. Select Smoothie program.

3. Switch machine to Start and allow machine to complete programmed cycle.

nutritional information

per 1 cup (240 ml) serving: *Calories: 100, Total Fat: 0 g, Saturated Fat: 0 g, Protein: 2 g, Fiber: 3 g, Carbohydrates: 25 g, Sodium: 18 mg, Cholesterol: 3 mg*

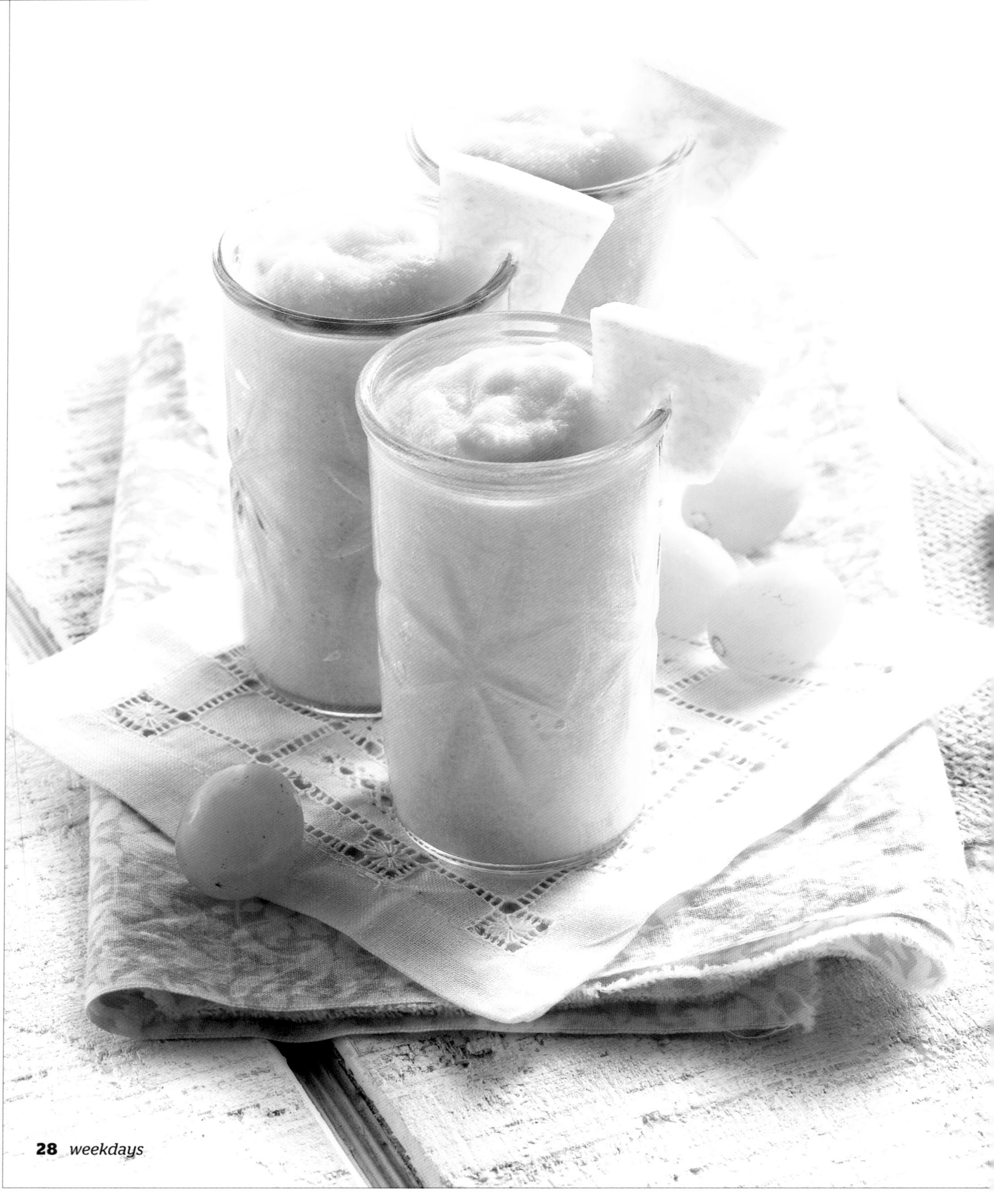

cucumber melon
smoothie

preparation: 10 minutes | **processing:** 1 minute
yield: 4 cups (960 ml)

¼ cup (60 ml) soy milk

1 cup (150 g) green grapes

1 ½ cups (240 g) cantaloupe chunks

½ cup (65 g) peeled and chopped cucumber

1 cup (170 g) honeydew chunks

1 small lime, peeled, halved

1 cup (240 ml) ice cubes

1. Place all ingredients into the Vitamix container in the order listed and secure lid.

2. Select Smoothie program.

3. Switch machine to Start and allow machine to complete programmed cycle.

nutritional information

per 1 cup (240 ml) serving: *Calories: 82, Total Fat: 1 g, Saturated Fat: 0 g, Protein: 2 g, Fiber: 2 g, Carbohydrates: 20 g, Sodium: 31 mg, Cholesterol: 0 mg*

bright idea

Very ripe melon is best for this recipe, and it's an ideal way to use up cantaloupe that's getting close to the 'overripe' stage.

garden green smoothie 💧

preparation: 10 minutes | ***processing:*** 1 minute
yield: 4 ¼ cups (1.0 L)

¼ cup (60 ml) water

1 orange, peeled,
halved, seeded

1 celery stalk, halved

1 small carrot, halved

1 green apple,
cored, quartered

½ medium zucchini,
cut into large chunks

1 cup (50 g) romaine lettuce

1 cup (67 g) kale,
spine removed

½ cup (30 g) parsley leaves

2 cups (480 ml) ice cubes

1. Place all ingredients into the Vitamix container
   in the order listed and secure lid.

2. Select Smoothie program.

3. Switch machine to Start and allow machine
   to complete programmed cycle, using the
   tamper to press the ingredients into the blades.

nutritional information

per 1 cup (240 ml) serving: *Calories: 60, Total Fat: 0 g,
Saturated Fat: 0 g, Protein: 2 g, Fiber: 3 g, Carbohydrates: 14 g,
Sodium: 37 mg, Cholesterol: 0 mg*

healthy choices

packing a punch

Dark leafy greens such
as kale, chard, dandelion
and spinach are, calorie
for calorie, some of the
most concentrated nutrient
sources of any food.
They're rich in both minerals
(iron, calcium, potassium
and magnesium) and
vitamins (K, C, E and
many of the Bs).

Knowing that greens are
good for you is a start.
The next step is to make
sure you eat plenty of them.
One easy way to increase
your consumption is to
add them to smoothies!
A powerful blender will
purée them, preserving all
of their nutrients, into any
smoothie recipe. Mix and
match your favorite greens
and fruits for a healthy and
delicious smoothie.

spinach cocktail 💧

preparation: 5 minutes | ***processing:*** 1 minute | ***yield:*** 3 ½ cups (840 ml)

1 ½ cups (360 ml) water

4 cups (120 g) fresh spinach leaves

4 small mint leaves

2 cups (300 g) frozen pineapple chunks

1. Place all ingredients into the Vitamix container in the order listed and secure lid.

2. Select Smoothie program.

3. Switch machine to Start and allow machine to complete programmed cycle.

nutritional information

per 1 cup (240 ml) serving: *Calories: 132, Total Fat: 0 g, Saturated Fat: 0 g, Protein: 1 g, Fiber: 3 g, Carbohydrates: 34 g, Sodium: 51 mg, Cholesterol: 0 mg*

green *pick me up* ◉

preparation: 5 minutes | **processing:** 1 minute
yield: 2 ½ cups (600 ml)

½ cup (75 g) green grapes

½ orange, peeled, seeded

½ green apple, seeded

2 cups (72 g) Swiss chard

2 cups (480 ml) ice cubes

1. Place all ingredients into the Vitamix container in the order listed and secure lid.

2. Select Smoothie program.

3. Switch machine to Start and allow machine to complete programmed cycle.

nutritional information

per 1 cup (240 ml) serving: *Calories: 70, Total Fat: 0 g, Saturated Fat: 0 g, Protein: 1 g, Fiber: 3 g, Carbohydrates: 18 g, Sodium: 66 mg, Cholesterol: 0 mg*

planning ahead

prep help *in the* kitchen

Once you have your Vitamix and ingredients ready, your smoothies almost make themselves. Many of our recipes call for unpeeled fruit, but when needed, it's nice to be prepared with the right tools. Here are a few kitchen items that speed up food prep:

vegetable peeler: These handheld swivel-bladed peelers make it quick to peel apples, carrots, cucumbers and potatoes. They're sold in right- and left-handed models. Also look for padded grips for maximum comfort.

chef's knife: These large knives are perfect for chopping fresh herbs and slicing fruits and vegetables. Keep yours sharp for the best (and safest) results.

apple corer: Shaped like a vegetable peeler, but with a hollow round blade instead of the swivel blade, this tool easily removes cores and seeds from apples, pears and tomatoes.

lemon ginger
muffins

preparation: 15 minutes | **processing:** 30 seconds
bake time: 15–20 minutes | **yield:** 12 muffins

2 cups (250 g)
all-purpose flour

1 Tablespoon freshly
grated lemon zest

1 ¾ teaspoons baking powder

¼ teaspoon salt

½ cup (100 g) sugar

¼ cup (60 g) crystallized
ginger, small pieces

⅓ cup (80 g) butter, softened

1 large egg

¾ cup (180 ml) milk

¼ cup (50 g) sugar

2 teaspoons freshly
grated lemon zest

3 Tablespoons (45 g)
butter, melted

1 Tablespoon freshly
squeezed lemon juice

1. Preheat oven to 350°F (180°C). Spray 12–cup
   muffin tin with cooking spray; set aside.

2. In a medium-sized mixing bowl mix together flour,
   1 Tablespoon lemon zest, baking powder and salt;
   set aside.

3. Place ½ cup (100 g) sugar and crystallized ginger
   into the Vitamix container and secure lid.

4. Select Variable 1.

» **lemon ginger muffins** continues on page 36

gifts from your kitchen

reinvent the breakfast basket

A tasty gift basket is
sure to brighten anyone's
morning—especially if the
goodies come straight from
your kitchen. Instead of
offering the usual cookie
assortment, fill mini cocottes
(or similar-sized crocks) with
homemade Honey Butter
(page 48) or Chocolate
Hazelnut Spread (page 50)
to accompany your Glorious
Morning Muffins (page 37)
or Peanut Butter Chocolate
Chip Scones (page 40).

Add a sampling of
seasonings to sprinkle on
a morning coffee cup. Go
gourmet with maple flakes,
ground vanilla or granulated
honey. Your thoughtfulness
will be appreciated long after
their morning coffee break.

continued from page 35

lemon ginger
muffins

5. Switch machine to Start and slowly increase speed to Variable 3.

6. Blend for 5 seconds. Stop machine and remove lid. Add ⅓ cup (80 g) butter to the Vitamix container and secure lid.

7. Select Variable 1.

8. Switch machine to Start and slowly increase speed to Variable 4.

9. Blend for 10 seconds. Stop machine and scrape sides of container with a spatula.

10. Add egg and milk to the Vitamix container and secure lid.

11. Select Variable 1.

12. Switch machine to Start and slowly increase speed to Variable 5.

13. Blend for 15 seconds.

14. Pour wet mixture into dry mixture and combine by hand until well mixed.

15. Spoon ¼ cup (60 ml) batter into each muffin cup. Bake until toothpick inserted in center comes out clean and edges are very lightly browned (15 to 20 minutes).

16. Meanwhile, in small bowl stir together ¼ cup (50 g) sugar and 2 teaspoons lemon zest; set aside.

17. In small bowl stir together 3 Tablespoons (45 ml) melted butter and lemon juice; set aside.

18. While muffins are still hot, roll tops in melted butter mixture, then in sugar and lemon zest mixture. Place muffins on wire rack to cool.

nutritional information

per muffin: *Calories: 217, Total Fat: 8 g, Saturated Fat: 5 g, Protein: 3 g, Fiber: 0 g, Carbohydrates: 33 g, Sodium: 183 mg, Cholesterol: 40 mg*

glorious morning muffins

preparation: 10 minutes | **processing:** 22 seconds + pulsing
bake time: 15–20 minutes | **yield:** 15 muffins

kitchen prep

Letting batter stand an additional 10 minutes in pan before baking allows ingredients to fully hydrate, giving muffins a richer texture. A little patience works wonders!

½ cup (50 g) pecan halves

¾ cup (132 g) steel-cut oats

1 ¼ cups (150 g) whole wheat flour

¼ cup (29 g) wheat germ

1 ¼ teaspoons baking soda

1 teaspoon baking powder

1 teaspoon ground cinnamon

½ teaspoon salt

1 carrot cut in 4 pieces,
about 1 ½ cups (140 g) chunks

1 cup (150 g) fresh pineapple chunks

½ cup (120 ml) honey

¼ cup (60 ml) vegetable oil

¼ cup (60 ml) milk

2 large eggs

½ cup (83 g) golden raisins,
if desired

1. Preheat oven to 400°F (200°C). Line 15 medium-sized muffin cups with paper liners.

2. Place pecans into the Vitamix container and secure lid.

3. Select Variable 2.

4. Pulse 3 times until finely chopped. Pour into large-sized mixing bowl.

5. Place steel-cut oats into the Vitamix container and secure lid.

6. Select Variable 1.

7. Switch machine to Start and slowly increase speed to Variable 4.

» **glorious morning muffins** continues on page 38

continued from page 37

glorious morning
muffins

8. Blend for 20 seconds or until flour texture. Tap sides and top of container to shake oat flour down.

9. Add flour, wheat germ, baking soda, baking powder, cinnamon and salt to the flour mixture in the Vitamix container and secure lid.

10. Select Variable 4.

11. Switch machine to Start and blend 2 seconds. Tap sides and top of container to shake flour down. Pour into bowl with pecans.

12. Place carrot chunks into the Vitamix container and secure lid.

13. Select Variable 7.

14. Pulse 4 times or until finely chopped.

15. Add pineapple, honey, oil, milk and eggs to the Vitamix container and secure lid.

16. Select Variable 4.

17. Pulse 3 times until mixture is blended.

18. Pour liquid mixture over dry ingredients. Stir by hand until moistened. If desired, fold in raisins. Let batter stand 10 minutes. Scoop mixture evenly into muffin cups, filling almost full.

19. Bake 15 to 20 minutes or until set. Let stand 10 minutes.

20. Remove from muffin pans. To store, cool completely and place in covered container at room temperature.

nutritional information

per muffin: *Calories: 200, Total Fat: 8 g, Saturated Fat: 1 g, Protein: 5 g, Fiber: 3 g, Carbohydrates: 30 g, Sodium: 227 mg, Cholesterol: 29 mg*

cherry and golden raisin bread

preparation: 10 minutes | **processing:** 20 seconds
bake time: 1 hour | **yield:** 1 loaf (16 slices)

to prepare lemon glaze:
Combine ½ cup (60 g) powdered sugar and 1 teaspoon lemon zest in a small bowl. Stir in 2 teaspoons lemon juice, adding more if needed to reach drizzling consistency.

2 cups (250 g) all-purpose flour

1 cup (100 g) sugar

1 teaspoon baking powder

½ teaspoon salt

¼ teaspoon baking soda

2 teaspoons lemon zest, freshly grated

1 large egg

1 cup (240 ml) milk

⅓ cup (80 ml) cooking oil

1 teaspoon vanilla extract

½ cup (83 g) coarsely snipped dried cherries

½ cup (83 g) golden raisins

Lemon Glaze

1. Preheat oven to 350°F (180°C). Spray a 9-inch x 5-inch (23 cm x 13 cm) loaf pan with cooking spray; set aside.

2. In a large-sized mixing bowl, combine flour, sugar, baking powder, salt, baking soda and zest by hand.

3. Place egg, milk, oil and vanilla into the Vitamix container in the order listed and secure lid.

4. Select Variable 1.

5. Switch machine to Start and slowly increase speed to Variable 6. Blend for 20 seconds or until smooth. Pour into dry mixture and stir by hand just until moistened. Fold in cherries and raisins.

6. Spoon into prepared loaf pan. Bake 1 hour or until a knife inserted into center comes out clean. Cool on a wire rack for 10 minutes. Remove from pan. Drizzle with Lemon Glaze. Cool on wire rack.

nutritional information

per glazed slice: Calories: 196, Total Fat: 5 g, Saturated Fat: 1 g, Protein: 3 g, Fiber: 2 g, Carbohydrates: 36 g, Sodium: 133 mg, Cholesterol: 14 mg

peanut butter chocolate chip scones

preparation: 10 minutes | **processing:** 12 seconds + pulsing
bake time: 15–18 minutes | **yield:** 8 scones

2 cups (250 g) all-purpose flour

¼ cup (50 g) sugar

2 teaspoons baking powder

¼ teaspoon baking soda

¼ teaspoon salt

¼ cup (60 g) cold butter
cut in 8 pieces

½ cup (120 g) miniature
chocolate chips

⅔ cup (160 ml) milk

1 large egg

½ cup (120 g) peanut butter
(page 55)

kitchen prep

Prepared scones are usually best reheated in the oven. But if you're short on time, they are still tasty warmed, one at a time, in the microwave for 10 seconds on High.

1. Preheat oven to 375°F (190°C). Line a cookie sheet with parchment paper.

2. Place flour, sugar, baking powder, soda and salt into the Vitamix container and secure lid.

3. Select Variable 4.

4. Switch machine to Start and blend for 2 seconds. Stop machine and remove lid.

5. Add butter to the Vitamix container and secure lid.

6. Select Variable 4.

7. Pulse 6 times. Pour mixture into large bowl. Stir in chocolate chips.

» **peanut butter chocolate chip scones** *continues on page 42*

continued from page 40

peanut butter
chocolate chip scones

8. Add milk, egg and peanut butter to the Vitamix container and secure lid.

9. Select Variable 2.

10. Switch machine to Start and blend for 10 seconds. Pour over dry ingredients.
Stir just until moistened.

11. Flour work surface. Scoop mixture onto floured surface and knead 5 or 6 times.
Form into 1 disk, 8 inches (20 cm) in diameter. Cut into 8 wedges.
Place 2 inches (5 cm) apart on cookie sheet.

12. Bake 15 to 18 minutes or until golden brown and set. Do not over bake.
Store at room temperature in closed container.

nutritional information

per scone: *Calories: 360, Total Fat: 18 g, Saturated Fat: 8 g, Protein: 10 g,
Fiber: 2 g, Carbohydrates: 43 g, Sodium: 356 mg, Cholesterol: 43 mg*

fruit granola
with cashew coating

preparation: 10 minutes | **processing:** 30 seconds
bake time: 35–40 minutes | **yield:** 8 ½ cups (2.0 kg)

coating:

⅓ cup (80 ml) honey

⅓ cup (80 ml) orange juice

¼ cup (55 g) firmly packed brown sugar

1 teaspoon freshly grated orange zest

1 teaspoon vanilla extract

1 cup (140 g) dry roasted salted cashews

granola:

3 cups (540 g) old-fashioned rolled oats

½ cup (54 g) slivered almonds

½ cup (65 g) snipped dried apricots

½ cup (83 g) dried cherries

½ cup (45 g) coconut flakes

½ cup (83 g) dried cranberries

½ cup (70 g) unsalted pumpkin seeds

1. Preheat oven to 350°F (180°C). Line a large baking sheet with parchment paper. Place all coating ingredients into the Vitamix container in the order listed and secure lid.

2. Select Variable 1.

3. Switch machine to Start and slowly increase speed to Variable 10.

» **fruit granola with cashew coating** continues on page 44

granola berry parfaits

For a breakfast treat, layer Fruit Granola with Cashew Coating in tall parfait glasses with plain Greek yogurt and lots of fresh blueberries. Serve with Glorious Morning Muffins (page 37) and Chocolate Hazelnut Spread (page 50).

If entertaining at breakfast time, add a tropical twist with Fruit Granola with Cashew Coating served in hollowed-out small pineapples or orange halves, topped with a dollop of pineapple yogurt and sprinkled with additional shredded coconut. Serve with Lemon Ginger Muffins (page 35) and Key Lime Kiwi Smoothies (page 22) garnished with skewered pineapple chunks and lime slices.

continued from page 43

fruit granola
with cashew coating

4. Blend for 30 seconds or until smooth. If necessary, scrape sides of the container with a spatula.

5. In mixing bowl stir together all granola ingredients. Pour cashew coating over granola mixture; mix well.

6. Pour cereal mixture onto prepared sheet pan. Bake for 35 to 40 minutes, stirring every 10 minutes, or until cereal is lightly browned.

7. Remove from oven; cool completely. Store cereal in covered container.

nutritional information

per 1 cup (240 g) serving: *Calories: 122, Total Fat: 5 g, Saturated Fat: 1 g, Protein: 4 g, Fiber: 2 g, Carbohydrates: 17 g, Sodium: 31 mg, Cholesterol: 0 mg*

fruit jelly 💧

preparation: 5 minutes | ***processing:*** 1 minute | ***yield:*** 6 cups (1.9 kg)

2 cups (480 g) fresh or frozen fruit,
cut into large pieces

3 cups (720 ml) water

1.75–ounce (50 g) package fruit pectin

4 ½ cups (900 g) sugar

1. Place the fruit and water into the Vitamix container and secure lid.

2. Select Smoothie program.

3. Switch machine to Start and allow machine to complete programmed cycle.

4. Pour contents into a 4–cup (960 ml) capacity measuring cup.
   Add additional water to equal 4 cups (960 ml) if necessary.

5. Transfer to a Dutch oven or similar size pot. Stir in fruit pectin.

6. Place pot over high heat, stirring constantly until mixture comes to a hard boil.

7. Add sugar and bring to a full rolling boil for 1 minute.

8. If canning: follow standard canning procedure. If storing in a refrigerator,
   place in airtight container. Product may be refrigerated for up to 4 weeks.

nutritional information

per 2 tablespoon (40 g) serving: *Calories: 80, Total Fat: 0 g, Saturated Fat: 0 g,
Protein: 0 g, Fiber: 0 g, Carbohydrates: 21 g, Sodium: 2 mg, Cholesterol: 0 mg*

monster **breakfast bars**

preparation: 15 minutes | *processing:* 20 seconds | *bake time:* 20–22 minutes | *yield:* 18 servings

topping:

½ cup (120 g) butter, melted

2 cups (516 g) creamy peanut butter

4 large eggs

1 ¾ cups (385 g) firmly packed brown sugar

2 teaspoons vanilla extract

oat mixture:

2 teaspoons baking soda

¾ teaspoon salt

1 ½ teaspoons ground cinnamon

3 ½ cups (630 g) old-fashioned rolled oats

fruits:

1 cup (130 g) snipped dried apricots

1 cup (165 g) dried cherries

1 cup (240 g) cinnamon chips

1 cup (90 g) flaked coconut

1 cup (165 g) dried cranberries

1 cup (165 g) golden raisins

1. Preheat oven to 350°F (180°C). Spray a 13-inch x 9-inch (33 cm x 23 cm) baking pan with cooking spray; set aside.

2. Place all Topping ingredients into the Vitamix container in the order listed and secure lid.

3. Select Variable 1.

4. Switch machine to Start and slowly increase speed to Variable 5.

5. Blend for 20 seconds or until smooth, using the tamper if necessary.

6. Meanwhile, in large-sized mixing bowl stir together Oat Mixture ingredients. Pour Topping Mixture over Oat Mixture; mix well with a sturdy wooden spoon. Mixture is very thick.

7. Stir in Fruits; mix well. Pour into prepared pan. Spread to even out top.

8. Bake for 20 to 22 minutes or until bars are lightly brown at edges. Pan will be heavy.

9. Cool completely; cut into desired bar size.

10. Store covered at room temperature.

nutritional information

per bar: *Calories: 570, Total Fat: 27 g, Saturated Fat: 10 g, Protein: 13 g, Fiber: 7 g, Carbohydrates: 76 g, Sodium: 476 mg, Cholesterol: 61 mg*

honey **butter**

preparation: 5 minutes | **processing:** 40 seconds
yield: 3 ½ cups (840 g)

on the menu

Serve with all your breakfast favorites. At dinner time, brush Honey Butter on salmon fillets during grilling; the honey will caramelize and create a tasty glaze.

1 pound (454 g) butter, softened

1 cup (240 ml) canola or light olive oil

½ cup (120 ml) honey (or to taste)

1. Place all ingredients into the Vitamix container in the order listed and secure lid.

2. Select Variable 1.

3. Switch machine to Start and slowly increase speed to Variable 5.

4. Blend for 30 seconds, using the tamper to press the ingredients into the blades. Stop machine and scrape sides with a spatula.

5. Reduce speed to Variable 3.

6. Switch machine to Start and blend for 10 seconds.

7. Cover and refrigerate or roll in plastic wrap and form a 6-inch (15 cm) log.

nutritional information

per 1 tablespoon serving: Calories: 104, Total Fat: 11 g, Saturated Fat: 5 g, Protein: 1 g, Fiber: 0 g, Carbohydrates: 2 g, Sodium: 47 mg, Cholesterol: 17 mg

almond butter

preparation: 5 minutes | **processing:** 2 minutes 30 seconds | **yield:** 2 cups (480 g)

4 cups (590 g) raw almonds

¼ cup (60 ml) canola oil

1. Place almonds into the Vitamix container and secure lid.

2. Select Variable 1.

3. Switch machine to Start and slowly increase speed to Variable 10.

4. Blend for 2 minutes, using the tamper to press the ingredients into the blades.

5. Stop machine and remove the lid plug. Add oil through the lid plug opening.

6. Select Variable 1.

7. Switch machine to Start and slowly increase speed to Variable 8.

8. Blend for an additional 30 seconds.

9. Store in an airtight container under refrigeration for up to a week. It can also be frozen for longer storage.

nutritional information

per 2 tablespoon (30 g) serving: *Calories: 236, Total Fat: 21 g, Saturated Fat: 2 g, Protein: 8 g, Fiber: 4 g, Carbohydrates: 8 g, Sodium: 0 mg, Cholesterol: 0 mg*

chocolate hazelnut
spread ⠵

preparation: 30 minutes | **processing:** 5–6 minutes
bake time: 15 minutes | **yield:** 1 ½ cups (360 g)

1 cup (200 g) sugar

½ cup (120 ml) water

4 cups (540 g) raw hazelnuts

½ cup (43 g) unsweetened cocoa powder

1 ½ teaspoons vanilla extract

2 Tablespoons (30 ml) light olive oil

⅛ teaspoon salt

1. Preheat oven to 350°F (180°C).
   Line a baking sheet with foil.

2. Combine sugar and water in a 3–4 cup saucepan. Cover
   and bring the mixture to a simmer over medium heat.
   Remove the lid and wipe down the sides of the pan
   with a wet pastry brush or a scrunched-up paper towel
   dipped in water. Cover and cook for 2 minutes or until
   the sugar is completely dissolved. Uncover and cook
   until the syrup looks like pale amber maple syrup.

3. Immediately pour the caramel onto the lined baking
   sheet. Tilt the sheet to spread the caramel as thinly
   as possible. Let harden completely, about 15 minutes.

» **chocolate hazelnut spread** continues on page 52

build a meal

spread *the* news

Chocolate Hazelnut Spread
is a delicious alternative to
butter or jam on toast and
croissants, and makes a
wonderful filling for pastries
and desserts.

Delight guests with a
breakfast menu of your
favorite crepes filled with
Chocolate Hazelnut Spread,
accompanied by Apricot
Breakfast Bread (page 193),
fresh strawberries and a
steaming mug of Cappuccino
(page 65).

Don't miss a chance to enjoy
sliced bananas dipped in
Chocolate Hazelnut Spread
for a snack. You'll also find
that a tablespoon or two of
Chocolate Hazelnut Spread
on slices of Mocha Tea
Bread (page 194), Cranberry
Nut Bread (page 183) or
Chocolate Chunk Banana
Bread (page 191) turns
these rich breads into
decadent desserts.

continued from page 50

chocolate hazelnut
spread

4. Place hazelnuts in a single layer on a baking sheet. Toast in the oven until the skins are almost black and the meat is dark brown, about 15 minutes. Stir the nuts halfway through baking to ensure an even color.

5. To remove skins, wrap cooled hazelnuts in a clean kitchen towel. Rub until most of the skins come off.

6. Break cooled caramel into small pieces and place into the Vitamix container and secure lid.

7. Select Variable 1.

8. Switch machine to Start and slowly increase speed to Variable 5.

9. Blend for 15 seconds. Stop machine and remove lid.

10. Add the nuts to the Vitamix container and secure lid.

11. Select Purée program.

12. Switch machine to Start and allow machine to complete programmed cycle, using the tamper to press the ingredients into the blades. Remove lid to scrape sides of the container with a spatula. Continue blending until nuts liquefy.

13. Add remaining ingredients to the Vitamix container and secure lid.

14. Select Variable 1.

15. Switch machine to Start and slowly increase speed to Variable 8.

16. Blend for 4 minutes using the tamper to press the ingredients into the blades.

nutritional information

per 1 tablespoon serving: *Calories: 189, Total Fat: 15 g, Saturated Fat: 1 g, Protein: 4 g, Fiber: 3 g, Carbohydrates: 13 g, Sodium: 13 mg, Cholesterol: 0 mg*

fresh fruit **syrup** ♨

preparation: 3 minute
processing: 5 minutes 45 seconds
yield: 2 cups (480 ml)

3 cups (454 g) fresh fruit of choice

¼ cup (50 g) sugar

1 teaspoon lemon juice

1. Place all ingredients into the Vitamix container in the order listed and secure lid.

2. Select Hot Soup program.

3. Switch machine to Start and allow machine to complete programmed cycle.

4. For a traditional thicker syrup, place mixture in a pot and cook on medium heat for 30 minutes.

nutritional information

per 1 tablespoon serving: *Calories: 14, Total Fat: 0 g, Saturated Fat: 0 g, Protein: 0 g, Fiber: 0 g, Carbohydrates: 4 g, Sodium: 0 mg, Cholesterol: 0 mg*

planning ahead

sensational syrups

Fresh fruit syrup gives you a base recipe from which to customize the flavors you enjoy most. Besides topping waffles, pancakes and desserts, these syrups make great beverage stir-ins.

Just mix 1 ounce (30 ml) of syrup with 8 to 12 ounces (240 to 360 ml) club soda. Pour the mixture over ice and you have a chilled and refreshing beverage. You could also add the syrup to a complementary fruit juice (strawberry or mango syrup mixed with orange juice, for example) to create a juice cocktail of your own.

peanut butter

preparation: 5 minutes | **processing:** 1 minute 30 seconds | **yield:** 2 cups (480 g)

4 cups (590 g) unsalted,
dry roasted peanuts

1. Place nuts into the Vitamix container and secure lid.

2. Select Variable 1.

3. Switch machine to Start and slowly increase speed
   to Variable 10.

4. Use the tamper to press the ingredients into the blades.

5. In 1 minute you will hear a high-pitched chugging sound.
   Once the butter begins to flow freely through the blades,
   reduce speed to Variable 7.

6. Blend for an additional 30 seconds.

7. Store in an airtight container under refrigeration for up
   to a week. It can also be frozen for longer storage.

nutritional information

per 2 tablespoon (30 g) serving: *Calories: 214, Total Fat: 18 g, Saturated Fat: 3 g,
Protein: 9 g, Fiber: 3 g, Carbohydrates: 8 g, Sodium: 2 mg, Cholesterol: 0 mg*

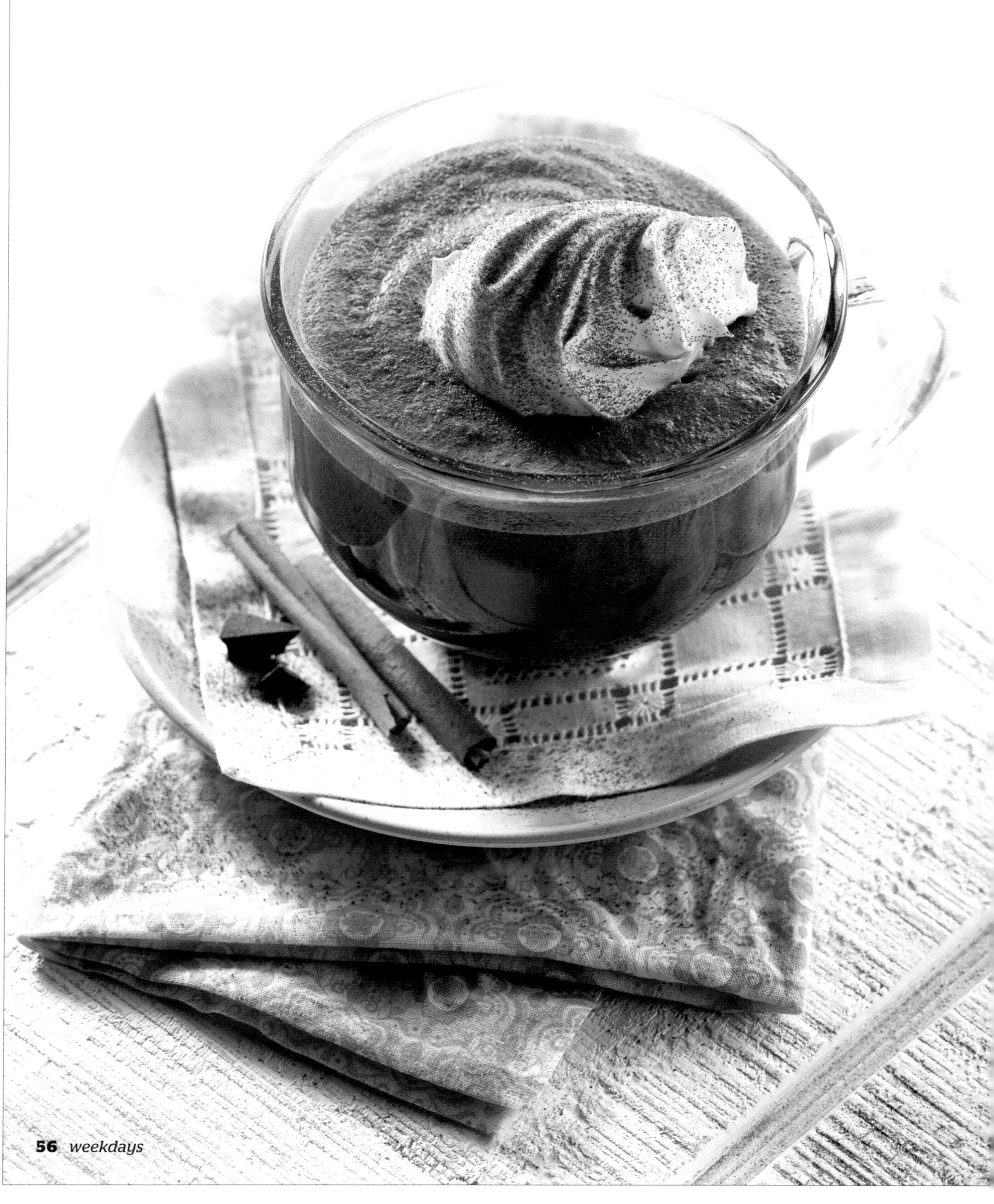

mocha spiced
hot cocoa ♨

preparation: 5 minutes | **processing:** 5 minutes 45 seconds
yield: 2 cups (480 ml)

1 ½ cups (360 ml) milk

½ cup (90 g) semisweet chocolate chips

¼ teaspoon ground cinnamon

2 teaspoons instant coffee granules

⅛ teaspoon chili powder

1. Place all ingredients into the Vitamix container in the order listed and secure lid.

2. Select Hot Soup program.

3. Switch machine to Start and allow machine to complete programmed cycle.

nutritional information

per 1 cup (240 ml) serving: *Calories: 365, Total Fat: 18 g, Saturated Fat: 11 g, Protein: 11 g, Fiber: 4 g, Carbohydrates: 46 g, Sodium: 98 mg, Cholesterol: 11 mg*

surprise visitors

instant coffee break

Be prepared for those moments when a friend stops by, a committee meeting is suddenly moved to your house, or your family decides to drop in on Sunday morning.

Stock your shelves with fresh spices: nutmeg, allspice, ginger, ground cinnamon, cinnamon sticks and cloves. Keep pure vanilla extract, chocolate chips, heavy cream and coconut on hand. You'll always be ready to whip up a delicious coffee treat that will impress your visitors.

Pair your specialty drink with Mocha Tea Bread (page 194) or Cranberry Nut Bread (page 183) that you've baked ahead of time and stored in the freezer, ready to defrost when needed.

mexican *coffee*

preparation: 5 minutes | ***processing:*** 10 seconds | ***yield:*** 6 cups (1.4 L)

6 cups (1.4 L) water

2 cinnamon sticks

4 whole cloves

6 Tablespoons (90 g)
ground coffee

2 ounces (56 g) bittersweet
chocolate, coarsely chopped

Whipped Cream (page 324)

6 cinnamon sticks

1. Add the cinnamon sticks and cloves to the coffee grounds.

2. Brew the coffee using all of the water.

3. Place coffee and chocolate into the Vitamix container
in the order listed and secure lid.

4. Select Variable 1.

5. Switch machine to Start and slowly increase
speed to Variable 10.

6. Blend for 10 seconds until chocolate is melted.

7. Top each serving with whipped cream and garnish
with cinnamon sticks.

nutritional information

per 1 cup (240 ml) serving (without whipped cream): *Calories: 54, Total Fat: 4 g,
Saturated Fat: 2 g, Protein: 1 g, Fiber: 1 g, Carbohydrates: 6 g, Sodium: 5 mg, Cholesterol: 0 mg*

vanilla coffee frappé

preparation: 5 minutes | **processing:** 10 seconds
yield: 2 ½ cups (600 ml)

¾ cup (180 ml) double strength
coffee or espresso, cooled

2 ounces (60 ml) espresso

½ cup (120 ml) half and half

3 Tablespoons (38 g) sugar

1 ½ Tablespoons vanilla extract

1 ¼ cups (300 ml) ice cubes

1. Place all ingredients into the Vitamix container
   in the order listed and secure lid.

2. Select Variable 1.

3. Switch machine to Start and slowly increase
   speed to Variable 8.

4. Blend for 10 seconds or until desired
   consistency is reached.

5. Top with Whipped Cream (page 324).

nutritional information

per 1 cup (240 ml) serving (without whipped cream):
*Calories: 195, Total Fat: 8 g, Saturated Fat: 5 g,
Protein: 3 g, Fiber: 0 g, Carbohydrates: 25 g,
Sodium: 48 mg, Cholesterol: 25 mg*

planning ahead

fix your morning fix — fast

On hot summer mornings, iced coffee drinks can be a real treat. You can still enjoy one, despite the got-to-get-to-work juggling, with a little bit of planning.

Fresh, cooled coffee is best in your Vanilla Coffee Frappé or other chilled coffee drinks, but since you don't often have time to wait for it to cool, simply place the brewed java in the freezer before you start your morning routine.

By the time you're dressed and ready, the coffee will be cold, but not frozen. Add ice and other ingredients when it's time to blend and you'll be out the door in no time!

pumpkin
spice syrup ☕

preparation: 5 minutes
processing: 5 minutes 45 seconds
yield: 2 cups (480 ml)

1 ¼ cups (300 ml) water

½ cup (120 g) pumpkin purée,
fresh or canned

½ cup (100 g) sugar

½ teaspoon vanilla extract

1 teaspoon ground cinnamon

½ teaspoon ground allspice

½ teaspoon ground ginger

1. Place all ingredients into the Vitamix container
   in the order listed and secure lid.

2. Select Hot Soup program.

3. Switch machine to Start and allow machine
   to complete programmed cycle.

nutritional information

per 2 tablespoon (30 ml) serving: *Calories: 28, Total Fat: 0 g,
Saturated Fat: 0 g, Protein: 0 g, Fiber: 0 g, Carbohydrates: 7 g,
Sodium: 1 mg, Cholesterol: 0 mg*

change it up

pumpkin spice for every season

Create a Pumpkin Pie Latte
by combining ½ cup (120 ml)
Pumpkin Spice Syrup with ½ cup
(120 ml) hot milk and 1 ½ cups
(360 ml) coffee and blend on
Variable 8 for 20 seconds.
Yield is 2 ½ cups.

You can also make a Pumpkin
Chai Latte by combining
½ cup (120 ml) Pumpkin Spice
Syrup with ½ cup (120 ml) chai
concentrate and 1 cup (240 ml)
hot milk and blend on Variable 8
for 20 seconds. Yield is 2 cups.

Add 1 cup Powdered Sugar (page
325) to 3 tablespoons Pumpkin
Spice Syrup to make a sweet
Pumpkin Spice Glaze for cakes,
breads and muffins.

For a quick dessert, heat the
Pumpkin Spice Syrup, pour over
vanilla ice cream, and top with
pecans. Or give a flavor blast to
plain yogurt by stirring in a swirl
of Pumpkin Spice Syrup.

bright idea

Enhance specialty coffee drinks with Whipped Cream (page 324) lightly sprinkled with freshly toasted shredded coconut and drizzled with chocolate syrup.

moco-coco
chilled coffee 💧

preparation: 5 minutes | **processing:** 1 minute
yield: 3 ½ cups (840 ml)

¾ cup (180 ml) double strength
coffee, cooled

1 cup (240 ml) milk

¼ cup (60 ml) chocolate syrup

1 ½ Tablespoons cream of coconut

2 Tablespoons (9 g) sweetened
shredded coconut

2 cups (480 ml) ice cubes

1. Place all ingredients into the Vitamix container in the order listed and secure lid.

2. Select Smoothie program.

3. Switch machine to Start and allow machine to complete programmed cycle.

nutritional information

per 1 cup (240 ml) serving: *Calories: 165, Total Fat: 4 g, Saturated Fat: 3 g, Protein: 4 g, Fiber: 0 g, Carbohydrates: 28 g, Sodium: 80 mg, Cholesterol: 10 mg*

eggnog coffee punch

preparation: 5 minutes | ***processing:*** 20 seconds | ***yield:*** 4 cups (960 ml)

2 cups (264 g) coffee
or vanilla ice cream

1 cup (240 ml) cold coffee

½ cup (120 ml) dairy eggnog

1 cup (240 ml) ice cubes

1. Place all ingredients into the Vitamix container in the order listed and secure lid.

2. Select Variable 1.

3. Switch machine to Start and slowly increase speed to Variable 8.

4. Blend for 20 seconds or until smooth.

5. Sprinkle each serving with cinnamon, if desired.

nutritional information

per 1 cup (240 ml) serving: *Calories: 283, Total Fat: 17 g, Saturated Fat: 11 g, Protein: 5 g, Fiber: 0 g, Carbohydrates: 25 g, Sodium: 78 mg, Cholesterol: 94 mg*

cappuccino

preparation: 10 minutes | **processing:** 10 seconds
yield: 1 ¼ cups (300 ml)

create your own

For a summer treat, try a Cappuccino or a Pumpkin Pie Latte (page 60) over ice — garnish with Whipped Cream (page 324), cinnamon and crushed graham crackers.

¾ cup (180 ml) hot double strength coffee

¼ cup (60 ml) milk

2 Tablespoons (30 g) white chocolate chips

¼ teaspoon vanilla extract

1. Place all ingredients into the Vitamix container in the order listed and secure lid.

2. Select Variable 1.

3. Switch machine to Start and slowly increase speed to Variable 8.

4. Blend for 10 seconds.

nutritional information

per recipe: Calories: 318, Total Fat: 14 g, Saturated Fat: 11 g, Protein: 8 g, Fiber: 0 g, Carbohydrates: 38 g, Sodium: 136 mg, Cholesterol: 23 mg

soups

salad dressings

wraps & sandwiches

PREPARE QUICK SOUPS that taste like they have been simmering on the stove all day. You can make our *Soups* (page 68) in minutes; serve with a crisp salad tossed with one of the recipes from *Salad Dressings* (page 93). Prepare a batch of soup and bring portions to work for a quick, healthy and cost-efficient alternative to eating out. In *Wraps & Sandwiches* (page 107) there are delightful ideas from around the world to add color and excitement to the noon hour.

weekdays

lunches

SOUPS / SALAD DRESSINGS / WRAPS & SANDWICHES

french onion *soup* ♨

preparation: 10 minutes | **processing:** 5 minutes 45 seconds
cook time: 15 minutes | **yield:** 3 ½ cups (840 ml)

3 Tablespoons (45 ml)
extra virgin olive oil

4 cups (560 g) onions, sliced

2 garlic cloves, peeled,
cut into 4 slices

1 teaspoon Kosher salt

½ teaspoon sugar

¼ teaspoon dried
thyme leaves

⅛ teaspoon freshly
cracked black pepper

2 cups (480 ml)
beef broth

¼ cup (60 ml) dry
white wine

8 slices baguette bread

4 slices Swiss cheese

1. In large nonstick skillet heat olive oil over medium heat.
   Add onions. Cook over medium heat, partially covered,
   stirring occasionally, until onions soften (10 to 12 minutes).

2. Add garlic, salt, sugar, thyme leaves and pepper.
   Continue cooking, stirring occasionally, until garlic
   softens (4 to 5 minutes).

3. Place onion mixture, beef broth and wine into the
   Vitamix container and secure lid.

4. Select Hot Soup program.

5. Switch machine to Start and allow machine to
   complete programmed cycle.

» **french onion soup** *continues on page 70*

herbology

there's an herb for that

If you find yourself staring
at the spice rack, not sure
which herb best complements
the soup you have whirling
in your blender, here are
some hints.

Basil is a great go-to herb;
it enhances beef, chicken,
fish and vegetable soups
like minestrone. Add it to a
tomato bisque or potato-
based soup as well.

To bring out the flavors
of onion, oyster or spinach
soups, reach for the marjoram.
For white beans, lamb and pea
soups, mint can add a delicate
and unexpected note. Oregano
often partners with basil to
spice tomato-based soups.

A more exotic choice,
saffron is perfect for
bouillabaisse, while tarragon
kicks up the flavor of
consommés. Thyme works
well in gumbos and clam
chowders. For a distinctly
Indian flavor, add turmeric
to coconut or potato curries
or pumpkin-based soups.

continued from page 69

french onion soup

6. Pour serving size of soup into oven/broiler-safe bowl.

7. Top each serving bowl with two baguette slices and one slice of cheese. Place under hot broiler for 45 to 60 seconds or until cheese is melted. Serve immediately.

8. Refrigerate leftovers.

nutritional information

per 1 cup (240 ml) serving (with baguette slices and cheese): *Calories: 485, Total Fat: 21 g, Saturated Fat: 6 g, Protein: 18 g, Fiber: 5 g, Carbohydrates: 55 g, Sodium: 1535 mg, Cholesterol: 23 mg*

camp napa culinary
chilled avocado soup ❄

preparation: 10 minutes | ***processing:*** 45 seconds | ***yield:*** 8 cups (1.9 L)

2 ripe avocados

¼ cup (55 g) sour cream

¼ cup (4 g) chopped cilantro sprigs

1 ½–inch x 1 ½–inch (4 cm x 4 cm)
cube of peeled fresh ginger or
1 Tablespoon chopped ginger

½ lime, peeled or 2 Tablespoons
(30 ml) fresh squeezed lime juice

1 teaspoon Asian chili sauce

1 teaspoon salt

5 cups (1.2 L) chicken broth

½ cup (70 g) finely chopped roasted
red bell pepper, store bought

dusting of freshly grated nutmeg

1. Cut the avocados in half, discard the seeds and scoop out the flesh.

2. Place avocados, sour cream, cilantro, ginger, lime, chili sauce, salt and
   chicken broth into the Vitamix container and secure lid.

3. Select Frozen Dessert program.

4. Switch machine to Start and allow machine to complete programmed cycle.

5. Transfer to a bowl and refrigerate until thoroughly chilled.
   Finely chop the red pepper and refrigerate.

6. Taste and adjust the seasonings for salt, lime juice and chili sauce.
   Transfer the soup to 2 to 4 chilled soup bowls. Place a little red pepper garnish
   in the center of each bowl. Grate nutmeg across surface. Serve at once.

nutritional information

per 1 cup (240 ml) serving: *Calories: 110, Total Fat: 9 g, Saturated Fat: 2 g,*
Protein: 2 g, Fiber: 4 g, Carbohydrates: 6 g, Sodium: 899 mg, Cholesterol: 5 mg

sweet potato soup
with seared tomatillos

preparation: 15 minutes | **processing:** 40 seconds
cook time: 30 – 35 minutes | **yield:** 6 cups (1.4 L)

2 Tablespoons (30 ml)
grapeseed oil

1 pound (454 g) smoked
pork bones or ham

1 pound (454 g) onions,
peeled, diced medium

1 jalapeño, seeded, diced

2 bay leaves

4 – inch (10 cm) cinnamon stick

3 garlic cloves, peeled, sliced

¼ pound (113 g) poblano
peppers, stemmed,
seeded, diced

1 Tablespoon ground
coriander seed

1 cup (240 ml) dry white wine

2 pounds (908 g)
sweet potatoes, peeled,
diced medium

7 cups (1.7 L) chicken broth

1 teaspoon Kosher salt

½ teaspoon fresh ground
black pepper

garnish:

1 ½ pounds (680 g) small
tomatillos, husks removed
and cut in small wedges

2 Tablespoons (30 ml)
grapeseed oil

2 jalapeños, seeded,
diced brunoise

2 Tablespoons (30 ml)
lime juice

2 Tablespoons (25 g) sugar

1 cup (16 g) cilantro leaves,
chopped coarsely

salt and pepper to taste

» **sweet potato soup with seared tomatillos**
continues on page 74

farmer's market

saving *at the* stands

A weekly visit to the local farmer's market is a summer treat for good cooks. What surprises will you find today? All that farm-fresh bounty is inspiring for soup lovers; but if you want to make the most of your farmer's market visit, don't be afraid to make substitutions to recipes.

If you don't see kale, try substituting cabbage. If you don't like the look of the potatoes, add fresh beans for carbs instead. If bell peppers aren't in season, add fresh carrots for sweetness.

Since you tend to buy in bulk at the market for the best prices, making big batches of soup to store in the freezer is a great way to make sure you use every last tomato, celery stalk and onion.

continued from page 72

sweet potato soup
with *seared tomatillos*

1. Add oil to a medium-hot large stockpot, add the smoked pork bones and render for 3 minutes. Add the onions, jalapeño, bay leaves, cinnamon stick, garlic and poblanos and sweat for 5 minutes.

2. Add the coriander and sauté for 1 minute.

3. Add the wine and reduce by two-thirds. Add potatoes and broth, salt and pepper and bring to a boil. Simmer for 25 to 30 minutes until potatoes are very tender.

4. Remove bay leaves, cinnamon stick and pork bones or ham. Set aside pork bones or ham. Let soup cool for 30 minutes.

5. Add half the mixture to the Vitamix container and secure lid.

6. Select Variable 1.

7. Switch machine to Start and slowly increase speed to Variable 10.

8. Blend for 20 seconds until all ingredients are blended. Repeat with remaining mixture. If necessary, return to pot to heat.

9. Heat a sauté pan until very hot. Toss the tomatillos with the oil, season with salt and pepper. Add to the pan and sear. Do not toss too much as you want to keep the pan hot. Cook for 1 minute.

10. Add the jalapeños and cook for 30 seconds. Add the lime juice and sugar, cooking an additional 3 minutes. Remove to a plate for garnish.

11. Divide tomatillos between 8 bowls. Sprinkle the cilantro leaves in the bowl. Ladle the hot soup over the leaves and around the tomatillos and serve. Remove meat from pork bones and dice brunoise. Garnish each bowl with the diced meat.

nutritional information

per 1 cup (240 ml) serving (with ham garnish): *Calories: 531, Total Fat: 13 g, Saturated Fat: 2 g, Protein: 33 g, Fiber: 13 g, Carbohydrates: 67 g, Sodium: 1516 mg, Cholesterol: 56 mg*

roasted *red pepper soup* ♨

preparation: 10 minutes | **processing:** 5 minutes 45 seconds | **cook time:** 6 minutes | **yield:** 4 cups (960 ml)

1 Tablespoon extra virgin olive oil

½ cup (50 g) chopped celery

¼ cup (40 g) chopped onion

2 garlic cloves, peeled, chopped

2 Tablespoons (15 g) all-purpose flour

8-ounce (227 g) jar roasted red peppers, drained, patted dry

1 cup (240 ml) low sodium chicken broth

1 cup (240 ml) half and half

½ teaspoon salt

2 dashes cayenne pepper

1. In a small 8-inch (20 cm) nonstick skillet heat olive oil; add celery and onions. Cook over medium heat, stirring occasionally for 4 minutes.

2. Add garlic pieces; continue cooking, stirring occasionally 1 more minute.

3. Stir in flour; cook for 30 to 60 seconds until very lightly browned.

4. Place cooked vegetable mixture, roasted pepper, chicken broth, half and half, salt and pepper into the Vitamix container and secure lid.

5. Select Hot Soup program.

6. Switch machine to Start and allow machine to complete programmed cycle.

7. Refrigerate leftovers.

nutritional information

per 1 cup (240 ml) serving: *Calories: 153, Total Fat: 11 g, Saturated Fat: 5 g, Protein: 4 g, Fiber: 1 g, Carbohydrates: 10 g, Sodium: 682 mg, Cholesterol: 23 mg*

gazpacho

preparation: 5 minutes | **processing:** 5 seconds | **yield:** 8 cups (1.9 L)

3 cups (720 ml) tomato juice, fresh or canned

⅓ cup (80 ml) red wine vinegar

1 pound (454 g) ripe tomatoes (4–5 large), quartered

2 ½ cups (332 g) cucumber, peeled, cut into chunks

¼ cup (60 ml) olive oil

2 ounces (56 g) chopped onion (about 1 small)

8 ounces (227 g) sweet green bell pepper, seeded, quartered (about 1 medium)

dash hot sauce

salt and black pepper to taste

1. Place all ingredients into the Vitamix container in the order listed and secure lid.

2. Select Variable 1.

3. Switch machine to Start and slowly increase speed to Variable 2.

4. Blend for 5 seconds.

5. Season soup and serve immediately.

nutritional information

per 1 cup (240 ml) serving: Calories: 105, Total Fat: 7 g, Saturated Fat: 1 g, Protein: 2 g, Fiber: 2 g, Carbohydrates: 9 g, Sodium: 262 mg, Cholesterol: 0 mg

holiday
squash soup

preparation: 30 minutes
processing: 6 minutes 15 seconds
yield: 4 cups (960 ml)

2 cups (480 ml) chicken
or vegetable broth

½ butternut squash,
freshly roasted, peeled
or 2 cups (410 g) freshly
cooked squash

2 Tablespoons (20 g)
chopped onion

¼ medium apple, seeded

¼ teaspoon ground nutmeg

¼ teaspoon dried sage

¼ teaspoon dried rosemary

⅛ teaspoon white pepper

½ teaspoon salt

¼ cup (60 ml) heavy
whipping cream

1. Place broth, squash, onion, apple, nutmeg, sage,
   rosemary, pepper and salt into the Vitamix container
   in the order listed and secure lid.

2. Select Hot Soup program.

3. Switch machine to Start and allow machine to
   complete programmed cycle.

4. Add heavy cream to the Vitamix container and secure lid.

5. Switch machine to Start and slowly increase
   speed to Variable 8.

6. Blend for an additional 30 seconds.

nutritional information

*per 1 cup (240 ml) serving: Calories: 109, Total Fat: 6 g,
Saturated Fat: 3 g, Protein: 2 g, Fiber: 3 g, Carbohydrates: 13 g,
Sodium: 766 mg, Cholesterol: 20 mg*

kitchen chemistry

sweeten the deal

Roasting any vegetable
is a great way to caramelize
sugars and increase flavor.
This slow browning brings
about a subtle sweetness
and slightly nutty flavor,
giving the squash an almost
candy-like quality.

To roast winter squash such as
buttercup, butternut or even
pumpkin, pierce the squash with
a knife and microwave briefly
just to soften slightly. Cut the
squash in half, cut off the stem
and scoop out seeds and any
stringy flesh. Prick the outsides
of the squash with a fork and
brush all surfaces with olive
oil. Place cut side down on a
baking sheet and roast at 400°F
(200°C) for 40 minutes or until
squash is fork-tender and just
beginning to brown. Scoop the
flesh out of the shell to cool
slightly, then use as directed.

thai **pumpkin soup**

preparation: 20 minutes | **processing:** 1 minute
yield: 8 cups (1.9 L)

looking good

>> For an appetizing
presentation, and
an authentic dash of
extra flavor, garnish
the soup with chopped
cilantro, chopped peanuts
and sour cream.

2 Tablespoons (30 ml) olive oil

1 cup (160 g) chopped onion

1 Tablespoon tomato paste

2 ½ cups (610 g)
canned pumpkin

2 Tablespoons (30 g)
chopped fresh ginger

1 garlic clove, peeled, chopped

3 cups (720 ml) chicken
or vegetable broth

¾ cup (180 ml) coconut cream

¾ cup (180 ml) coconut milk

1 Tablespoon chopped
green chilies

1 Tablespoon lemon juice

salt and pepper

1. Sauté onion in olive oil until soft. Add tomato paste, pumpkin,
   ginger, garlic, broth, coconut cream and coconut milk.
   Combine until thoroughly heated through.

2. Place mixture into the Vitamix container. Add chilies and
   lemon juice and secure lid.

3. Select Purée program.

4. Switch machine to Start and allow machine to complete
   programmed cycle.

5. Season to taste with salt and pepper.

nutritional information

per 1 cup (240 ml) serving: *Calories: 216, Total Fat: 13 g, Saturated Fat: 9 g,
Protein: 2 g, Fiber: 3 g, Carbohydrates: 24 g, Sodium: 375 mg, Cholesterol: 0 mg*

warm *hummus soup* ❄

preparation: 10 minutes | ***processing:*** 1 minute 30 seconds | ***cook time:*** 15–20 minutes | ***yield:*** 9 cups (2.1 L)

6 cups (1.4 L) vegetable broth

3 15-ounce (426 g) cans chickpeas, drained

¼ cup (60 ml) lemon juice or 1 large lemon, peeled, halved, seeded

3 Tablespoons (45 g) tahini paste

2 Tablespoons (17 g) chopped garlic

5–6 teaspoons ground cumin

2 teaspoons ground coriander

2 teaspoons turmeric

1 ½ teaspoons salt

½ teaspoon black pepper

1. Combine half of all ingredients into the Vitamix container and secure lid.

2. Select Frozen Dessert program.

3. Switch machine to Start and allow machine to complete programmed cycle.

4. Pour into a stockpot. Repeat with remaining half of ingredients.

5. Bring soup to a simmer over medium-low heat and cook for 15 to 20 minutes. Serve garnished with cilantro and pita chips.

nutritional information

per 1 cup (240 ml) serving: *Calories: 167, Total Fat: 5 g, Saturated Fat: 0 g, Protein: 8 g, Fiber: 5 g, Carbohydrates: 23 g, Sodium: 1388 mg, Cholesterol: 0 mg*

cream of **asparagus soup**

preparation: 25 minutes | **processing:** 4 minutes
yield: 4 cups (960 ml)

1 ½ pounds (680 g) asparagus spears, cooked
(reserve 1 cup (180 g) pieces for garnish)

1 ½ cups (360 ml) chicken broth

⅛ teaspoon salt

⅛ teaspoon black pepper

½ cup (120 ml) heavy cream

1. Place asparagus, chicken broth, salt and pepper into the Vitamix container and secure lid.

2. Select Variable 1.

3. Switch machine to Start and slowly increase speed to Variable 10.

4. Blend for 3 ½ minutes or until smooth.

5. Reduce speed to Variable 1 and remove the lid plug. Pour in heavy cream through the lid plug opening.

6. Slowly increase speed to Variable 8 and blend for an additional 30 seconds. Serve immediately over reserved asparagus pieces.

nutritional information

per 1 cup (240 ml) serving: *Calories: 146, Total Fat: 12 g, Saturated Fat: 7 g, Protein: 5 g, Fiber: 3 g, Carbohydrates: 8 g, Sodium: 457 mg, Cholesterol: 41 mg*

wild rice soup ☕

preparation: 10 minutes | ***processing:*** 5 minutes 50 seconds | ***cook time:*** 6 minutes | ***yield:*** 4 cups (960 ml)

2 Tablespoons (30 g) butter

1 cup (70 g) sliced mushrooms

¼ cup (40 g) chopped onions

2 Tablespoons (15 g) all-purpose flour

½ teaspoon salt

⅛ teaspoon black pepper

1 cup (164 g) cooked wild rice, divided use

¼ cup (23 g) sliced almonds, divided use

1 cup (240 ml) chicken broth

1 cup (240 ml) half and half

⅓ cup (20 g) fresh parsley, washed, dried

6 ounces (170 g) cooked chicken,
cut into pieces

1 to 2 Tablespoons dry sherry, optional

1. In small nonstick skillet, melt butter over medium heat. Add mushrooms and onions; continue cooking, stirring occasionally, until mushrooms begin to brown and onions are softened (5 to 6 minutes).

2. Add flour, salt and pepper. Continue cooking, stirring occasionally, until flour turns light brown (1 minute).

3. Add onion mixture, ½ of wild rice, ½ of almonds, chicken broth and half and half to the Vitamix container and secure lid.

4. Select Hot Soup program.

5. Switch machine to Start and allow machine to complete programmed cycle.

6. Select Variable 2. Switch machine to Start and remove the lid plug. Drop in remaining wild rice, almonds, parsley, chicken and sherry through the lid plug opening. Blend an additional 5 seconds. Serve immediately.

nutritional information

per 1 cup (240 ml) serving (without sherry): *Calories: 353, Total Fat: 23 g, Saturated Fat: 10 g, Protein: 13 g, Fiber: 3 g, Carbohydrates: 24 g, Sodium: 788 mg, Cholesterol: 56 mg*

cabbage *soup*

preparation: 10 minutes | **processing:** 5 minutes 45 seconds
cook time: 10 minutes | **yield:** 4 cups (960 ml)

2 cups (480 ml)
chicken broth

2 Tablespoons (30 ml)
white wine

1 medium onion (100 g),
peeled, quartered

½ medium carrot

1 large potato (370 g),
baked, quartered

¼ teaspoon caraway seed

1 teaspoon dill seed

¼ teaspoon hot sauce

½ teaspoon salt

⅛ teaspoon black pepper

4 cups (350 g) cabbage,
wet chopped

1. Place broth, wine, onion, carrot, potato, caraway, dill, hot sauce, salt and pepper into the Vitamix container in the order listed and secure lid.

2. Select Hot Soup program.

3. Switch machine to Start and allow machine to complete programmed cycle.

4. Meanwhile, cook cabbage in large skillet with ½–1 cup (120–240 ml) water until tender, about 10 minutes.

5. Drain excess water. Place cooked cabbage in serving bowls. Pour soup over cabbage.

nutritional information

per 1 cup (240 ml) serving: Calories: 123, Total Fat: 1 g, Saturated Fat: 0 g, Protein: 4 g, Fiber: 5 g, Carbohydrates: 25 g, Sodium: 788 mg, Cholesterol: 0 mg

savory soups with less salt

Making soup from scratch is already an improvement, health-wise, over the canned varieties. Swapping out regular, store-bought broth for a low sodium variety is an easy way to lower a soup recipe's salt content.

For a base that is both low in sodium and low in fat, make your own vegetable broth. Simply gather potatoes, onions, celery stalks, parsnips, carrots or anything else you have lying around, and toss them in a pot with enough water to cover the veggies. Add garlic, fresh herbs and just a pinch of sea salt and let simmer for about an hour, then strain. Herbs—fresh and dried—are also a great substitute for salt in any soup recipe. Many, like rosemary, turmeric and oregano, have big antioxidant and disease-fighting benefits to boot.

bacon cheddar
potato soup ☕

preparation: 15 minutes | **processing:** 5 minutes 55 seconds
yield: 4 cups (960 ml)

2 cups (480 ml) milk

12 ounces (340 g)
Russet potatoes, baked,
halved (about 2 medium),
divided use

⅔ cup (80 g) shredded
cheddar cheese, divided use

2 Tablespoons (20 g)
chopped onion, sautéed

½ teaspoon dried dill weed

½ teaspoon salt

1 ounce (28 g)
bacon, cooked

1. Place milk, one potato, half of the cheese, onion,
   dill and salt into the Vitamix container in the order
   listed and secure lid.

2. Select Hot Soup program.

3. Switch machine to Start and allow machine
   to complete programmed cycle.

4. Select Variable 1.

5. Switch machine to Start and remove lid plug.
   Add remaining potato, bacon and cheese through
   the lid plug opening.

6. Blend an additional 10 seconds.

nutritional information

per 1 cup (240 ml) serving: *Calories: 254, Total Fat: 11 g,
Saturated Fat: 6 g, Protein: 14 g, Fiber: 2 g, Carbohydrates: 26 g,
Sodium: 649 mg, Cholesterol: 35 mg*

---

planning ahead

just heat *and* serve

When you're strapped
for time or don't feel
like cooking, a freezer
stocked with homemade
soup is a lifesaver.

Remember to only freeze
soup in packages sized for
single use, whether that's
a cup for a quick lunch or
a quart for a quick family
meal. Stored in an airtight
container, most soups can be
frozen for up to two months.
For best results, place frozen
quart-size containers in the
fridge to thaw for 24 hours
before preparing.

If you're running out the
door and realize you forgot
to pack a lunch, grab one
of those single-serving
containers and let it thaw
in the fridge at work until
heating at lunchtime.

clam bisque provençale

preparation: 10 minutes | ***processing:*** 25 seconds | ***cook time:*** 25 minutes | ***yield:*** 4 ¼ cups (1.0 L)

½ cup (80 g) chopped onion

¼ cup (25 g) chopped celery

¼ cup (32 g) chopped carrot

1 cup (150 g) peeled, diced potato

1 garlic clove, peeled, chopped

2 ½ Tablespoons (40 ml) olive oil

2 Tablespoons (30 g) tomato paste

1 pound (454 g) clam meat, divided use

1 ½ cups (360 ml) chicken broth

½ cup (120 ml) dry white wine

1 bay leaf

½ teaspoon dried oregano

1 teaspoon dried thyme

1 cup (240 ml) heavy whipping cream

salt and black pepper

1. Sauté chopped onion, celery, carrot, potato and garlic in olive oil until soft. Add tomato paste and stir well.

2. Add half of the clam meat, chicken broth, white wine, bay leaf, oregano and thyme; simmer for 15 minutes.

3. Stir in cream. Bring mixture back up to a simmer. Heat for an additional 5 minutes; do not boil. Remove bay leaf and remove from heat. Let mixture cool 15 minutes. Add soup mixture to the Vitamix container and secure lid.

4. Select Variable 1.

5. Switch machine to Start and slowly increase speed to Variable 8.

6. Blend for 20 seconds.

7. Stop machine and remove lid. Add remaining clam meat, salt and pepper. Secure lid.

8. Select Variable 1.

9. Switch machine to Start and slowly increase speed to Variable 5.

10. Blend for 5 seconds.

nutritional information

per 1 cup (240 ml) serving: *Calories: 382, Total Fat: 29 g, Saturated Fat: 14 g, Protein: 11 g, Fiber: 2 g, Carbohydrates: 15 g, Sodium: 1065 mg, Cholesterol: 96 mg*

planning ahead

freeze leftover canned broth for quick flavor

Canned broth makes it possible to use smaller amounts of broth without having to invest the time in making large batches of chicken, beef or vegetable stock. Soups, stews and chili are obvious solutions for leftover broth. But you can also freeze unused broth in ice cube trays; pull these cubes out in the amounts you need to add moisture and flavor when sautéing vegetables or cooking rice or potatoes.

Broth cubes can also be used to poach chicken and fish, preventing these lean proteins from drying out while they cook. Add a splash of wine as well and you'll have the base for a tasty sauce to spoon over the finished dish.

tortilla *soup* ⊗

preparation: 5 minutes | ***processing:*** 5 minutes 55 seconds | ***yield:*** 2 ½ cups (600 ml)

soup base:

1 cup (240 ml) low sodium
chicken, beef or vegetable broth

1 Roma tomato, halved

1 carrot, halved

1 stalk celery, halved

1 thin slice of onion, peeled

1 garlic clove, peeled

1 thin slice of yellow squash

1 thin slice of red bell pepper

1 thin slice of cabbage

1 mushroom

salt and black pepper, to taste

1 teaspoon taco seasoning

dash cumin

optional ingredients:

½ cup (70 g) cooked chicken,
breast meat

½ fresh jalapeño

¼ cup (30 g) pitted olives

¼ cup (50 g) unsalted canned corn, drained

2 ounces (60 g) baked tortilla chips

1. Place all Soup Base ingredients into the Vitamix container in the order listed and secure lid.

2. Select Hot Soup program.

3. Switch machine to Start and allow machine to complete programmed cycle.

4. If adding Optional Ingredients, select Variable 2. Switch machine to Start and remove
   the lid plug. Drop in chicken, jalapeños, olives, corn and chips through the lid plug opening.

5. Blend for an additional 10 seconds.

nutritional information

per serving (with optional ingredients): *Calories: 276, Total Fat: 12 g, Saturated Fat: 2 g,
Protein: 9 g, Fiber: 4 g, Carbohydrates: 34 g, Sodium: 918 mg, Cholesterol: 15 mg*

chicken potato
spinach soup ♨

preparation: 15 minutes | **processing:** 6 minutes
yield: 5 ¼ cups (1.2 L)

1 cup (240 ml) chicken broth	⅛ teaspoon dried rosemary
1 ½ cups (360 ml) milk	1 Tablespoon spinach, cooked or frozen, thawed
¼ cup (40 g) chopped onion	
3 medium Russet potatoes (640 g), scrubbed, baked, halved, divided use	5 ounces (140 g) skinless, boneless chicken breast, cooked and diced
	salt to taste

1. Place broth, milk, onion, two potatoes and rosemary into the Vitamix container in the order listed and secure lid.

2. Select Hot Soup program.

3. Switch machine to Start and allow machine to complete programmed cycle.

4. Select Variable 1. Switch machine to Start and remove the lid plug. Add spinach, remaining potato and chicken through the lid plug opening.

5. Blend an additional 10 to 15 seconds.

nutritional information

per 1 cup (240 ml) serving: *Calories: 213, Total Fat: 6 g, Saturated Fat: 1 g, Protein: 10 g, Fiber: 3 g, Carbohydrates: 30 g, Sodium: 353 mg, Cholesterol: 16 mg*

---

surprise visitors

soup solutions *in a* hurry

It's a cold, wintry day, unexpected company is on the way, and you're in charge of lunch. No problem, just mix up a hearty dish like this Chicken Potato Spinach Soup. With 15 minutes of prep and just 6 minutes to process, you'll have time to make a batch of Rosemary Focaccia (page 189) to serve on the side. Fresh bread from the oven plus a warm bowl of homemade soup will delight anyone.

For warm weather drop-ins, mix up a batch of Gazpacho (page 76) in minutes that will convince guests you've been prepping all day. Serve with a side of Bacon Cheddar Cornbread (page 186).

root vegetable *soup* ♨

preparation: 15 minutes | ***processing:*** 5 minutes 50 seconds | ***cook time:*** 6 minutes | ***yield:*** 4 cups (960 ml)

1 Tablespoon extra virgin olive oil

⅓ cup (52 g) sliced onions

1 garlic clove, peeled, cut into 4 pieces

⅔ cup (85 g) chopped carrots

⅓ cup (50 g) peeled, chopped parsnips

2 small red potatoes, cooked, divided use

½ cup (65 g) peeled, cubed turnips

1-inch (2.5 cm) piece peeled, fresh ginger root, cut into pieces

2 Tablespoons (6 g) fresh dill weed

½ teaspoon salt

¼ teaspoon freshly cracked black pepper

1 cup (240 ml) reduced sodium chicken broth

1 cup (240 ml) half and half

1. In a small 8-inch (20 cm) nonstick skillet heat olive oil; add onions. Cook over medium heat, stirring occasionally for 4 minutes.

2. Add garlic pieces; continue cooking, stirring occasionally 1 more minute.

3. Place cooked onion mixture, carrots, parsnips, 1 red potato, turnips, ginger, dill, salt, pepper, broth and half and half into the Vitamix container and secure lid.

4. Select Hot Soup program.

5. Switch machine to Start and allow machine to complete programmed cycle.

6. Select Variable 2. Switch machine to Start and remove the lid plug. Drop in remaining cooked potato through the lid plug opening.

7. Blend an additional 5 seconds or until smooth. Stop machine. Serve immediately.

nutritional information

per 1 cup (240 ml) serving: *Calories: 206, Total Fat: 11 g, Saturated Fat: 5 g, Protein: 5 g, Fiber: 3 g, Carbohydrates: 24 g, Sodium: 504 mg, Cholesterol: 23 mg*

orange vanilla
vinaigrette

preparation: 10 minutes | **processing:** 20 seconds
yield: 3 cups (720 ml)

2 oranges, peeled,
halved, seeded

1 Tablespoon apple
cider vinegar

1 ½ teaspoons
vanilla extract

1 Tablespoon honey

1 lemon, peeled,
halved, seeded

1 dash hot sauce

¼ teaspoon salt

⅛ teaspoon black pepper

1 ½ cups (360 ml)
extra virgin olive oil

1. Place oranges, vinegar, vanilla, honey, lemon,
   hot sauce, salt and pepper into the Vitamix container
   in the order listed and secure lid.

2. Select Variable 1.

3. Switch machine to Start and slowly increase
   speed to Variable 4.

4. Blend for 20 seconds or until smooth.
   Reduce speed to Variable 1 and remove the lid plug.

5. Slowly pour olive oil through the lid plug opening
   until emulsified.

nutritional information

per 2 tablespoon (30 ml) serving: *Calories: 135, Total Fat: 14 g,
Saturated Fat: 2 g, Protein: 0 g, Fiber: 0 g, Carbohydrates: 2 g,
Sodium: 25 mg, Cholesterol: 0 mg*

bright idea

Salad dressings make
wonderful marinades
for fish or poultry. You
can also brush a salad
dressing on fish or
poultry during grilling.

farmer's market

dress your salads
with *fresh fruit*

Sure, you hit the farmer's
market to stock up on salad
fixings like summer greens
and heirloom tomatoes, but
next time you're perusing
the stands, keep your eye out
for ingredients to dress your
salads as well. As with any
farmer's market purchase,
seasonality is key, both for
availability of ingredients
and overall freshness.

Raspberries make a delicious
mid-summer dressing
when blended with olive oil
and basil in our Raspberry
Vinaigrette (page 94).
Try Fresh Apple and Pear
Dressing (page 98) as a
salad topper in the fall, when
you're sure to find bushels
of sweet McIntosh and tart
Granny Smith apples.

raspberry vinaigrette

preparation: 5 minutes | ***processing:*** 30 seconds | ***yield:*** 1 ¾ cups (420 ml)

¾ cup (180 ml) olive oil

¼ cup (60 ml) apple cider or raspberry vinegar

1 teaspoon salt

1 teaspoon dried basil

½ cup (60 g) fresh or frozen red raspberries

¼ cup (60 ml) water

2 Tablespoons (30 ml) honey

1. Place olive oil, vinegar, salt, basil, raspberries and water into the Vitamix container in the order listed and secure lid.

2. Select Variable 1.

3. Switch machine to Start and remove the lid plug.
   Add honey through the lid plug opening and replace lid plug.

4. Slowly increase speed to Variable 4.

5. Blend for 30 seconds.

nutritional information

per 2 tablespoon (30 ml) serving: *Calories: 120, Total Fat: 12 g, Saturated Fat: 2 g, Protein: 0 g, Fiber: 0 g, Carbohydrates: 3 g, Sodium: 167 mg, Cholesterol: 0 mg*

dark cherry
balsamic vinaigrette

preparation: 15 minutes | **processing:** 20 seconds
cook time: 10–15 minutes | **yield:** 4 cups (960 ml)

1 cup (240 ml) balsamic vinegar

½ cup (100 g) granulated sugar

2 garlic cloves, peeled

1 cup (240 g) cherry preserves

½ cup (120 ml) red wine vinegar

2 cups (480 ml) canola oil

Kosher salt

black pepper

1. In a medium saucepan on medium high heat, add balsamic vinegar, sugar and garlic until boiling. Simmer and reduce by half. Remove from heat and let cool 20 minutes.

2. Place vinegar mixture, cherry preserves and red wine vinegar into the Vitamix container and secure lid.

3. Select Variable 1.

4. Switch machine to Start and slowly increase speed to Variable 4.

5. Blend for 20 seconds.

6. Remove the lid plug and slowly pour oil through the lid plug opening until emulsified. Season to taste with salt and pepper.

nutritional information

per 2 tablespoon (30 ml) serving: *Calories: 165, Total Fat: 14 g, Saturated Fat: 1 g, Protein: 0 g, Fiber: 0 g, Carbohydrates: 11 g, Sodium: 6 mg, Cholesterol: 0 mg*

raspberry maple
dressing

preparation: 5 minutes | **processing:** 10 seconds
yield: 2 ½ cups (600 ml)

1 cup (240 ml) raspberry vinegar

4 Tablespoons (60 ml) maple syrup

pinch salt

pinch black pepper

1 ¼ cups (300 ml) olive oil

1. Place vinegar, maple syrup, salt and pepper into the Vitamix container in the order listed and secure lid.

2. Select Variable 1.

3. Switch machine to Start and slowly increase speed to Variable 5.

4. Remove the lid plug and slowly pour olive oil through the lid plug opening.

5. Once all the oil is incorporated, slowly increase speed to Variable 8.

6. Blend for 10 seconds.

nutritional information

per 2 tablespoon (30 ml) serving: Calories: 136, Total Fat: 14 g, Saturated Fat: 2 g, Protein: 0 g, Fiber: 0 g, Carbohydrates: 3 g, Sodium: 8 mg, Cholesterol: 0 mg

build a meal

soup and salad

Mix and match soups and salads for satisfying, flavorful meals. Here are some suggestions that combine soup and salad recipes with complementary profiles. All you need is fresh bread and butter to complete the feast.

Toss romaine lettuce with Caesar Salad Dressing (page 103) and serve with French Onion Soup (page 69). Drizzle Orange Basil Vinaigrette (page 97) on arugula to accompany Thai Pumpkin Soup (page 78). Raspberry Maple Dressing spooned over a mixture of butter lettuce, walnuts and sliced pears is wonderful with Holiday Squash Soup (page 77).

orange basil
vinaigrette

preparation: 15 minutes | ***processing:*** 30 seconds | ***yield:*** 3 ¼ cups (780 ml)

½ cup (120 ml) orange juice

½ cup (120 ml) white wine vinegar

2 Tablespoons (31 g) Dijon mustard

2 Tablespoons (12 g) freshly
grated orange zest

½ Tablespoon salt

1 teaspoon black pepper

2 cups (480 ml) light olive oil

2 Tablespoons (5 g) fresh basil leaves

1. Place orange juice, vinegar, mustard, zest, salt and pepper into the
   Vitamix container in the order listed and secure lid.

2. Select Variable 1.

3. Switch machine to Start and slowly increase speed to Variable 5.

4. Blend for 20 seconds.

5. Reduce speed to Variable 1 and remove the lid plug. Gradually add
   the oil through the lid plug opening. Once all the oil is incorporated,
   add the basil. Replace the lid plug.

6. Blend for 10 seconds until smooth.

nutritional information

per 2 tablespoon (30 ml) serving: *Calories: 152, Total Fat: 17 g, Saturated Fat: 2 g,
Protein: 0 g, Fiber: 0 g, Carbohydrates: 1 g, Sodium: 162 mg, Cholesterol: 0 mg*

on the menu

This fresh fruit dressing is perfect for mixed greens. Add a few apple slices, slivered almonds and crumbled feta or blue cheese.

fresh apple and *pear dressing*

preparation: 5 minutes | **processing:** 20 seconds
cook time: 4–6 minutes | **yield:** 2 ½ cups (600 ml)

1 ripe apple, cored, chopped

1 ripe pear, cored, chopped

½ cup (100 g) granulated sugar

⅔ cup (160 ml) water

1 teaspoon fresh tarragon leaves

4 Tablespoons (60 ml) cider vinegar, divided use

3 Tablespoons (45 ml) fresh lemon juice, divided use

1. Place fruit, sugar, water and tarragon in a medium saucepan and simmer, covered, over medium heat until very soft, about 4 to 6 minutes depending on ripeness of fruit.

2. Let water evaporate. There should be about 1 ¾ cups (420 ml) fruit and liquid when finished cooking. Allow the mixture to cool.

3. Pour fruit mixture into the Vitamix container and secure lid.

4. Select Variable 1.

5. Switch machine to Start and slowly increase speed to Variable 10.

6. Blend for 20 seconds or until smooth.

7. Remove mixture to a medium-sized bowl. Whisk in half of the cider vinegar and lemon juice. Taste; dressing should be a pleasant blend of sweet tart. If desired, add remaining cider vinegar and lemon juice.

nutritional information

per 2 tablespoon (30 ml) serving: *Calories: 32, Total Fat: 0 g, Saturated Fat: 0 g, Protein: 0 g, Fiber: 1 g, Carbohydrates: 8 g, Sodium: 1 mg, Cholesterol: 0 mg*

balsamic fig
dressing

preparation: 10 minutes | ***processing:*** 30 seconds | ***yield:*** 1 ¾ cups (420 ml)

½ cup (120 ml) balsamic vinegar

⅓ cup (8 small) dried Mission figs

3 Tablespoons (45 ml) orange juice

1 Tablespoon water

1 teaspoon coarsely
chopped shallots

½ teaspoon fresh orange zest

½ teaspoon vanilla extract

¼ teaspoon salt

⅛ teaspoon freshly cracked
black pepper

1 cup (240 ml) vegetable oil

1. Place vinegar, figs, orange juice, water, shallots, zest, vanilla, salt and
   pepper into the Vitamix container in the order listed and secure lid.

2. Select Variable 1.

3. Switch machine to Start and slowly increase speed to Variable 10.

4. Blend for 30 seconds or until smooth.

5. Reduce speed to Variable 4 and remove lid plug.

6. Pour oil in a thin stream through the lid plug opening until thoroughly emulsified
   (1 minute). If necessary, scrape sides of the container with a spatula.

7. Refrigerate leftovers.

nutritional information

per 2 tablespoon (30 ml) serving: *Calories: 156, Total Fat: 16 g, Saturated Fat: 2 g,
Protein: 0 g, Fiber: 0 g, Carbohydrates: 4 g, Sodium: 44 mg, Cholesterol: 0 mg*

greek salad
dressing

preparation: 10 minutes | **processing:** 20 seconds
yield: 1 ½ cups (360 ml)

2 large lemons, peeled with white removed, halved, seeded	¾ teaspoon sugar
¾ cup (180 ml) extra virgin olive oil	¼ teaspoon salt
1 ½ teaspoons dried oregano leaves	⅛ teaspoon freshly cracked black pepper
2 garlic cloves, peeled	⅓ cup (50 g) crumbled feta cheese
	6 Kalamata olives, pitted

1. Place lemons, oil, oregano, garlic, sugar, salt and pepper into the Vitamix container in the order listed and secure lid.

2. Select Variable 1.

3. Switch machine to Start and slowly increase speed to Variable 5.

4. Blend for 15 seconds or until smooth. Stop machine and remove lid. Add feta cheese and olives and secure lid.

5. Select Variable 1.

6. Switch machine to Start and slowly increase speed to Variable 3. Blend an additional 5 seconds. If necessary, scrape sides of the container with a spatula.

nutritional information

per 2 tablespoon (30 ml) serving: *Calories: 148, Total Fat: 15 g, Saturated Fat: 3 g, Protein: 1 g, Fiber: 0 g, Carbohydrates: 2 g, Sodium: 126 mg, Cholesterol: 4 mg*

herbology

herbal remedies

Fresh herbs add special punch to salad dressings, often in surprising combinations. They can help balance spicy flavors, take the edge off acidity, add color, and sweeten when necessary.

Fresh tarragon lends an anise-scented touch to the sweet crunch of apples and pears in our Fresh Apple and Pear Dressing recipe (page 98). Fresh, pungent basil kicks up the spicy flavor of Dijon mustard in the Orange Basil Vinaigrette recipe (page 97) while softening the acidity of the orange juice. Cool, refreshing dill and sweetly fragrant marjoram offset the sharpness of green onion in our creamy Fresh Herb Ranch Dressing recipe (page 105).

tomato vinaigrette

preparation: 5 minutes | ***processing:*** 20 seconds | ***yield:*** 2 cups (480 ml)

½ cup (120 ml) white
balsamic vinegar

¼ cup (60 ml) water

¾ cup + 2 Tablespoons
(210 ml) extra virgin olive oil

½ teaspoon salt

¼ teaspoon black pepper

6 Tablespoons (18 g)
chopped fresh chives

1 Roma tomato, halved

1. Place all ingredients into the Vitamix container
   in the order listed and secure lid.

2. Select Variable 1.

3. Switch machine to Start and slowly increase
   speed to Variable 5.

4. Blend for 20 seconds until emulsified.

nutritional information

per 2 tablespoon (30 ml) serving: *Calories: 118, Total Fat: 12 g, Saturated Fat: 2 g,
Protein: 0 g, Fiber: 0 g, Carbohydrates: 2 g, Sodium: 75 mg, Cholesterol: 0 mg*

caesar salad dressing

preparation: 10 minutes | ***processing:*** 25 seconds | ***yield:*** 4 cups (960 ml)

6 large eggs

2 Tablespoons (30 ml) red
wine vinegar

1 ½ small garlic cloves, peeled

½ cup + 1 Tablespoon (135 ml)
lemon juice

1 cup (100 g) grated Parmesan cheese

½ teaspoon salt

1 Tablespoon + 1 ½ teaspoons
anchovy filets

⅓ teaspoon dry mustard

1 cup + 2 Tablespoons (270 ml)
extra virgin olive oil

1. Place eggs, vinegar, garlic, lemon juice, cheese, salt, anchovy and mustard into the Vitamix container in the order listed and secure lid.

2. Select Variable 1.

3. Switch machine to Start and slowly increase speed to Variable 5.

4. Blend for 25 seconds or until smooth. Reduce speed to Variable 1 and remove the lid plug.

5. Slowly pour olive oil through the lid plug opening and blend an additional 10 seconds.

nutritional information

per 2 tablespoon (30 ml) serving: *Calories: 105, Total Fat: 10 g, Saturated Fat: 2 g, Protein: 2 g, Fiber: 0 g, Carbohydrates: 1 g, Sodium: 373 mg, Cholesterol: 46 mg*

fresh herb
ranch dressing

preparation: 10 minutes | **processing:** 20 seconds
yield: 2 ½ cups (600 ml)

1 cup (240 g)
real mayonnaise

1 cup (240 g) sour cream

¾ cup (18 g) mixed
favorite fresh herbs
(dill, marjoram, basil, etc.)

2 Tablespoons (12 g)
chopped green onion

2 Tablespoons (30 ml)
white vinegar

½ teaspoon garlic powder

½ teaspoon salt

¼ teaspoon freshly
cracked black pepper

1. Place all ingredients into the Vitamix container
   in the order listed and secure lid.

2. Select Variable 1.

3. Switch machine to Start and slowly increase
   speed to Variable 5.

4. Blend for 20 seconds or until smooth.
   Use tamper if necessary.

5. Refrigerate leftovers.

nutritional information

per 2 tablespoon (30 ml) serving: *Calories: 107, Total Fat: 11 g,
Saturated Fat: 3 g, Protein: 1 g, Fiber: 0 g, Carbohydrates: 1 g,
Sodium: 123 mg, Cholesterol: 12 mg*

build a meal

cool, spicy and frosty

Choosing a variety of
textures, colors and
seasonings is the secret
to putting together a
memorable meal from
intriguing recipes. Try this
summer menu with a cool
beginning, spicy middle
and frosty ending.

For a chilled salad, combine
generous portions of mixed
greens with fresh corn
kernels (blanched), broccoli
florets, cherry tomatoes,
chopped cucumber and
chopped green onion.
Toss with Fresh Herb Ranch
Dressing. Next, serve up
a spicy second course of
Jamaican Pulled Pork
(page 134) alongside
Creamy Polenta with
Mushrooms and Chives
(page 172). Offer guests
a chance to refresh
their palates with Pink
Grapefruit Granita
(page 291) for dessert.

chop chop pocket
sandwiches

preparation: 15 minutes | **processing:** pulsing
yield: 8 sandwiches

1 cup (100 g) walnut halves

1 carrot (110 g), quartered

6 large radishes

6-inch (15 cm) zucchini, cut in 1 ½-inch (4 cm) sections

2 4 ½-ounce (128 g) cooked boneless skinless chicken breasts, each cut in 3 pieces

2 cups (140 g) chopped iceberg lettuce

1 cup (240 g) homemade or purchased blue cheese dressing

½ teaspoon Kosher salt

¼ teaspoon black pepper

8 soft flax, oat and whole wheat pita pocket halves

1. Place walnuts into the Vitamix container and secure lid.

2. Select Variable 4. Pulse 3 times. Pour into large bowl.

3. Place carrots into the Vitamix container and secure lid.

4. Select Variable 5. Pulse 3 times. Place in bowl with nuts.

5. Place radishes and zucchini into the Vitamix container and secure lid.

» **chop chop pocket sandwiches** continues on page 108

send in a sub!

amp up your sandwich

Instead of using typical burger buns or sliced bread, try new options. Brioche is a rich, pastry-like bread with enough substance to stand in for a bun. Toasted slices from a ciabatta loaf can turn any sandwich into a panini.

Spelt bread has a nutty, hearty taste. If you're cooking for someone with a gluten intolerance, turn your sandwich into a lettuce wrap by using large-leaf greens such as radicchio, romaine, red lettuce or collard greens.

If you love wraps, but crave something with more bite, try swapping out your flaxseed wrap with irresistibly chewy naan flatbread.

continued from page 107

chop chop pocket
sandwiches

6. Select Variable 4. Pulse 4 times. Add to bowl.

7. Place chicken into the Vitamix container and secure lid.

8. Select Variable 4. Pulse 3 times. Add to bowl.

9. Add lettuce and dressing to bowl. Add salt and pepper.
   Toss to mix well. Spoon into pita halves.

nutritional information

per sandwich: Calories: 355, Total Fat: 26 g, Saturated Fat: 4 g, Protein: 12 g, Fiber: 4 g, Carbohydrates: 24 g, Sodium: 739 mg, Cholesterol: 16 mg

salmon *patties*

preparation: 10 minutes | **processing:** pulsing
cook time: 10–12 minutes | **yield:** 4 patties

create your own

Here's a variation for tuna melt lovers: use tuna in place of salmon and garnish the patties with shredded cheddar.

3 slices firm wheat sandwich bread, torn into quarters

½ celery stalk, cut into 1 ½-inch (4 cm) sections, approximately ⅓ cup (30 g)

¼ small green bell pepper, cut crosswise in half

¼ cup (40 g) diced onion, large dice

1 large egg

2 5-ounce (142 g) cans boneless skinless pink salmon, well drained

2 Tablespoons (30 ml) vegetable oil

Kosher salt and pepper

1. Place bread into the Vitamix container and secure lid.

2. Select Variable 4. Pulse 2 times. Pour into small bowl; set aside.

3. Place celery, green pepper and onion into the Vitamix container and secure lid.

4. Select Variable 6. Pulse 3 times. Stop machine and remove the lid.

5. Add egg, salmon and ¾ cup (80 g) breadcrumbs to the chopped vegetables in the container and secure lid.

6. Select Variable 3. Pulse 10 times, stopping machine to scrape sides of the container with a spatula, if necessary. Form 4 balls from salmon mixture and roll in remaining breadcrumbs. Flatten patties and dip into breadcrumbs again.

7. Heat oil in 10-inch (25 cm) nonstick skillet over medium-low to medium heat. Add patties. Cook 5 to 6 minutes per side or until browned and thoroughly cooked. Season to taste with salt and pepper.

nutritional information

per patty: *Calories: 245, Total Fat: 12 g, Saturated Fat: 13 g, Protein: 17 g, Fiber: 1 g, Carbohydrates: 18 g, Sodium: 493 mg, Cholesterol: 101 mg*

black bean *burgers*

preparation: 20 minutes | ***processing:*** 15 seconds + pulsing | ***yield:*** 7 patties

½ green pepper, seeded, rough chopped

¼ medium onion (25 g), peeled

3 garlic cloves, peeled

2 15-ounce (426 g) cans black beans, drained and rinsed well, divided use

1 teaspoon Italian seasoning

1 teaspoon dried basil

1 ¼ teaspoons salt

2 Tablespoons (30 ml) pizza sauce

1 large egg

1 cup (108 g) plain breadcrumbs

¾ cup (180 ml) canola oil

1. Place pepper, onion and garlic into the Vitamix container and secure lid.

2. Select Variable 5.

3. Pulse 3 to 4 times. Stop and scrape sides of the container with a spatula. Pulse several more times until chopped.

4. Add half of the black beans, Italian seasoning, basil, salt and pizza sauce to the Vitamix container and secure lid.

5. Select Variable 1.

6. Switch machine to Start and blend for 10 seconds. Stop and scrape sides of the container with a spatula. Continue to blend for 5 seconds. Mixture will resemble the consistency of guacamole.

7. Transfer to a mixing bowl and add the remaining black beans, egg and breadcrumbs. Combine by hand. Divide into 7 balls and flatten into patties. Make sure mixture is not too wet or too crumbly. If mixture sticks to your hands, add more breadcrumbs 1 Tablespoon at a time.

8. Place a 12–inch (30 cm) heavy-bottomed skillet over medium-high heat and pour in canola oil. Once oil is hot, cook patties 3 to 4 minutes on each side, until deep brown. Transfer to a paper towel-lined plate.

nutritional information

per patty: *Calories: 286, Total Fat: 15 g, Saturated Fat: 1 g, Protein: 10 g, Fiber: 8 g, Carbohydrates: 29 g, Sodium: 929 mg, Cholesterol: 31 mg*

on the menu

 For a sweet and tangy accent, top your burger with Pineapple Cranberry Relish (page 270) and refresh with Brazilian Lemonade (page 221).

healthy choices

no one will wonder "where's the beef?"

Black Bean Burgers, Salmon Patties (page 109) and Zucchini Burgers (page 115) are a great choice when you're craving a hamburger but still want to watch your fat and cholesterol intake. All three are deliciously high in protein, yet lower in fat, and full of fresh veggies that are good for you. (Adding chopped cashews to the Black Bean Burger recipe will add even more texture and protein!)

Eating smaller portions is also an important part of a healthy diet, and these burger recipes are perfect for making sliders. Form smaller patties, place on mini buns and serve as an appetizer the next time you entertain.

bbq beef sandwiches ♨

preparation: 20 minutes | **processing:** 5 minutes 45 seconds + pulsing
cook time: 8 hours 15 minutes | **yield:** 8 sandwiches

14 ½-ounce (412 g) can fire roasted diced tomatoes

½ medium onion, halved (about ⅓ cup or 60 g)

1 garlic clove, peeled

3 Tablespoons (14 g) brown sugar

1 Tablespoon cornstarch

6-ounce (170 g) can tomato paste

4 Tablespoons (60 ml) cider vinegar, divided use

1 Tablespoon Worcestershire sauce

½ teaspoon dry mustard

1 teaspoon salt

1 boneless beef chuck roast (about 2 ½ pounds or 1.1 kg)

1 Tablespoon vegetable oil

1 pound (454 g) cabbage cut in 4, then in 1 ½-inch (4 cm) pieces (½ small head)

1 carrot (110 g), quartered

¼ red onion (85 g), halved

¾ cup (180 g) homemade or purchased mayonnaise

1 Tablespoon sugar

8 sandwich buns, split

1. Place tomatoes, onion, garlic, brown sugar, cornstarch, tomato paste, 2 Tablespoons (30 ml) vinegar, Worcestershire sauce, mustard and salt into the Vitamix container and secure lid.

2. Select Hot Soup program.

3. Switch machine to Start and allow machine to complete programmed cycle.

4. Meanwhile, if desired, brown roast on all sides in oil in nonstick skillet. Spray inside of 3 ½ to 4-quart slow cooker with cooking spray. Place roast in cooker. Pour sauce over roast; cover. Cook on Low heat setting 8 to 10 hours or until meat is fork-tender.

5. Before serving time, place cabbage, carrot and onion into the Vitamix container and add water just to cover and secure lid.

6. Select Variable 8.

7. Pulse 4 times. Drain well.

8. In large bowl, mix mayonnaise, remaining 2 Tablespoons (30 ml) vinegar and sugar. Add cabbage mixture and stir to mix well. Add salt and pepper to taste.

9. Remove roast to a cutting board. Increase heat setting to High. Pull meat apart with 2 forks, removing visible fat. Add to sauce in slow cooker, cover and cook 15 minutes or until thoroughly heated. With slotted spoon, pile meat on bottoms of buns, top with coleslaw and bun tops. Store leftover meat and coleslaw covered in refrigerator.

nutritional information

per sandwich: *Calories: 576, Total Fat: 29 g, Saturated Fat: 6 g, Protein: 39 g, Fiber: 4 g, Carbohydrates: 41 g, Sodium: 786 mg, Cholesterol: 84 mg*

thai spring rolls
with dipping sauce

preparation: 20 minutes | ***processing:*** 20 seconds | ***yield:*** 4 servings (2 ½ cups (600 ml) sauce)

dipping sauce:

¼ cup (60 ml) extra virgin olive oil

4 kaffir lime leaves or 2 teaspoons freshly grated lime zest

1 Tablespoon Nama Shoyu

2 Thai red chilies

½ cup (125 g) raw Almond Butter (page 49)

lemon juice, about 2 Tablespoons (30 ml)

1 cup (240 ml) filtered water

fillings:

1 zucchini, julienned

1 cup (105 g) mung bean sprouts

½ bunch basil leaves

¼ bunch mint leaves

1 to 2 Thai chilies, finely chopped

wrapper:

2 large collard green leaves, ribs removed, and leaves halved

1. Place all Dipping Sauce ingredients into the Vitamix container and secure lid.

2. Select Variable 1.

3. Switch machine to Start and slowly increase speed to Variable 10.

4. Blend for 20 seconds, until smooth. Set aside.

5. To fill wrapper, lay a collard leaf flat, darker green side down, and layer filling ingredients along the bottom edge of each leaf.

6. To serve, roll up each collard leaf from the bottom into a tight cylinder. Serve with Thai Dipping Sauce.

nutritional information

per serving (1 spring roll and 2 tablespoons (30 ml) sauce): *Calories: 88, Total Fat: 7 g, Saturated Fat: 1 g, Protein: 3 g, Fiber: 2 g, Carbohydrates: 6 g, Sodium: 146 mg, Cholesterol: 0 mg*

zucchini *burgers*

preparation: 15 minutes | **processing:** pulsing | **cook time:** 6 minutes | **yield:** 17 patties

2 pounds (908 g) zucchini, cut into large chunks

1 large onion, peeled, quartered, about 1 ¼ cups (195 g) chopped

1 ½ cups (180 g) Italian seasoned dry breadcrumbs

3 large eggs

½ cup (50 g) shredded Romano or Parmesan cheese

½ teaspoon garlic powder

½ teaspoon onion powder

½ teaspoon dried parsley

½ teaspoon dried basil

½ teaspoon dried oregano

Canola oil for frying

1. Place zucchini into the Vitamix container, float with water and secure lid.

2. Select Variable 8.

3. Pulse 5 times until chopped. Strain in a colander. Place towel or paper towel over top to pat dry.

4. Place onion into the Vitamix container and secure lid.

5. Select Variable 3.

6. Pulse 4 to 5 times to evenly chop. Combine zucchini, onion, breadcrumbs, eggs, cheese and spices in a large bowl and stir until evenly combined.

7. Heat a large 12–inch (30 cm) heavy-bottomed skillet over medium high heat. Pour ¼ cup (60 ml) oil in pan. When oil is hot, measure ¼ cup (60 g) portions of the zucchini mixture into pan. Spread gently to form a patty. Cook 3 minutes or until the underside is crispy and dark brown. Flip and cook an additional 3 minutes. Remove to a paper towel-lined plate.

nutritional information

per patty: *Calories: 87, Total Fat: 4 g, Saturated Fat: 1 g, Protein: 4 g, Fiber: 1 g, Carbohydrates: 10 g, Sodium: 325 mg, Cholesterol: 40 mg*

falafel

preparation: 15 minutes | *processing:* pulsing | *cook time:* 8–10 minutes | *yield:* 24 balls

2 cups (344 g) dried chickpeas

⅔ cup (105 g) rough chopped onion

¼ cup (60 ml) water

¼ cup (15 g) flat leaf parsley

¼ cup (15 g) fresh cilantro leaves

8 garlic cloves, peeled

2 teaspoons dried cumin

1 teaspoon ground cayenne pepper

2 teaspoons Kosher salt

1 ½ teaspoons baking soda

½ cup (62 g) all-purpose flour, divided use

Canola oil for frying

1. Rinse and pick over chickpeas, removing any debris. Place in a bowl and cover with cool water. Cover and place in refrigerator for 12 to 24 hours.

2. Drain chickpeas. Place chickpeas, onion, water, parsley, cilantro, garlic, cumin, cayenne and salt into the Vitamix container and secure lid.

3. Select Variable 4.

4. Pulse several times until well mixed and finely ground. Sprinkle the baking soda and 1 Tablespoon flour over the mixture.

5. Pulse several times until evenly combined. Scrape mixture into a mixing bowl. Add remaining flour and mix by hand to combine. Refrigerate overnight before cooking.

6. Heat 3 inches (7.5 cm) of oil to 375°F (190°C) in a high-sided, heavy-bottomed pan. Form mixture into balls using 1 ½ Tablespoons at a time. When oil reaches the right temperature, drop about 6 balls in at a time. Fry for 1 minute, turn and fry for an additional minute. Use a slotted spoon or tongs to transfer to a paper towel-lined plate.

nutritional information

per serving (4 falafel balls): Calories: 345, Total Fat: 13 g, Saturated Fat: 1 g, Protein: 14 g, Fiber: 12 g, Carbohydrates: 47 g, Sodium: 973 mg, Cholesterol: 0 mg

greek chicken pockets

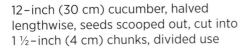

preparation: 20 minutes | ***processing:*** 3 seconds + pulsing
yield: 4 sandwiches

12-inch (30 cm) cucumber, halved lengthwise, seeds scooped out, cut into 1½-inch (4 cm) chunks, divided use

1½ cups (360 g) Greek yogurt

½ cup (120 g) sour cream

2 large garlic cloves, peeled

1 teaspoon dried dill weed

½ teaspoon salt

¼ teaspoon white or black pepper

¼ red onion, cut in 2 wedges and then in half, approximately ½ cup (85 g)

¼ cup (33 g) pitted Kalamata olives

2 4½-ounce (128 g) rotisserie chicken breast halves, skin and bones removed, each cut in 3 pieces

4 soft flax, oat and whole wheat pita pocket halves

4 large leaf lettuce leaves

1. Place ½ of the cucumber chunks into the Vitamix container and secure lid.

2. Select Variable 4.

3. Pulse 3 times. Stop machine and remove lid.

4. Add yogurt, sour cream, garlic, dill, salt and pepper to the Vitamix container and secure lid.

5. Select Variable 1.

6. Switch machine to Start and slowly increase speed to Variable 5.

7. Blend for 3 seconds. Scoop into medium bowl; set aside.

8. Rinse container. Place remaining cucumber into the Vitamix container and secure lid.

9. Select Variable 4.

10. Pulse 2 times. If necessary, use rubber scraper to move larger pieces to top; cover and Pulse once more. Drain and pour into another medium bowl.

11. Add onion to the Vitamix container and secure lid.

12. Select Variable 6.

13. Pulse 2 times. Use rubber scraper to move larger pieces to top and add olives. Secure lid and Pulse 2 times. Scrape into bowl with cucumber.

14. Add chicken to the Vitamix container and secure lid.

15. Select Variable 4.

16. Pulse 3 times. Add to vegetables in bowl.

17. Line each pita pocket with lettuce leaf. Spoon chicken mixture into pocket and drizzle yogurt mixture over the top. Serve additional sauce on the side. Store leftover sauce covered in refrigerator.

nutritional information

per sandwich (with 2 tablespoons sauce): *Calories: 230, Total Fat: 7 g, Saturated Fat: 2 g, Protein: 20 g, Fiber: 3 g, Carbohydrates: 23 g, Sodium: 669 mg, Cholesterol: 56 mg*

YOU'LL FIND QUICK AND HEALTHY DINNERS for hectic weekdays in *Meals* (page 123). Discover the wonderful variety of choices in *Sauces, Purées & Marinades* (page 143). *Side Dishes* (page 165) brings you satisfying side recipes and menu-building ideas, as well as ways kids can help in the kitchen. Get everyone involved and meal time is more fun.

weekdays

dinners

MEALS / SAUCES, PURÉES & MARINADES / SIDE DISHES

thin crust
pizza dough

preparation: 5 minutes | **processing:** 1 minute
bake time: 12–15 minutes | **yield:** 1 large or 2 very thin crusts

3 cups (375 g)
all-purpose flour

11 ounces (325 ml)
hot water

1 ¾ teaspoons instant
fast-rise yeast

3 ¾ teaspoons olive oil

1 ¼ teaspoons salt

1. Preheat oven to 425°F (220°C).

2. Place flour, yeast and salt into the Vitamix container and secure lid.

3. Select Variable 1.

4. Switch machine to Start and slowly increase speed to Variable 8. Blend for 5 seconds. Turn machine off and remove lid plug.

5. Select Variable 3.

6. Pulse about 60 short times in 45 seconds while slowly adding oil and water through the lid plug opening until a ball forms.

7. After ball has formed, Pulse continuously for 10 to 15 seconds.

8. With floured hands, remove dough and form into a round ball. Place in a greased bowl, turning over to grease all around. Let rise 10 minutes for a thin crust. Stretch into pizza and top as desired. Bake for 12 to 15 minutes.

nutritional information

per serving (⅛ of large pizza without toppings):
*Calories: 172, Total Fat: 2 g, Saturated Fat: 0 g, Protein: 5 g,
Fiber: 1 g, Carbohydrates: 33 g, Sodium: 366 mg, Cholesterol: 0 mg*

bright idea

Prepare two batches. Shape unused dough, place on cookie sheet in freezer until firm, remove, wrap well and freeze up to 1 month. Ready to bake any time!

family time

make-your-own-pizza night

Fridays are for family fun. Instead of ordering in, turn your kitchen into a pizza parlor. Set up prep stations where everyone can roll out Pizza Dough and assemble their own made-to-order pies.

Have Spicy Tomato Sauce (page 150) or Fresh Tomato Sauce (page 153) on hand, along with sliced pepperoni, chopped onions and mushrooms, sliced black olives, fresh basil and plenty of shredded mozzarella cheese. For more adventurous palates, try something new: diced cooked chicken, mild banana peppers, roasted red peppers, artichoke hearts, spinach leaves or feta cheese. Add a salad with Caesar Salad Dressing (page 103) to make it a meal.

spaghetti _with_ roasted vegetable sauce 💧

preparation: 20 minutes | **processing:** 1 minute 10 seconds | **bake time:** 20 minutes | **yield:** 6 servings

2 pounds (908 g) Roma tomatoes, halved

3 garlic cloves, peeled

½ large carrot, halved, about ½ cup (72 g)

1 ½ cups (144 g) button mushrooms

1 wedge red onion, peeled, 1 ½-inches (4 cm) thick

3 Tablespoons (45 ml) extra virgin olive oil

1 teaspoon salt

¼ teaspoon black pepper

4 ounces (113 g) Parmigiano-Reggiano or Parmesan cheese, cut in 1-inch (2.5 cm) chunks

12 ounces (340 g) whole wheat spaghetti

6-ounce (170 g) can tomato paste

¼ cup (6 g) firmly packed fresh basil leaves

¼ cup (6 g) firmly packed fresh oregano leaves

1. Preheat oven to 450°F (230°C). Place tomatoes, garlic, carrot, mushrooms and onion on an 11-inch x 17-inch (28 cm x 43 cm) cookie sheet. Drizzle with olive oil and sprinkle with salt and pepper. Roast 20 minutes or until tomatoes are very tender, stirring mushrooms and garlic once.

2. Meanwhile, place cheese into the Vitamix container and secure lid.

3. Select Variable 1.

4. Switch machine to Start and slowly increase speed to Variable 4.

5. Blend for 5 seconds or until finely grated. Remove to small bowl.

6. Cook pasta as directed on package while vegetables are roasting. Drain well, reserving ½ cup (120 ml) of cooking water. Keep warm.

7. Place all vegetables, liquid from pan and tomato paste into the Vitamix container and secure lid.

8. Select Smoothie program.

9. Switch machine to Start and allow machine to complete programmed cycle.

10. Add basil and oregano to the Vitamix container and secure lid.

11. Select Variable 1.

12. Switch machine to Start and slowly increase speed to Variable 3.

13. Blend for 5 seconds. If a thinner sauce is desired, add pasta cooking water 1 Tablespoon at a time. Serve sauce over pasta. Sprinkle with cheese.

nutritional information

per serving: *Calories: 403, Total Fat: 14 g, Saturated Fat: 4 g, Protein: 18 g, Fiber: 12 g, Carbohydrates: 60 g, Sodium: 684 mg, Cholesterol: 0 mg*

create your own

Simply add two tablespoons of vodka along with the ingredients in Step 7 to turn this zesty tomato sauce into a flavorful rendition of Vodka Marinara.

quick *lasagna bake*

preparation: 25 minutes | **processing:** 30 seconds + pulsing
bake time: 30 – 40 minutes | **yield:** 6 servings

12 ounces (340 g) penne pasta

4 ounces (113 g) Parmesan cheese,
cut in 1–inch (2.5 cm) cubes

1 large egg

1 ½ cups (360 g) cottage cheese

¼ cup (16 g) firmly packed
fresh parsley leaves

28–ounce (795 g) can whole
peeled tomatoes, well-drained

6–ounce (170 g) can tomato paste

1–inch (2.5 cm) wedge
medium onion, peeled

2 garlic cloves, peeled

½ teaspoon salt

¼ teaspoon black pepper

4 ounces (113 g) whole mushrooms

¼ cup (6 g) firmly packed
fresh basil leaves

2 cups (224 g) shredded
mozzarella cheese

1. Preheat oven to 375°F (190°C). Spray a 9–inch x 13–inch (23 cm x 33 cm)
   baking dish with cooking spray.

2. Cook pasta as directed on package. Drain; return to pot.

3. Place Parmesan cheese into the Vitamix container and secure lid.

4. Select Variable 1.

5. Switch machine to Start and slowly increase speed to Variable 4.

6. Blend for 5 seconds or until finely grated. Remove to a small bowl.

» **quick lasagna bake** continues on page 128

continued from page 126

quick **lasagna bake**

7. Add egg, cottage cheese and ½ cup (50 g) grated cheese to the Vitamix container and secure lid.

8. Select Variable 1.

9. Switch machine to Start and slowly increase speed to Variable 4.

10. Blend for 20 seconds. Turn machine off, remove lid, add parsley to the Vitamix container and secure lid.

11. Select Variable 3.

12. Pulse 3 times or until parsley is chopped. Scoop into a medium-sized bowl. Rinse container.

13. Place tomatoes, tomato paste, onion, garlic, salt and pepper into the Vitamix container and secure lid.

14. Select Variable 1.

15. Switch machine to Start and slowly increase speed to Variable 4.

16. Blend for 5 seconds. Stop machine and remove lid. Add mushrooms and basil to the Vitamix container and secure lid.

17. Select Variable 5.

18. Pulse 4 times until finely chopped. Add 1 cup (240 ml) of the sauce to cooked pasta; toss to coat.

19. Spoon half of the pasta into baking dish. Drop 1 cup (240 g) of cheese mixture by spoonfuls over pasta; spread to cover. Sprinkle with ¾ cup (84 g) mozzarella cheese. Spoon half of the remaining tomato sauce over cheese layer; spread to cover. Repeat layers. Sprinkle with remaining shredded and grated cheeses.

20. Bake 30 to 40 minutes or until hot and bubbly. If desired, garnish with additional fresh basil.

nutritional information

per serving: *Calories: 508, Total Fat: 17 g, Saturated Fat: 9 g, Protein: 35 g, Fiber: 3 g, Carbohydrates: 57 g, Sodium: 1172 mg, Cholesterol: 77 mg*

mediterranean
pita pizzas 🌢

preparation: 25 minutes | **processing:** 1 minute + pulsing
bake time: 12–15 minutes | **yield:** 8 pizzas

8 soft pita breads

½ small red onion, cut in 1 ½–inch (4 cm) chunks, approximately ½ cup (65 g)

¾ cup (100 g) pitted Kalamata olives

½ cup (120 g) plain Greek yogurt

⅓ cup (80 ml) chicken broth

¼ cup (60 ml) olive oil

2 15–ounce (426 g) cans garbanzo beans, drained, rinsed

¼ cup (36 g) toasted sesame seeds

½ lemon, seeded, thinly sliced

2 garlic cloves, peeled

4 Roma tomatoes, thinly sliced

8 ounces (227 g) feta cheese, crumbled

¼ cup (6 g) firmly packed, chopped mint leaves

¼ cup (6 g) firmly packed, chopped oregano leaves

1. Preheat oven to 400°F (200°C). Place pitas on 2 cookie sheets. Bake 5 minutes. Remove from oven.

2. Place onion into the Vitamix container and secure lid.

3. Select Variable 6.

4. Pulse 2 times. Scrape into small bowl.

5. Place olives into the Vitamix container and secure lid.

6. Select Variable 4.

7. Pulse 2 times. Scrape into another small bowl. Set aside. (No need to rinse container.)

» **mediterranean pita pizzas** *continues on page 130*

continued from page 129

mediterranean
pita pizzas

8. Place yogurt, broth, olive oil, beans, sesame seeds, lemon and garlic into the Vitamix container and secure lid.

9. Select Smoothie program.

10. Switch machine to Start and allow machine to complete programmed cycle, using the tamper to push ingredients into the blades if necessary.

11. Divide bean mixture evenly among pitas (about ½ cup (120 g) each) and spread evenly. Top with onion and olives. Arrange tomatoes on top and sprinkle with cheese, mint and oregano. Bake 7 to 10 minutes or until crisp and thoroughly heated. Cut in wedges to serve.

nutritional information

per pizza: *Calories: 491, Total Fat: 21 g, Saturated Fat: 6 g, Protein: 17 g, Fiber: 8 g, Carbohydrates: 57 g, Sodium: 1211 mg, Cholesterol: 27 mg*

feta-stuffed
chicken breasts

preparation: 20 minutes | ***processing:*** 10 seconds + pulsing
bake time: 40–50 minutes | ***yield:*** 5 servings

2 ounces (56 g) Parmesan cheese cut in 1–inch (2.5 cm) pieces

4 ounces (113 g) feta cheese, broken in 2 pieces

2 Tablespoons (11 g) fresh oregano leaves

2 Tablespoons (30 ml) olive oil

5 boneless skinless chicken breasts, 5 to 6 ounces (142–170 g) each

½ teaspoon salt

¼ teaspoon black pepper

1 pound (454 g) Roma tomatoes (5 large)

4 Tablespoons (60 g) tomato paste

½–inch (1.3 cm) wedge red onion, peeled

1 garlic clove, peeled

2 Tablespoons (11 g) fresh oregano leaves

1. Preheat oven to 375°F (190°C). Spray an 8–inch x 8–inch (20 cm x 20 cm) square baking dish with cooking spray.

2. Place Parmesan cheese into the Vitamix container and secure lid.

3. Select Variable 1.

4. Switch machine to Start and slowly increase speed to Variable 4.

5. Blend for 5 seconds. Stop machine and remove lid. Add feta cheese, oregano and oil to the Vitamix container and secure lid.

6. Select Variable 4.

7. Pulse 4 times for 1 second each time until coarsely chopped. Stop machine and scrape down sides with rubber scraper if necessary. Pulse once more.

» ***feta-stuffed chicken breasts*** continues on page 132

continued from page 131

feta-stuffed chicken breasts

8. Cut a pocket in thicker side of each chicken breast; season inside with salt and pepper. Spoon filling into each pocket. Secure with toothpicks or small metal skewers. Place in baking dish.

9. Place tomatoes, tomato paste, onion, garlic and oregano into the Vitamix container and secure lid.

10. Select Variable 1.

11. Switch machine to Start and slowly increase speed to Variable 4.

12. Blend for 5 seconds. Pour over chicken.

13. Bake 40 to 50 minutes or until chicken is no longer pink in center and meat thermometer inserted in thickest part of chicken reads 165°F (74°C). Remove picks or skewers. Stir sauce and serve over chicken.

nutritional information

per serving: *Calories: 307, Total Fat: 14 g, Saturated Fat: 5 g, Protein: 37 g, Fiber: 3 g, Carbohydrates: 9 g, Sodium: 758 mg, Cholesterol: 84 mg*

oven-braised round steak
in *vegetable gravy*

preparation: 10 minutes | **processing:** 2 seconds + pulsing
bake time: 1 ½–2 hours | **yield:** 6 servings

on the menu

This recipe makes a
generous amount
of gravy that would
be delicious served
over mashed potatoes
or wide egg noodles.

1 ½–2 pounds (908 g) eye of
beef round cut in serving pieces

1 Tablespoon vegetable oil

14 ½–ounce (412 g) can fire
roasted tomatoes

2 chunks onion, peeled,
1–inch (2.5 cm) each

2 sprigs fresh parsley

½ teaspoon salt

¼ teaspoon black pepper

½ cup (120 ml) milk

3 Tablespoons (24 g) all-purpose flour

4 ounces (113 g) whole
button mushrooms

chopped parsley, if desired

1. Preheat oven to 325°F (160°C). Heat oil in a 12–inch (30 cm) ovenproof skillet
   or chafing dish. Brown steaks over medium-high heat in oil on both sides. Set aside.

2. Meanwhile, place tomatoes, onion, parsley, salt, pepper, milk and flour
   into the Vitamix container and secure lid.

3. Select Variable 1.

4. Switch machine to Start and slowly increase speed to Variable 3.

5. Blend for 2 seconds. Stop machine and remove lid. Add mushrooms to the
   Vitamix container and secure lid.

6. Pulse 3 times. Pour tomato mixture over browned steaks. Cover and place in oven.

7. Bake 1 ½ to 2 hours or until meat is fork-tender. Garnish with chopped parsley if desired.

nutritional information

per serving: *Calories: 310, Total Fat: 14 g, Saturated Fat: 4 g, Protein: 36 g,
Fiber: 2 g, Carbohydrates: 10 g, Sodium: 302 mg, Cholesterol: 91 mg*

jamaican pulled pork

preparation: 15 minutes | **processing:** 43 seconds | **cook time:** 4–5 hours | **yield:** 4 cups pulled pork

1 ⅓ cups (195 g) chopped onion

2 garlic cloves, peeled

2 thin slices fresh ginger

1 Tablespoon Jerk Seasoning (page 162)

8–ounce (227 g) can pineapple chunks in juice, drained, reserve juice

1 Tablespoon vegetable oil

2 ½ pounds (1.1 kg) boneless pork shoulder roast, trimmed of outside fat

¾ cup (180 ml) barbecue sauce

1. Place onion, garlic, ginger, jerk seasoning, reserved pineapple juice (reserve pineapple chunks) and oil into the Vitamix container and secure lid.

2. Select Variable 1.

3. Switch machine to Start and slowly increase speed to Variable 4.

4. Blend for 20 seconds. If necessary, stop machine and use rubber spatula to scrape sides of container. Secure lid and blend on Variable 4 an additional 3 seconds.

5. Spray 3 ½ to 4–quart slow cooker with cooking spray. Place meat in cooker. Pour onion mixture over meat, turning to coat all sides. Cover and cook on High heat setting 4 ½ to 5 hours or until fork-tender. (If desired, roast can be cooked on Low heat setting for 9 to 10 hours.)

6. Just before meat is done, place drained pineapple chunks and barbecue sauce into the Vitamix container and secure lid.

7. Select Variable 1.

8. Switch machine to Start and slowly increase speed to Variable 4.

9. Blend for 20 seconds.

10. Remove meat to cutting board. Pour juices into medium-sized bowl. Shred meat using 2 forks, discarding any fat. Place back in slow cooker and pour ¾ cup (180 ml) of the meat juices over pork. Pour pineapple barbecue sauce over meat and stir to coat. Cover and cook on High heat setting 20 minutes or until thoroughly heated.

11. Serve as an entrée with fried plantains, or fill sandwich buns for pulled pork sandwiches.

nutritional information

per ½ cup (224 g) serving: *Calories: 261, Total Fat: 12 g, Saturated Fat: 4 g, Protein: 28 g, Fiber: 1 g, Carbohydrates: 9 g, Sodium: 470 mg, Cholesterol: 95 mg*

ingredient IQ

Canned pineapple is used in this recipe because the pork is prepared in a slow cooker; fresh pineapple contains a powerful enzyme that would over-tenderize the meat.

build a meal

big bold barbecue

For an updated summer barbecue menu, make a big batch of Jamaican Pulled Pork and add some out-of-the-ordinary fixings.

Instead of coleslaw, prepare Fennel, Apple and Radish Chopped Salad (page 165). Serve Bacon Cheddar Cornbread (page 186) alongside, rather than sandwich buns. Cut colorful watermelon in wedges and pile on big white platters. Washtubs filled with ice can hold plenty of cold beer or apple cider.

Serve up the feast on metal plates, along with utensils wrapped in red or blue bandanas and tied with sturdy twine. For dessert, spoon simple Strawberry Yogurt Freeze (page 297) into tin cups.

potato cheese **pierogies**

preparation: 20 minutes | **processing:** 10 seconds + pulsing | **cook time:** 40–60 minutes | **yield:** 4 dozen

2 cups (240 g) whole wheat flour

2 ½ cups (312 g) all-purpose unbleached flour

½ teaspoon salt

⅓ cup (80 ml) extra virgin olive oil

2 large eggs

1–1 ½ cups (240–360 ml) water

1 pound (454 g) russet potatoes, peeled, cut into chunks

1 ½ teaspoons extra virgin olive oil

⅔ cup (106 g) finely chopped onion

½ cup (120 g) low fat cottage cheese

2 cups (280 g) sauerkraut, rinsed, chopped

½ cup (56 g) shredded sharp Cheddar cheese

½ teaspoon salt

½ teaspoon freshly ground black pepper

5 Tablespoons (75 ml) extra virgin olive oil, divided use

5 Tablespoons (75 ml) water

1. Mix flours and salt in a large mixing bowl. Set aside.

2. Place olive oil, eggs and water into the Vitamix container and secure lid.

3. Select Variable 1.

4. Switch machine to Start and slowly increase speed to Variable 5.

5. Blend for 10 seconds. Stop machine and remove lid.

6. Pour into dry ingredients and mix by hand to combine.
   Set aside on a well floured surface.

» **potato cheese pierogies** continues on page 138

continued from page 136

potato cheese **pierogies**

7. To prepare the filling, place potatoes in a large saucepan and cover with water. Bring to a boil and cook until tender, 15 to 17 minutes. Drain well.

8. Heat 1 ½ teaspoons olive oil in a large skillet over medium heat. Add onion and cook until tender, about 5 minutes.

9. Place potatoes, onion, cottage cheese, sauerkraut, cheddar, salt and pepper into the Vitamix container.

10. Select Variable 2.

11. Pulse 10 to 12 times to thoroughly blend.

12. Put a large pot of water on to boil. Coat 1 large baking sheet with cooking spray. Place next to the stove. Very generously dust 2 more large baking sheets with flour.

13. Roll out one disk of dough on a well floured surface until it's about ⅟₁₆–inch (.2 cm) thick, approximately 16–inch x 20–inch (40 cm x 50 cm) oval. Use a 3 ½–inch (9 cm) round cutter to cut out dough. Moisten the edges of each round with water. Place 1 Tablespoon of the filling in the center of each round. Fold the dough over the filling and press the edges; crimp with fork to seal completely. Place on a well floured baking sheet. Repeat with the remaining disks of dough.

14. Cook the pierogies in 5 batches in the boiling water until they float to the top. Transfer with a slotted spoon to the baking sheet coated with cooking spray.

15. Preheat oven to 200°F (93°C).

16. Heat 1 Tablespoon of oil and water in a large nonstick skillet over medium heat. Add 8 to 10 pierogies and cook until browned on both sides, 6 to 10 minutes total. Transfer to a baking sheet and keep warm in the oven while you repeat the process with the remaining pierogies.

nutritional information

per serving (4 pierogies): *Calories: 343, Total Fat: 15 g, Saturated Fat: 3 g, Protein: 10 g, Fiber: 5 g, Carbohydrates: 42 g, Sodium: 517 mg, Cholesterol: 41 mg*

thai peanut
chicken stir-fry

preparation: 10 minutes | **processing:** 1 minute
cook time: 8 minutes | **yield:** 4 servings

looking good

» Use half of a red pepper and half of a green pepper in recipe. Spoon extra peanut sauce into remaining pepper halves to create a garnish for platter of rice.

16-ounce (480 ml) can lite coconut milk

2 Tablespoons (30 ml) soy sauce

2 Tablespoons (30 ml) rice wine vinegar

2 garlic cloves, peeled

1 teaspoon brown sugar

1 teaspoon sesame oil

½ jalapeño pepper, seeds removed

1 cup (144 g) cocktail peanuts

1 Tablespoon vegetable oil

1 pound (454 g) boneless chicken breast cut in ¾-inch (2 cm) cubes

1 bell pepper, any color, cut in bite-size pieces

4 cups (632 g) hot cooked rice

1. Place coconut milk, soy sauce, vinegar, garlic, brown sugar, sesame oil, jalapeño and peanuts into the Vitamix container in the order listed and secure lid.

2. Select Smoothie program.

3. Switch machine to Start and allow machine to complete programmed cycle. (Stop machine after 45 seconds if you prefer a chunky peanut sauce.)

4. Heat oil in a medium-sized nonstick skillet over medium-high heat. Add chicken; cook and stir 4 minutes or until browned. Add bell pepper; cook and stir 3 minutes or until chicken is no longer pink and peppers are crisp-tender.

5. Reduce heat to low. Stir in 1 cup (240 ml) of the peanut sauce. Cook over low heat just until heated. For thinner sauce, add water one Tablespoon at a time. Serve over rice.

nutritional information

per serving: Calories: 567, Total Fat: 28 g, Saturated Fat: 13 g, Protein: 36 g, Fiber: 4 g, Carbohydrates: 45 g, Sodium: 496 mg, Cholesterol: 66 mg

pork tenderloin in orange-ginger sauce

preparation: 10 minutes | **processing:** 10 seconds | **cook time:** 13–15 minutes | **yield:** 5 servings

1 ¼–1 ½ pounds (568–680 g) pork tenderloin

½ teaspoon salt

¼ teaspoon black pepper

1 orange, peeled, halved, plus 1-inch x 2-inch (2.5 cm x 5 cm) strip orange zest

2 thin slices fresh ginger

1 teaspoon dark sesame oil

1 cup (240 ml) chicken broth

2 Tablespoons (30 ml) honey

1 Tablespoon cornstarch

1 Tablespoon vegetable oil

1 small red bell pepper cut in thin bite-size strips

2 Tablespoons (12 g) sliced green onions

1. Cut tenderloin crosswise into 5 pieces. Place each piece cut side down between pieces of plastic wrap. Pound to ¼-inch (.6 cm) thickness with meat mallet or rolling pin, starting at center. Season with salt and pepper. Set aside.

2. Place orange, ginger, sesame oil, broth, honey and cornstarch into the Vitamix container and secure lid.

3. Select Variable 1.

4. Switch machine to Start and slowly increase speed to Variable 6. Blend for 10 seconds.

5. Heat oil in 12-inch (30 cm) nonstick skillet over medium-high heat. Add pork. Cook 8 to 10 minutes or until deep golden brown, turning once. Remove from skillet; add bell pepper. Cook 2 minutes. Add pork back to skillet. Pour orange mixture into skillet. Cook 3 minutes or until bubbly and thickened, and pork is no longer pink, stirring occasionally. Serve sauce over pork. Sprinkle with green onions.

nutritional information

per serving: *Calories: 233, Total Fat: 9 g, Saturated Fat: 2 g, Protein: 26 g, Fiber: 1 g, Carbohydrates: 13 g, Sodium: 496 mg, Cholesterol: 80 mg*

fish with *cilantro sauce*

preparation: 15 minutes | *processing:* 10 seconds | *cook time:* 10-12 minutes | *yield:* 4 servings

½ cup (120 ml) plus 1 Tablespoon extra virgin olive oil, divided use

¼ cup (60 ml) chicken or vegetable broth

2 Tablespoons (30 ml) white or regular balsamic vinegar

2 Tablespoons (30 ml) honey

3 cups (48 g) firmly packed cilantro, long stems removed

2 cups (60 g) firmly packed fresh spinach leaves

½ cup (8 g) firmly packed parsley sprigs, long stems removed

½ lime, cut in thin slices

1 thin slice jalapeño

1 large garlic clove, peeled

½ teaspoon salt

1 ½ pounds (608 g) white fish (about 4 filets)

1. Place ½ cup (120 ml) olive oil, broth, vinegar, honey, cilantro, spinach, parsley, lime, jalapeño, garlic and salt into the Vitamix container in the order given and secure lid.

2. Select Variable 1.

3. Switch machine to Start and slowly increase speed to Variable 5. Blend for 10 seconds, using the tamper to push ingredients into the blades.

4. Heat 1 Tablespoon of the oil in a large nonstick skillet over medium heat. Add fish. Cook 10 to 12 minutes, depending on thickness of filets, turning over once, until fish flakes easily with fork. Serve sauce over fish. Store leftover sauce covered in refrigerator.

nutritional information

per serving (1 filet and ¼ cup (60 ml) sauce): Calories: 422, Total Fat: 28 g, Saturated Fat: 4 g, Protein: 35 g, Fiber: 1 g, Carbohydrates: 10 g, Sodium: 392 mg, Cholesterol: 85 mg

kale *and* **basil** *pesto*

preparation: 5 minutes | **processing:** 30 seconds
yield: 1 ¾ cups (420 ml)

1 cup (240 ml) olive oil

1 cup (100 g) grated Parmesan cheese

3 medium garlic cloves, peeled

2 cups (80 g) fresh basil leaves

2 cups (135 g) fresh kale leaves

3 Tablespoons (25 g) pine nuts

¼ teaspoon salt

pinch black pepper

1. Place all ingredients into the Vitamix container in the order listed and secure lid.

2. Select Variable 1.

3. Switch machine to Start and slowly increase speed to Variable 3.

4. Blend for 30 seconds or until desired consistency is reached.

nutritional information

per 2 tablespoon (30 ml) serving: *Calories: 96, Total Fat: 10 g, Saturated Fat: 2 g, Protein: 2 g, Fiber: 0 g, Carbohydrates: 1 g, Sodium: 85 mg, Cholesterol: 3 mg*

build a meal

breadsticks *and* pesto

Use leftovers from the Thin Crust Pizza Dough recipe (page 123) (or make a double batch) to create your own breadsticks.

Instead of stretching the dough into a pizza pan after the initial rise, roll it into breadsticks and place on a cookie sheet. Add a sprinkle of coarse salt and bake as directed, checking periodically for doneness.

Serve the hot sticks with a side of Kale and Basil Pesto. Now you have a delicious accompaniment for Spaghetti with Roasted Vegetable Sauce (page 124) and mixed greens dressed with Tomato Vinaigrette (page 102).

citrus marinade

preparation: 7 minutes | **processing:** 30 seconds
yield: 2 cups (480 ml)

¼ cup (60 ml) white
wine vinegar

1 Tablespoon honey
or agave nectar

1 medium orange, peeled,
halved, seeded

½ lime, peeled, halved

1 Tablespoon chopped
green onion

1 Tablespoon chopped
fresh ginger

½ teaspoon salt

½ cup (120 ml) canola oil

¼ cup (60 ml) olive oil

2 teaspoons sesame oil

¼ cup (15 g) fresh
parsley leaves

¼ cup (5 g) fresh
cilantro leaves

1. Place vinegar, honey, orange, lime, onion, ginger and salt into the Vitamix container in the order listed and secure lid.

2. Select Variable 1.

3. Switch machine to Start and slowly increase speed to Variable 4.

4. Blend for 20 seconds. Reduce speed to Variable 1 and remove the lid plug.

5. Slowly add oils in a thin stream through the lid plug opening. Add parsley and cilantro. Blend for 10 seconds.

nutritional information

per 2 tablespoon (30 ml) serving: Calories: 53, Total Fat: 6 g, Saturated Fat: 1 g, Protein: 0 g, Fiber: 0 g, Carbohydrates: 1 g, Sodium: 37 mg, Cholesterol: 0 mg

bright idea

This tangy accent is more than just a marinade for chicken or pork. Brush it on vegetables, pineapple, pears or apples while grilling to add some extra pizazz.

kitchen chemistry

guiltless flavor enhancer

Agave nectar is a syrupy liquid that comes from the agave plant—the same succulent used to make tequila. It is slightly sweeter than honey or sugar, and can be substituted in recipes for honey, maple syrup or corn syrup on a 1–1 basis. Agave nectar has a low glycemic index, so it doesn't cause a spike in your blood sugar. When used in place of granulated sugar, use ⅔ cup nectar for every 1 cup sugar, and reduce other liquids by ¼ to ⅓. You can find agave nectar in your grocer's baking or health food aisle.

green *curry sauce*

preparation: 10 minutes | **processing:** 15 seconds
yield: 1 ½ cups (360 ml)

2 teaspoons sesame oil

¼ cup (24 g) peeled, chopped
ginger root

2 garlic cloves, peeled, sliced

¼ cup (60 ml) dry white wine

1 Tablespoon lime juice

2 teaspoon green curry paste

13 ½–ounce (383 ml)
can coconut milk

½ teaspoon fish sauce
(preferably Nam Pla)

½ cup (8 g) cilantro leaves

Kosher salt, freshly ground
black pepper and lime, to taste

on the menu

Drizzle this Green
Curry Sauce over seared
striped bass, or serve it
as a dip to provide a spicy
Thai kick for Crab Cakes
with Sweet Chilli Dipping
Sauce (page 254).

1. In a small saucepan, heat sesame oil over medium heat. Add the
   ginger and garlic and sauté for 30 seconds. Add the white wine and
   the lime juice and reduce to almost dry. Add the curry paste, coconut milk
   and fish sauce and reduce to 1 cup (240 ml) liquid. Let cool 10 minutes.

2. Place the cooked mixture and the cilantro into the Vitamix container
   and secure lid.

3. Select Variable 1.

4. Switch machine to Start and slowly increase speed to Variable 10.

5. Blend for 15 seconds.

nutritional information

per ¼ cup (60 ml) serving: *Calories: 154, Total Fat: 15 g, Saturated Fat: 12 g,
Protein: 2 g, Fiber: 1 g, Carbohydrates: 3 g, Sodium: 54 mg, Cholesterol: 0 mg*

sun-dried
tomato pesto

preparation: 10 minutes | ***processing:*** 15–20 seconds | ***yield:*** 3 cups (720 g)

2 garlic cloves, peeled

1 teaspoon Kosher salt

⅔ cup (90 g) pine nuts

8 oil-packed sun-dried
tomato halves

1 cup (24 g) fresh basil leaves

½ cup (24 g) fresh
oregano leaves

⅔ cup (180 ml) extra
virgin olive oil

2 tomatoes (250 g), seeded

2 Tablespoons (12 g)
grated Romano cheese

1. Place all ingredients into the Vitamix container
   in the order listed and secure lid.

2. Select Variable 1.

3. Switch machine to Start and slowly increase
   speed to Variable 5.

4. Blend for 15 to 20 seconds, using the tamper to press
   the ingredients into the blades.

nutritional information

per 2 tablespoon (30 g) serving: *Calories: 92, Total Fat: 9 g, Saturated Fat: 2 g,
Protein: 1 g, Fiber: 1 g, Carbohydrates: 2 g, Sodium: 93 mg, Cholesterol: 0 mg*

asian pesto *sauce*

preparation: 10 minutes | **processing:** 15 seconds
yield: 1 cup (240 ml)

¼ cup (60 ml) orange juice, freshly squeezed

2 Tablespoons (30 ml) wine vinegar, any type

2 Tablespoons (30 ml) dark sesame oil

1 Tablespoon low sodium soy sauce

2 teaspoons hoisin sauce

½ teaspoon Asian chili sauce

2 cups (60 g) fresh spinach leaves, washed, dried

¼ cup (4 g) cilantro sprigs

8 fresh basil leaves

1 garlic clove, peeled

2 Tablespoons (12 g) ginger, peeled

½ teaspoon orange peel, grated

1. Place all ingredients into the Vitamix container in the order listed and secure lid.

2. Select Variable 1.

3. Switch machine to Start and slowly increase speed to Variable 10.

4. Blend for 15 seconds, using the tamper to press the ingredients into the blades.

nutritional information

per ¼ cup (60 ml) serving: *Calories: 85, Total Fat: 7 g, Saturated Fat: 1 g, Protein: 1 g, Fiber: 1 g, Carbohydrates: 6 g, Sodium: 228 mg, Cholesterol: 0 mg*

build a meal

citrus sensation menu

Oranges take center stage from entrée to dessert. Start with Asian Pesto Sauce, a perfect complement to grilled swordfish or salmon. Prepare fish with a simple rub of olive oil, salt and pepper, then place in a wire fish screen basket and grill over medium-high heat, turning about every two minutes. You'll know it's done when it just begins to flake when prodded with a fork.

Pour the Asian Pesto Sauce over each piece of fish and serve alongside white rice. For a light vegetable side that echoes the orange notes of the sauce, grill asparagus spears and top with Orange Basil Vinaigrette (page 97). Serve Orange Sorbet (page 293) for a refreshing light and sweet finish.

red pepper *walnut pesto*

preparation: 5 minutes | **processing:** 30 seconds
bake time: 15–20 minutes | **yield:** 4 cups (1.0 L)

on the menu

Toss this Red Pepper Walnut Pesto with hot fettuccine or linguini and cooked, peeled, tail-off shrimp for a fantastic lunch or dinner entrée.

6 ounces (270 g) red bell pepper	⅔ cup (20 g) fresh basil leaves
2 medium garlic cloves, peeled	½ cup (50 g) grated Parmesan cheese
¾ cup (75 g) walnuts, toasted	½ teaspoon salt
	¼ teaspoon black pepper
½ cup (27 g) sun-dried tomatoes	½ cup (120 ml) olive oil

1. Preheat oven to 400°F (200°C). Halve and trim red pepper, place skin side down on oven rack. Roast 15 to 20 minutes or until skin is well shriveled but not blackened. Place in plastic bag for 15 minutes to steam.

2. Place garlic cloves in medium-sized saucepan, add cold water to cover and bring to a boil. Reduce heat and simmer for 5 minutes or until soft enough to pierce with a fork. Remove using a slotted spoon and set aside to drain.

3. Place all ingredients into the Vitamix container in the order listed and secure lid.

4. Select Variable 1.

5. Switch machine to Start and slowly increase speed to Variable 3. Blend for 30 seconds or until desired consistency is reached.

nutritional information

per 2 tablespoon (30 g) serving: *Calories: 30, Total Fat: 3 g, Saturated Fat: 1 g, Protein: 1 g, Fiber: 0 g, Carbohydrates: 1 g, Sodium: 40 mg, Cholesterol: 1 mg*

gifts from your kitchen

pesto to go

Make your own Italian foodie gift by starting with a jar of homemade pesto. After sealing the pesto inside a glass jar, cover the lid with a square of fabric or tissue paper. Secure with a rubber band and tie with a coordinating ribbon or raffia. Pair your pretty pesto with a jar of dried, tri-color pasta, a loaf of Rosemary Focaccia (page 189) wrapped in parchment and tied with twine, and a wedge of Parmigiano-Reggiano. Arrange the items in a large colander, wrap in cellophane and finish with a colorful ribbon. Be sure to keep pesto refrigerated until just before gifting.

spicy **tomato sauce** ⚉

preparation: 5 minutes | **processing:** 1 minute | **cook time:** 30 minutes | **yield:** 2 cups (480 ml)

4 medium Roma tomatoes
(270 g), halved

3 Tablespoons (45 g) tomato paste

2 Tablespoons (25 g) cream cheese

½ teaspoon salt

½ teaspoon black pepper

½ jalapeño pepper

½ teaspoon dried basil

1 garlic clove, peeled

¼ teaspoon dried oregano

1 ½ teaspoons cornstarch mixed
in 1 Tablespoon cool water

1. Place tomatoes, tomato paste, cream cheese, salt, pepper,
   jalapeño, basil, garlic and oregano into the Vitamix container
   in the order listed and secure lid.

2. Select Purée program.

3. Switch machine to Start and allow machine to complete
   programmed cycle, using the tamper to press the
   ingredients into the blades.

4. Pour into saucepan, stir in the cornstarch mixture,
   and simmer for 30 minutes.

nutritional information

per ¼ cup (60 ml) serving: *Calories: 28, Total Fat: 1 g, Saturated Fat: 1 g,
Protein: 1 g, Fiber: 1 g, Carbohydrates: 3 g, Sodium: 168 mg, Cholesterol: 4 mg*

roasted creamy
basil tomato sauce 💧

preparation: 1 hour | **processing:** 1 minute 15 seconds | **roast time:** 1 hour | **yield:** 5 ½ cups (1.3 L)

6 large Roma tomatoes (450 g), quartered

2 ½ ounces (70 g) onion, peeled, halved

6 garlic cloves, peeled

2 Tablespoons (30 ml) olive oil

2 Tablespoons (8 g) chopped fresh parsley

1 cup (240 ml) milk

4 ounces (113 g) mascarpone cheese

1 teaspoon chipotle pepper sauce

1 ½ teaspoons salt

½ teaspoon black pepper

¼ cup (24 g) fresh basil leaves

¼ cup (14 g) sun-dried tomatoes

1. Preheat oven to 350°F (180°C).

2. Toss tomatoes, onion and garlic in olive oil and place in baking pan, cover with foil.

3. Roast in oven for 1 hour. Cool 15 minutes.

4. After roasting, place tomato mixture, parsley, milk, mascarpone, pepper sauce, salt and pepper into the Vitamix container in the order listed and secure lid.

5. Select Smoothie program.

6. Switch machine to Start and allow machine to complete programmed cycle.

7. Select Variable 1. Switch machine to Start and remove the lid plug. Add basil and sun-dried tomatoes through the lid plug opening.

8. Blend an additional 15 seconds.

nutritional information

per ¼ cup (60 ml) serving: Calories: 46, Total Fat: 4 g, Saturated Fat: 2 g, Protein: 1 g, Fiber: 0 g, Carbohydrates: 2 g, Sodium: 187 mg, Cholesterol: 7 mg

*fresh **tomato sauce*** 💧

preparation: 5 minutes | ***processing:*** 1 minute
cook time: 35–40 minutes | ***yield:*** 3 ½ cups (840 ml)

6 medium Roma tomatoes (400 g), halved

¼ cup (40 g) chopped onion

½ cup (65 g) chopped carrot

2 Tablespoons (30 g) tomato paste

1 garlic clove, peeled

½ teaspoon dried basil

½ teaspoon dried oregano

½ teaspoon fresh lemon juice

½ teaspoon brown sugar

¼ teaspoon salt

1. Place all ingredients into the Vitamix container in the order listed and secure lid.

2. Select Smoothie program.

3. Switch machine to Start and allow machine to complete programmed cycle.

4. Pour into saucepan and simmer for 35 to 40 minutes. Season to taste with additional salt and pepper if necessary.

nutritional information

per ¼ cup (60 ml) serving: *Calories: 12, Total Fat: 0 g, Saturated Fat: 0 g, Protein: 0 g, Fiber: 1 g, Carbohydrates: 3 g, Sodium: 48 mg, Cholesterol: 0 mg*

macaroni *with* **cheese sauce**

preparation: 5 minutes | **processing:** 4–5 minutes | **bake time:** 30 minutes | **yield:** 6 cups (1.4 kg)

2 cups (210 g) elbow
macaroni, uncooked

¼ cup (60 g) butter

¼ cup (30 g) all-purpose flour

¼ teaspoon salt

1 ⅓ cups (320 ml) milk

½ teaspoon yellow mustard

1 ½ cups (173 g) cubed American
cheese or other mild yellow cheese

crumb topping:

2 slices bread, white or wheat

1 teaspoon butter

dash garlic powder

dash black pepper

dash dried oregano

dash onion powder

dash cayenne pepper

1. Preheat oven to 350°F (180°C).

2. Cook macaroni as directed on package. Drain.

3. Spray an 8-inch x 8-inch (20 cm x 20 cm) baking dish with vegetable cooking spray then add macaroni to dish.

4. Place butter, flour, salt, milk and mustard into the Vitamix container in the order listed and secure lid.

5. Select Variable 1.

6. Switch machine to Start and slowly increase speed to Variable 8.

7. Blend for 4 minutes or until steam escapes from the vented lid. As mixture thickens, it will not splash as much.

» **macaroni with cheese sauce** continues on page 156

continued from page 154

macaroni with *cheese sauce*

8. Reduce speed to Variable 1 and remove the lid plug.
Add cheese through the lid plug opening.

9. Blend for 30 seconds.

10. Pour mixture over macaroni and mix thoroughly. Cover with crumb
topping mixture and bake until top is golden brown, about 30 minutes.

11. To make crumb topping:

12. Toast and butter 2 pieces of bread and cut into quarters.

13. Select Variable 2.

14. Switch machine to Start and remove the lid plug.

15. Drop bread through the lid plug opening. Blend until you
have crumbs. Add seasonings to the crumbs.

nutritional information

per 1 cup (240 g) serving: *Calories: 363, Total Fat: 17 g, Saturated Fat: 10 g,
Protein: 13 g, Fiber: 2 g, Carbohydrates: 40 g, Sodium: 593 mg, Cholesterol: 47 mg*

fajita marinade

preparation: 5 minutes | **processing:** 1 minute
yield: 2 cups (480 ml)

kitchen prep

This marinade is mild enough that you can marinate chicken, steak or pork overnight. Achieve extra flavor without that "over-tenderized" effect.

½ cup (120 ml) olive oil

¼ cup (60 ml) red wine vinegar

½ cup (120 ml) Worcestershire sauce

½ cup (120 ml) soy sauce

2 limes, peeled, halved

¼ teaspoon dried oregano

¼ teaspoon hot sauce

2 garlic cloves, peeled

1. Place all ingredients into the Vitamix container in the order listed and secure lid.

2. Select Smoothie program.

3. Switch machine to Start and allow machine to complete programmed cycle.

nutritional information

per 2 tablespoon (30 ml) serving: Calories: 40, Total Fat: 4 g, Saturated Fat: 0 g, Protein: 0 g, Fiber: 0 g, Carbohydrates: 2 g, Sodium: 375 mg, Cholesterol: 0 mg

planning ahead

marinating 101

Besides tenderizing meat and adding flavor, another benefit of marinades is they can be made ahead of time. Marinades can be stored in the refrigerator up to 2 days if they contain fresh produce, or up to a month if they do not. Most marinades can be frozen up to 2 months.

Always marinate in the refrigerator. Marinate beef, veal, pork and lamb in roast, steak or chop form up to 2 days. Marinate poultry and cubed meat from 2 hours up to overnight, if the marinade is only mildly acidic.

Another handy way to save time: freeze meat in a container with a marinade. The day before you plan to cook it, move the covered container from the freezer to the refrigerator. As it thaws, the meat will absorb the marinade.

ingredient IQ

Ginger Paste keeps
refrigerated for 3 weeks
or frozen for 6 months.
Use in equal amounts to
substitute for fresh ginger,
or half the amount for
ground ginger.

ginger *paste*

preparation: 5 minutes | **processing:** 20 seconds
yield: 2 ½ cups (600 g)

3 cups (300 g) fresh
ginger root, unpeeled

1 cup (240 ml) water

1. Place ginger and water into the Vitamix container
   and secure lid.

2. Select Variable 1.

3. Switch machine to Start and slowly increase
   speed to Variable 6.

4. Blend for 20 seconds, using the tamper to press the
   ingredients into the blades.

5. If not using immediately, strain. Cover a baking sheet with plastic
   wrap and place rounded teaspoons ½–inch (1.3 cm) apart.
   Freeze until solid and store in plastic bag.

nutritional information

per 2 tablespoon (30 g) serving: *Calories: 12, Total Fat: 0 g, Saturated Fat: 0 g,
Protein: 0 g, Fiber: 0 g, Carbohydrates: 3 g, Sodium: 3 mg, Cholesterol: 0 mg*

fresh ginger peanut teriyaki marinade 💧

preparation: 5 minutes | ***processing:*** 1 minute | ***yield:*** 3 cups (720 ml)

¾ cup (180 ml) soy sauce

¼ cup (60 ml) rice vinegar

1 Tablespoon sesame oil

1 medium orange, peeled, halved, seeded

½ lime, peeled

1 Tablespoon honey or agave nectar

¼ cup (40 g) fresh pineapple, core included or canned pineapple

1 garlic clove, peeled

1 teaspoon chopped fresh ginger

¼ cup (55 g) brown sugar

1 cup (145 g) peanuts or ½ cup (130 g) Peanut Butter (page 55)

1. Place all ingredients into the Vitamix container in the order listed and secure lid.

2. Select Smoothie program.

3. Switch machine to Start and allow machine to complete programmed cycle, using the tamper to press the ingredients into the blades.

nutritional information

per 2 tablespoon (30 ml) serving: *Calories: 30, Total Fat: 2 g, Saturated Fat: 0 g, Protein: 1 g, Fiber: 0 g, Carbohydrates: 3 g, Sodium: 329 mg, Cholesterol: 0 mg*

ginger beet purée

preparation: 15 minutes | *processing:* 20–25 seconds | *bake time:* 2 hours | *yield:* 2 ¼ cups (540 g)

2 ¾ pounds (1.2 kg) fresh beets, about 3 large

2 Tablespoons (30 ml) olive oil

½ cup (72 g) almonds

1 ½ Tablespoons fresh chopped ginger

1 Tablespoon fresh cilantro leaves

1 teaspoon ground ginger

⅛ teaspoon salt

⅛ teaspoon pepper

1. Preheat oven to 425°F (220°C). Clean and cut beets to leave 1–inch (2.5 cm) of stem. Double wrap beets in foil and roast for 2 hours. Cool.

2. Peel beets, trim ends and cut into quarters.

3. Place oil, beets, almonds, fresh ginger, cilantro, ground ginger, salt and pepper into the Vitamix container in the order listed and secure lid.

4. Select Variable 1.

5. Switch machine to Start and slowly increase speed to Variable 8.

6. Blend for 20 to 25 seconds, using the tamper if necessary to push the ingredients into the blades.

7. Serve as an accompaniment to grilled vegetables, fish, poultry or meat.

nutritional information

per ¼ cup (60 ml) serving: Calories: 136, Total Fat: 7 g, Saturated Fat: 1 g, Protein: 4 g, Fiber: 5 g, Carbohydrates: 15 g, Sodium: 143 mg, Cholesterol: 0 mg

jerk seasoning

preparation: 5 minutes | ***processing:*** 13 seconds | ***yield:*** ¾ cup (180 g)

3 Tablespoons (30 g) whole allspice

1 Tablespoon black peppercorns

2 teaspoons whole cloves

2 teaspoons crushed red pepper flakes

1 Tablespoon dried thyme leaves

1 Tablespoon salt

1 teaspoon ground cinnamon

¼ cup (55 g) firmly packed brown sugar

1. Place allspice, peppercorns, cloves and pepper flakes into the Vitamix container and secure lid.

2. Select Variable 1.

3. Switch machine to Start and slowly increase speed to Variable 4.

4. Blend for 10 seconds or until mixture is a medium-fine powder. Add remaining ingredients and secure lid.

5. Select Variable 1.

6. Switch machine to Start and slowly increase speed to Variable 3.

7. Blend for 3 seconds.

8. Store in covered container at room temperature. Use as a rub on grilled pork, shrimp or chicken, or any Jamaican-influenced recipe.

nutritional information

per tablespoon: *Calories: 22, Total Fat: 0 g, Saturated Fat: 0 g, Protein: 0 g, Fiber: 1 g, Carbohydrates: 5 g, Sodium: 600 mg, Cholesterol: 0 mg*

roasted celery root *and* **pear purée**

preparation: 15 minutes | ***processing:*** 5–10 seconds | ***bake time:*** 35–40 minutes | ***yield:*** 6 servings

vegetables:

¾ pound (340 g) celery root, peeled, cut into 1-inch (2.5 cm) chunks

1 ½ cups (240 g) yellow pear, cut into 1-inch (2.5 cm) chunks

3 Tablespoons (45 ml) walnut oil

½ teaspoon salt

sauce:

⅔ cup (160 ml) pear juice

¼ cup (60 ml) half and half

2 Tablespoons (30 ml) walnut oil

1 garlic clove, roasted, peeled

garnish:

Nutmeg, freshly grated

Toasted walnuts

1. Preheat oven to 400°F (200°C). In a 13-inch x 9-inch (33 cm x 23 cm) baking pan stir together all vegetable ingredients.

2. Bake for 35 to 40 minutes, stirring occasionally, until celery root is tender. Remove from oven.

3. Meanwhile, place sauce ingredients into the Vitamix container in the order listed; add roasted vegetables and secure lid.

4. Select Variable 1.

5. Switch machine to Start and slowly increase speed to Variable 3. Blend for 5 to 10 seconds or until slightly smooth.

6. Pour celery root purée into bowl. Garnish with sprinkles of fresh nutmeg and a handful of toasted walnuts.

nutritional information

per serving: Calories: 174, Total Fat: 13 g, Saturated Fat: 2 g, Protein: 1 g, Fiber: 2 g, Carbohydrates: 15 g, Sodium: 255 mg, Cholesterol: 4 mg

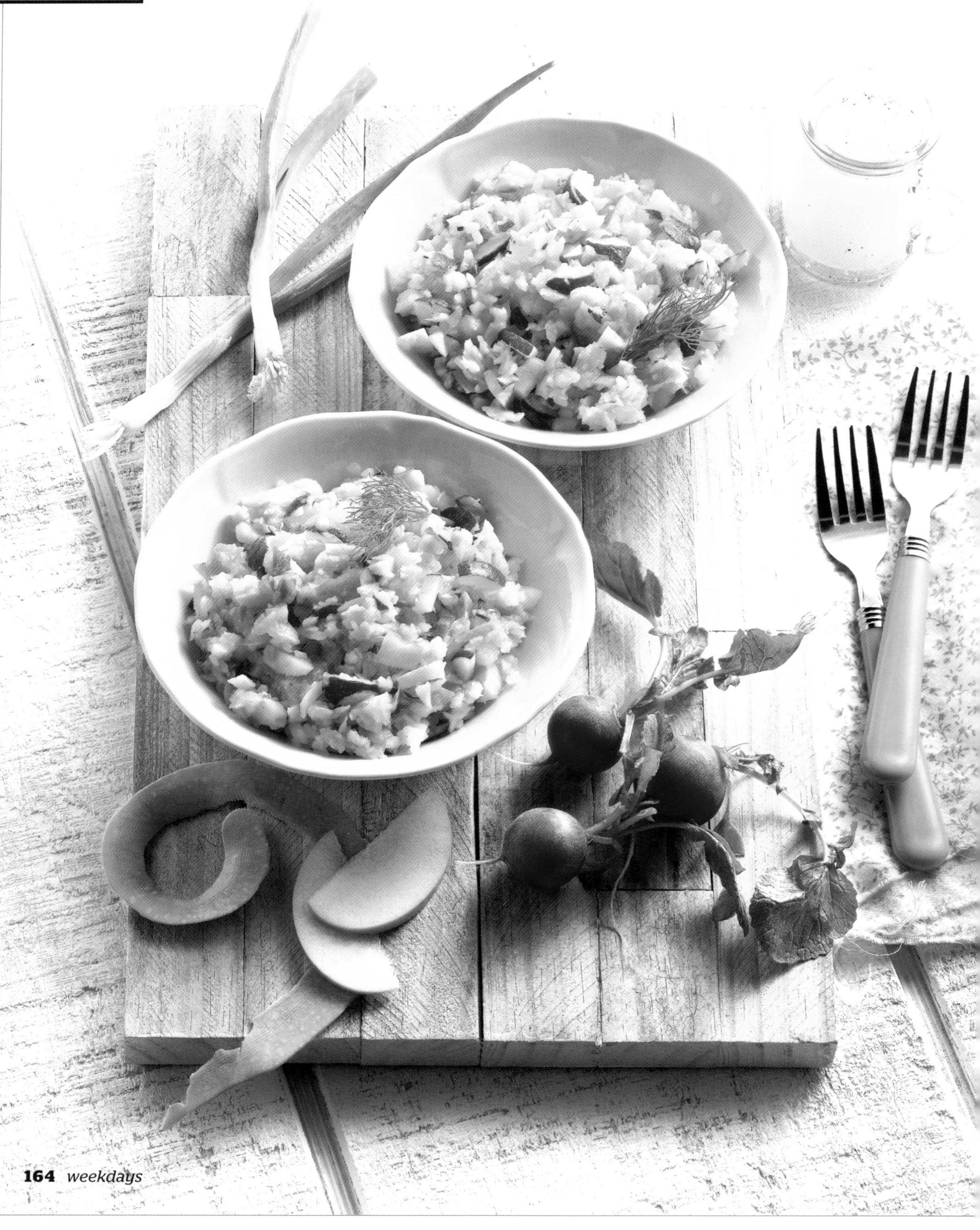

fennel, apple and radish chopped salad

preparation: 10 minutes | **processing:** 10 seconds + pulsing
yield: 5 servings

fruits and vegetables:

4 cups (350 g) fennel, trimmed, sliced into 1–inch (2.5 cm) pieces (1 large head)

½ large green apple, cored, cut into 4 wedges

½ large red apple, cored, cut into 4 wedges

8 small radishes, trimmed

4 scallions, cut into 1–inch (2.5 cm) pieces

1 cup (165 g) thinly sliced apricots

dressing:

¼ cup (60 ml) apricot oil or walnut oil

3 Tablespoons (45 ml) rice vinegar

½ teaspoon salt

¼ teaspoon freshly cracked black pepper

1. Place ½ of the fruits and vegetables into the Vitamix container in the order listed and secure lid.

2. Select Variable 5.

3. Pulse up to 10 times or until coarsely chopped; place into colander.

4. Repeat with remaining fruits and vegetables. Drain vegetables for 5 minutes in colander to remove excess liquid; discard liquid.

» **fennel, apple and radish chopped salad**
continues on page 166

freshen up

Fresh plums or ripe Anjou pears can be used if fresh apricots aren't available; you'll just be trading a bit of the tartness for more sweetness.

family time

sous chefs in training

Getting the kids involved in cooking helps them learn healthy eating habits and is a fun activity to bring the family together.

Washing veggies is an easy task to give younger children while you get organized. Then, while you head up the slicing, chopping and heating duties, designate your assistants to measuring detail. They can measure each ingredient into individual bowls before adding to your Vitamix container. After you select the correct setting for your recipe, and make sure the lid is secure, let them do the all-important job of pressing the button.

continued from page 165

fennel, apple and radish chopped salad

5. Pour fruits and vegetables into serving bowl.

6. Place all dressing ingredients into the Vitamix container in the order listed and secure lid.

7. Select Variable 1.

8. Switch machine to Start and slowly increase speed to Variable 5.

9. Blend for 10 seconds.

10. Pour dressing over vegetable mixture; mix well.

11. Refrigerate leftovers.

nutritional information

per serving: *Calories: 161, Total Fat: 11 g, Saturated Fat: 1 g, Protein: 2 g, Fiber: 4 g, Carbohydrates: 16 g, Sodium: 273 mg, Cholesterol: 0 mg*

barbecued artichokes
with **green goddess dressing**

preparation: 3 hours | **processing:** 35 seconds | **cook time:** 50 minutes
yield: 2 cups (480 ml) marinade | 3 cups (720 ml) dressing

4 artichokes

1 teaspoon whole cloves

marinade:

½ cup (120 ml) freshly squeezed
lemon juice

½ cup (120 ml) soy sauce

⅓ cup (80 ml) extra virgin olive oil

¼ cup (60 g) Dijon mustard

2-inch x 2-inch (5 cm x 5 cm) cube
of unpeeled ginger

⅓ cup (8 g) fresh chopped basil,
about 26 leaves

1 Tablespoon of your favorite chili sauce

green goddess dressing:

1 cup (240 g) mayonnaise

½ cup (110 g) sour cream

2 lemons, peeled, seeded, or 2
Tablespoons (30 ml) lemon juice

½ cup (30 g) fresh tarragon leaves

½ cup (30 g) fresh chopped parsley

½ cup (30 g) fresh chopped chives

2 garlic cloves, peeled, minced

2 anchovies

½ teaspoon salt

1. Trim sharp ends off all the exposed artichoke leaves. Bring a large
amount of water to a boil. Add cloves and artichokes. Cover and
cook at a low boil until a leaf pulls off easily and tastes tender, about
40 minutes. Drain and split in half. Scrape out thistle.

» **barbecued artichokes with green goddess dressing**
continues on page 168

continued from page 167

barbecued artichokes
with *green goddess dressing*

2. Place all marinade ingredients into the Vitamix container in the order listed and secure lid.

3. Select Variable 1.

4. Switch machine to Start and slowly increase speed to Variable 5.

5. Blend for 15 seconds.

6. Marinate the artichokes for 2 hours. Clean and dry the Vitamix container.

7. Place all Green Goddess Dressing ingredients into the Vitamix container in the order listed and secure lid.

8. Select Variable 1.

9. Switch machine to Start and slowly increase speed to Variable 10.

10. Blend for 20 seconds.

11. Grill artichokes until lightly charred on both sides, about 10 minutes of cooking. Transfer to dinner plates and serve with the Green Goddess Dressing.

nutritional information

per serving (1 artichoke and 2 tablespoons (30 ml) dressing):
Calories: 276, Total Fat: 19 g, Saturated Fat: 3 g, Protein: 8 g, Fiber: 10 g, Carbohydrates: 25 g, Sodium: 1236 mg, Cholesterol: 7 mg

sweet potato purée with maple bacon and sage

preparation: 15 minutes | **processing:** 20 – 25 seconds | **bake time:** 25 – 30 minutes | **yield:** 5 servings

vegetables:

4 cups (530 g) sweet potatoes or yams, peeled, cut into 1–inch (2.5 cm) chunks

1 large onion, peeled, cut into 8 wedges (150 g)

3 Tablespoons (45 ml) extra virgin olive oil

sauce:

¾ cup (180 ml) chicken stock, hot

2 Tablespoons (8 g) fresh chervil

2 Tablespoons (30 ml) real maple syrup

¾ teaspoon pumpkin pie spice

¼ teaspoon dried marjoram leaves

garnish:

3 ounces (85 g) maple flavored bacon, cooked, crumbled

1 Tablespoon chopped fresh sage

1 Tablespoon real maple syrup

1. Preheat oven to 400°F (200°C). In a 13–inch x 9–inch (33 cm x 23 cm) baking pan stir together all vegetable ingredients. Bake for 25 to 30 minutes, stirring occasionally, until sweet potatoes are tender. Remove from oven.

2. Meanwhile, place sauce ingredients in Vitamix container in the order listed; add roasted sweet potato mixture and secure lid.

3. Select Variable 1.

4. Switch machine to Start and slowly increase speed to Variable 4.

5. Blend for 20 to 25 seconds or until smooth, using tamper if necessary.

6. Place in serving bowl. Garnish with bacon, fresh sage and a drizzle of maple syrup.

nutritional information

per serving: *Calories: 320, Total Fat: 16 g, Saturated Fat: 4 g, Protein: 9 g, Fiber: 4 g, Carbohydrates: 35 g, Sodium: 506 mg, Cholesterol: 20 mg*

zucchini, summer squash
and scallions pancakes

preparation: 10 minutes | **processing:** 15–20 seconds | **cook time:** 10–12 minutes
yield: 12 (3 ½–inch (9 cm)) pancakes

pancakes:

2 cups (250 g) yellow summer squash
cut into 1–inch (2.5 cm) pieces

2 cups (250 g) zucchini cut into
1–inch (2.5 cm) pieces

3 scallions cut into 1–inch (2.5 cm) pieces

2 large eggs

¾ cup (94 g) all-purpose flour

1 teaspoon baking powder

¾ teaspoon salt

¼ teaspoon freshly cracked
black pepper

garnish:

Sour cream

Chives

1. Place summer squash, zucchini and scallions into the Vitamix container in the order listed and secure lid.

2. Select Variable 1.

3. Switch machine to Start and slowly increase speed to Variable 3.

4. Blend for 5 to 10 seconds, using tamper if necessary. Stop machine and remove lid.

5. Add eggs, flour, baking powder, salt and pepper into the Vitamix container and secure lid.

6. Switch machine to Start and slowly increase speed to Variable 3.

7. Blend for 5 to 10 seconds, using tamper if necessary. Mixture will be bright green and mostly smooth.

8. Heat a nonstick skillet over medium heat. Scoop out desired amount of pancake batter. Cook until first side is golden brown (5 to 6 minutes).

9. Turn pancakes over; continue cooking until second side is golden brown (5 to 6 minutes). Inside of cooked pancakes will be bright green and soft.

10. Repeat with remaining batter.

11. Serve pancakes with a dollop of sour cream and chives.

12. Refrigerate leftovers.

nutritional information

per 3 ½-inch (9 cm) pancake (without garnish): *Calories: 45, Total Fat: 1 g, Saturated Fat: 0 g, Protein: 2 g, Fiber: 1 g, Carbohydrates: 8 g, Sodium: 196 mg, Cholesterol: 36 mg*

creamy polenta with *mushrooms* and *chives*

preparation: 10 minutes | **processing:** 5–10 seconds
cook time: 5–6 minutes | **yield:** 4 servings

polenta:

1 ½ cups (360 ml) chicken broth

½ cup (120 ml) whipping cream

½ cup (80 g) roasted corn

¾ teaspoon salt

1 garlic clove, roasted, peeled

1-inch (2.5 cm) shallot piece

⅔ cup (80 g) quick
cooking polenta

mushrooms:

3 Tablespoons (45 g) butter

2 ½ cups (180 g) sliced
mushrooms, such as Shiitake,
button or Portobello

1 Tablespoon chopped shallots

garnish:

2 Tablespoons (30 g) butter

1 Tablespoon chopped
fresh chives

1. Place broth, cream, corn, salt, garlic and shallot into the Vitamix container in the order listed and secure lid.

2. Select Variable 1.

3. Switch machine to Start and slowly increase speed to Variable 3.

4. Blend for 5 seconds; there should be small pieces of roasted corn evident.

5. Pour mixture into 2-quart saucepan. Bring to a boil over medium-high heat; reduce heat to medium and add polenta.

6. Stir constantly until polenta thickens to desired texture (5 to 6 minutes).

7. Pour into serving bowl; keep warm.

8. Meanwhile, in a 12-inch (30 cm) skillet, melt butter over medium heat. Add mushrooms and shallots. (Mushrooms should be in a single layer.)

9. Cook, stirring occasionally, until mushrooms are light brown; set aside.

10. For garnish, in small skillet, over medium heat, melt butter. Heat until butter turns golden brown, about 2 minutes; set aside.

11. To serve, scoop out a portion of polenta, top with small amount of mushroom shallot mixture, then drizzle with melted butter and sprinkle with chives.

12. Refrigerate leftovers.

nutritional information

per serving: *Calories: 419, Total Fat: 29 g, Saturated Fat: 17 g, Protein: 9 g, Fiber: 3 g, Carbohydrates: 33 g, Sodium: 1011 mg, Cholesterol: 83 mg*

build a meal

rich and comforting

Just right for a cozy winter's night or a day in need of comfort food, this menu is elaborate enough to impress your foodie friends at a dinner party, but easy enough to make on a weeknight for the family.

Start with a salad of butter and romaine lettuce topped with Raspberry Maple Dressing (page 96). Serve wedges of Rosemary Focaccia (page 189) alongside your main course of Oven-Braised Round Steak in Vegetable Gravy (page 133) with a side dish of Creamy Polenta with Mushrooms and Chives.

To keep it simple, opt for button mushrooms in the polenta as you'll also use them in the vegetable gravy.

coconut milk, curry *and* chili paste *with* vegetables ☕

preparation: 15 minutes | **processing:** 5 minutes 45 seconds
bake time: 25–30 minutes | **yield:** 6 servings

vegetables:

1 pound (454 g) fingerling potatoes, washed, cut into 2-inch (5 cm) pieces

2 cups (200 g) cauliflower pieces, trimmed

2 cups (220 g) green beans, trimmed

1 ½ cups (240 g) yellow onion, cut into wedges

¼ cup (60 ml) vegetable oil

½ teaspoon salt

¼ teaspoon freshly cracked black pepper

sauce:

⅔ cup (160 ml) coconut milk

1 teaspoon roasted chili paste

¼ teaspoon curry powder

¼ teaspoon salt

⅛ teaspoon freshly cracked black pepper

1. Preheat oven to 400°F (200°C). In a 13-inch x 9-inch (33 cm x 23 cm) baking pan stir together all vegetable ingredients.

2. Bake for 25 to 30 minutes, stirring occasionally, until potatoes are tender. Remove from oven; keep warm.

3. Select Hot Soup program.

4. Switch machine to Start and allow machine to complete programmed cycle.

5. Pour hot sauce over vegetables; mix well.

6. Refrigerate leftovers.

nutritional information

per serving: *Calories: 217, Total Fat: 15 g, Saturated Fat: 6 g, Protein: 3 g, Fiber: 5 g, Carbohydrates: 21 g, Sodium: 310 mg, Cholesterol: 0 mg*

build a meal

coconut craving

Carrying one ingredient throughout a menu is a good way to make sure your flavors complement one another. It's always a good idea to check that your guests like that particular ingredient, though, just in case.

Coconut milk is used in each recipe of this spicy menu that mixes a variety of textures and colors. Decorate the table with bright tropical colors and serve Coconut Milk, Curry and Chili Paste with Vegetables alongside Thai Peanut Chicken Stir-Fry (page 139). Cut the heat with an icy Piña Colada (page 346).

ingredient IQ

Russet potatoes contain more starch than red potatoes, making them ideal for mashing. They are also high in protein and have almost no fat.

garlicky potatoes with tomatoes and basil

preparation: 10 minutes | **processing:** 2–5 seconds
cook time: 20 minutes | **yield:** 5 servings

3 cups (450 g) Russet potatoes, cut into 1-inch (2.5 cm) chunks

⅓ cup (80 ml) milk

⅓ cup (80 g) sour cream

2 Tablespoons (30 ml) extra virgin olive oil

2 garlic cloves, roasted, peeled

½ teaspoon salt

¼ teaspoon freshly cracked black pepper

1 cup (155 g) seeded, finely chopped tomatoes (red, yellow, orange)

¼ cup (10 g) finely chopped fresh basil leaves

1. In a 4-quart saucepan place potatoes; add water just to cover potatoes. Over high heat, bring to a boil (7 to 8 minutes).

2. Reduce heat to medium; continue cooking until potatoes are softened (10 to 12 minutes). Drain.

3. Place cooked potatoes, milk, sour cream, olive oil, garlic, salt and pepper into the Vitamix container and secure lid.

4. Select Variable 1.

5. Switch machine to Start and blend for 2 to 5 seconds or until slightly chunky. Use tamper if necessary.

6. DO NOT over process as potatoes will get gummy.

7. Scrape potatoes into serving bowl; carefully fold in tomatoes and basil. Serve warm.

nutritional information

per serving: *Calories: 163, Total Fat: 9 g, Saturated Fat: 3 g, Protein: 3 g, Fiber: 1 g, Carbohydrates: 18 g, Sodium: 251 mg, Cholesterol: 12 mg*

relax and entertain on

weekends

BRUNCHES / APPETIZERS / DESSERTS / COCKTAILS

LEISURELY WEEKEND BRUNCHES bring to mind good friends, indulgent treats and, most importantly, the extra time to enjoy them both. Enhance your brunch menus with recipes from *Breads* (page 183), *Brunch Mains* (page 197) and *Juices & Milks* (page 213). You'll also find gift-giving ideas for sharing baked treats from your kitchen, and creative ways frozen juices and smoothies can add to the fun.

weekends

brunches

BREADS / BRUNCH MAINS / JUICES & MILKS

cranberry nut bread

preparation: 10 minutes | **processing:** 15 seconds
bake time: 60 minutes | **yield:** 1 loaf (16 slices)

1 ½ teaspoons
baking powder

½ teaspoon baking soda

1 teaspoon salt

1 cup (120 g) whole
wheat flour

1 cup (125 g)
all-purpose flour

1 orange, peeled,
halved, seeded

2-inch (5 cm) strip of
orange peel

¼ cup (60 ml) light
olive oil or vegetable oil

¾ cup (180 ml) milk

1 cup (200 g) sugar

1 large egg

1 cup (100 g)
fresh cranberries

½ cup (60 g)
chopped walnuts

1. Preheat oven to 350°F (180°C). Spray an 8 ½–inch x 4 ½–inch (21 cm x 11 cm) loaf pan with cooking spray.

2. Combine baking powder, baking soda, salt and flours in a large-sized mixing bowl. Set aside.

3. Place orange, orange peel, oil, milk, sugar and egg into the Vitamix container in the order listed and secure lid.

4. Select Variable 1.

» **cranberry nut bread** *continues on page 184*

What better way to warm the hearts of friends and family than with fresh baked bread? Small loaves are perfect for hostess gifts, showers and holiday or housewarming parties.

Bake Cranberry Nut Bread or Chocolate Chunk Banana Bread (page 191) in charming mini loaf pans; fill mini loaf pans ⅔ full and place on a cookie sheet before putting them in the oven. Keep your oven temperature true to the baking instructions, but check for doneness after 20 to 30 minutes. Allow the loaves to cool in the pans, then wrap each loaf in a large sheet of cellophane and tie with a colorful ribbon. Place a mini loaf of each bread variety in a gift bag or basket.

continued from page 183

cranberry nut bread

5. Switch machine to Start and slowly increase speed to Variable 8.

6. Blend for 15 seconds.

7. Pour orange juice mixture into the dry ingredients, mixing by hand until ingredients are just combined.

8. Gently fold in cranberries and walnuts.

9. Spread the batter in the prepared loaf pan.

10. Bake for 60 minutes or until a knife inserted into the center comes out clean.

nutritional information

per slice: *Calories: 171, Total Fat: 6 g, Saturated Fat: 1 g, Protein: 3 g, Fiber: 2 g, Carbohydrates: 27 g, Sodium: 236 mg, Cholesterol: 14 mg*

almond zucchini *pineapple bread*

preparation: 15 minutes | ***processing:*** 10–15 seconds | ***bake time:*** 60 minutes | ***yield:*** 1 loaf (16 slices)

1 cup (120 g) whole wheat flour	½ cup (60 g) chopped almonds
½ cup (62 g) all-purpose unbleached flour	½ cup (75 g) raisins
1 teaspoon baking soda	1 large egg
¼ teaspoon baking powder	⅔ cup (130 g) sugar
¼ teaspoon salt	1 teaspoon vanilla extract
¼ teaspoon nutmeg	½ teaspoon almond extract
½ teaspoon ground cinnamon	¼ cup (38 g) fresh pineapple chunks
½ teaspoon allspice	1 ½ cups (190 g) zucchini chunks

1. Preheat oven to 350°F (180°C). Spray an 8 ½–inch x 4 ½–inch (21 cm x 11 cm) loaf pan with cooking spray.

2. Combine flours, baking soda, baking powder, salt, nutmeg, cinnamon and allspice in a medium-sized mixing bowl. Stir in almonds and raisins. Set aside.

3. Place egg, sugar, vanilla extract, almond extract, pineapple and zucchini into the Vitamix container and secure lid.

4. Select Variable 1.

5. Switch machine to Start and slowly increase speed to Variable 4. Blend for 10 to 15 seconds. Pour batter into dry mixture and mix gently by hand to combine.

6. Pour into prepared loaf pan. Bake for 60 minutes or until a knife inserted into the center comes out clean.

nutritional information

per slice: *Calories: 126, Total Fat: 3 g, Saturated Fat: 0 g, Protein: 3 g, Fiber: 2 g, Carbohydrates: 23 g, Sodium: 130 mg, Cholesterol: 13 mg*

bacon cheddar
cornbread

preparation: 10 minutes | ***processing:*** 15 seconds + pulsing
bake time: 23–28 minutes | ***yield:*** 9 servings

1 cup (125 g) all-purpose flour

1 cup (150 g) cornmeal

2 teaspoons baking powder

½ teaspoon baking soda

¼ teaspoon coarse salt

1 cup (240 ml) buttermilk

¼ cup (50 g) sugar

2 large eggs

3 Tablespoons (45 ml) canola oil

4 ounces (113 g) cheddar
cheese, cut into chunks

3 slices bacon,
cooked, crumbled

on the menu

 Serve this savory cornbread with an Onion Cheese Frittata (page 208) and a salad of strawberries and spinach in a Balsamic Fig Dressing (page 100).

1. Preheat oven to 375°F (190°C). Spray an 8–inch x 8–inch (20 cm x 20 cm) baking pan with nonstick cooking spray.

2. Combine flour, cornmeal, baking powder, baking soda and salt in a medium-sized mixing bowl. Set aside.

3. Place buttermilk, sugar, eggs and oil into the Vitamix container in the order listed and secure lid.

4. Select Variable 1.

5. Switch machine to Start and slowly increase speed to Variable 4.

6. Blend for 10 seconds until smooth. Stop machine and remove lid.

7. Add cheese to the Vitamix container and secure lid.

8. Select Variable 3.

9. Pulse 8 to 10 times until cheese is chopped. Remove lid.

10. Add flour mixture to the Vitamix container and secure lid.

11. Switch machine to Start and blend for 5 seconds until smooth. Remove lid plug.

12. Add bacon through the lid plug opening and replace lid plug.

13. Pulse 5 to 6 times to mix. Pour into prepared pan.

14. Bake 23 to 28 minutes until lightly browned.

nutritional information

per serving: *Calories: 248, Total Fat: 11 g, Saturated Fat: 3 g, Protein: 9 g, Fiber: 1 g, Carbohydrates: 29 g, Sodium: 394 mg, Cholesterol: 66 mg*

rosemary *focaccia*

preparation: 10 minutes | ***processing:*** 15 seconds + pulsing
bake time: 18 – 25 minutes | ***yield:*** 8 servings

1 cup (240 ml) warm water,
105 – 115°F (40 – 46°C)

1 Tablespoon honey

1 package (¼ ounce)
rapid rising yeast

2 Tablespoons (30 ml)
light olive oil, divided use

2 cups (250 g) all-purpose flour

½ cup (60 g) whole wheat flour

1 teaspoon coarse salt

2 Tablespoons (4 g) fresh
rosemary, divided use

2 Tablespoons (10 g) grated
Parmesan cheese

1. Combine water and honey in a small bowl. Sprinkle yeast over
   warm water and let stand 5 minutes. Stir in 1 Tablespoon olive oil.

2. Place flours, salt and 1 Tablespoon rosemary into the Vitamix container
   and secure lid.

3. Select Variable 1.

4. Switch machine to Start and blend until a hole forms in the center,
   about 5 seconds. Remove lid plug.

5. Add yeast mixture through the lid plug opening and slowly increase
   speed to Variable 3. Mix until dough forms, about 10 seconds.

6. To knead dough, scrape the sides of the container with a rubber
   spatula pulling dough to the center.

7. Select Variable 3.

» **rosemary focaccia** *continues on page 190*

continued from page 189

rosemary *focaccia*

8. Pulse 10 times. Scrape the sides of the container and repeat this step 4 times until dough is elastic.

9. Allow dough to drop onto lightly floured surface and shape into a ball. (Use a rubber spatula to remove any remaining dough.) Cover loosely and let stand 10 minutes.

10. Preheat oven to 400°F (200°C). Line a baking sheet with silpat mat.

11. Press dough onto baking sheet to ½-inch (1.3 cm) thickness. Lightly cover dough with a clean towel and let rise 15 to 20 minutes. Use the bottom of a wooden spoon or your knuckles to press indentations into the dough. Drizzle with the remaining olive oil, rosemary and Parmesan cheese. Sprinkle with salt, if desired.

12. Bake 18 to 25 minutes or until edges are browned.

nutritional information

per serving: *Calories: 174, Total Fat: 4 g, Saturated Fat: 1 g, Protein: 5 g, Fiber: 2 g, Carbohydrates: 30 g, Sodium: 270 mg, Cholesterol: 1 mg*

chocolate chunk
banana bread

preparation: 10 minutes | **processing:** 35 seconds + pulsing
bake time: 50–55 minutes | **yield:** 1 loaf (16 slices)

ingredient IQ

Greek–style yogurt gives this bread an unusually dense, rich texture. It is thicker and creamier than other yogurts because it is strained to remove the whey.

1 ½ cups (190 g) all-purpose flour

½ cup (60 g) whole wheat flour

1 Tablespoon baking powder

½ teaspoon coarse salt

⅓ cup (80 ml) canola oil

½ cup (100 g) sugar

1 large egg

3 ounces (85 g) semisweet chocolate, coarsely chopped

¾ cup (180 ml) milk

½ cup (120 g) vanilla Greek-style yogurt

2 medium bananas, peeled, cut into chunks

1. Preheat oven to 350°F (180°C). Spray a 9–inch x 5–inch (23 cm x 13 cm) loaf pan with nonstick cooking spray.

2. Combine flours, baking powder and salt in medium-sized mixing bowl.

3. Place oil, sugar and egg into the Vitamix container in the order listed and secure lid.

4. Select Variable 1.

5. Switch machine to Start and slowly increase speed to Variable 3. Blend for 15 seconds until smooth. Stop machine and remove lid. Add chocolate to the Vitamix container and secure lid.

6. Select Variable 3.

7. Pulse 4 times until chocolate is chopped. Remove lid. Add milk and yogurt to the Vitamix container and secure lid.

» **chocolate chunk banana bread** continues on page 192

continued from page 191

chocolate chunk
banana bread

8. Select Variable 1.

9. Switch machine to Start and slowly increase speed to Variable 3. Blend for 5 seconds. Stop machine and remove lid.

10. Add flour mixture to the Vitamix container and secure lid.

11. Select Variable 1.

12. Switch machine to Start and slowly increase speed to Variable 3. Blend an additional 5 seconds.

13. Reduce speed to Variable 3 and remove the lid plug. Add bananas through the lid plug opening.

14. Blend for 10 seconds until chopped.

15. Pour into prepared pan. Bake 50 to 55 minutes or until golden brown.

nutritional information

per slice: *Calories: 171, Total Fat: 7 g, Saturated Fat: 2 g, Protein: 3 g, Fiber: 1 g, Carbohydrates: 26 g, Sodium: 156 mg, Cholesterol: 15 mg*

apricot breakfast bread

preparation: 15 minutes | ***processing:*** 15–25 seconds
bake time: 45–60 minutes | ***yield:*** 1 loaf (16 slices)

1 cup (120 g) whole wheat flour

1 cup (125 g) all-purpose flour

¼ teaspoon baking soda

2 teaspoons baking powder

¼ teaspoon salt

¼ cup (60 ml) water

1 orange, peeled, halved, seeded

1 large egg

¾ cup (150 g) sugar

2 Tablespoons (30 g) butter

1 cup (130 g) chopped dried apricots

½ cup (60 g) chopped pecans

1. Preheat oven to 350°F (180°C). Spray an 8 ½–inch x 4 ½–inch (21 cm x 11 cm) loaf pan with cooking spray.

2. Combine flours, baking soda, baking powder and salt in a medium-sized mixing bowl. Set aside.

3. Place water, orange, egg, sugar and butter into the Vitamix container in the order listed and secure lid.

4. Select Variable 1.

5. Switch machine to Start and slowly increase speed to Variable 6. Blend for 15 to 25 seconds. Stop machine.

6. Pour batter into dry mixture and mix gently by hand to combine. Fold in apricots and pecans.

7. Pour mixture into prepared loaf pan. Bake for 45 to 60 minutes or until a knife inserted into the center comes out clean.

nutritional information

per slice: *Calories: 154, Total Fat: 5 g, Saturated Fat: 1 g, Protein: 3 g, Fiber: 2 g, Carbohydrates: 27 g, Sodium: 126 mg, Cholesterol: 17 mg*

mocha tea *bread*

preparation: 10 minutes | **processing:** 15 – 20 seconds
bake time: 40 – 50 minutes | **yield:** 1 loaf (16 slices)

1 cup (125 g) all-purpose flour

1 cup (120 g) whole wheat flour

1 teaspoon baking powder

1 teaspoon baking soda

4 teaspoons instant coffee granules

½ teaspoon salt

2 large eggs

½ cup (110 g) butter, softened

¾ cup (150 g) sugar

½ cup (120 ml) milk

½ cup (120 g) vanilla low fat yogurt

1 teaspoon vanilla extract

5 ounces (142 g) coarsely chopped semisweet chocolate

½ cup (70 g) chopped almonds, toasted

1. Preheat oven to 325°F (160°C). Spray a 9–inch x 5–inch (23 cm x 13 cm) loaf pan with cooking spray.

2. Combine flours, baking powder, baking soda, coffee and salt in a medium-sized mixing bowl. Set aside.

3. Place eggs, butter, sugar, milk, yogurt and vanilla extract into the Vitamix container in the order listed and secure lid.

4. Select Variable 1.

5. Switch machine to Start and slowly increase speed to Variable 5.

6. Blend for 15 to 20 seconds.

7. Pour wet mixture into dry ingredients and mix gently by hand to combine. Fold in chocolate and almonds.

8. Pour batter into prepared loaf pan.

9. Bake for 40 to 50 minutes or until a knife inserted into the center comes out clean. Cool in pan for 20 minutes before slicing.

nutritional information

per slice: *Calories: 233, Total Fat: 12 g, Saturated Fat: 6 g, Protein: 5 g, Fiber: 2 g, Carbohydrates: 29 g, Sodium: 238 mg, Cholesterol: 43 mg*

kitchen chemistry

roasted and ready to eat

Exposing almonds to dry heat causes their natural sugars to break down and caramelize; that's why the extra step of roasting adds such satisfying crunch and intensified flavor.

You can roast almonds easily at home to use in recipes like Mocha Tea Bread. Spread a single layer of raw almonds on an ungreased cookie sheet. Bake in a 300°F (150°C) oven about 20 minutes, stirring halfway through, until fragrant and browned. Stir again and let cool completely before using in recipes.

carrot raisin
muffins

preparation: 10 minutes | **processing:** 30 seconds
bake time: 20 – 25 minutes | **yield:** 12 muffins

1 ⅔ cups (200 g)
self-rising flour

½ teaspoon
baking soda

1 teaspoon ground
cinnamon

1 teaspoon pumpkin
pie spice

1 cup (165 g) raisins

¾ cup (100 g)
chopped carrots

2 large eggs

¾ cup (150 g) sugar

⅔ cup (160 ml)
light olive oil

1. Preheat oven to 350°F (180°C). Spray a 12-cup muffin tin with cooking spray or line cups with paper liners.

2. Place flour, baking soda, cinnamon and pumpkin pie spice in a medium-sized mixing bowl and stir lightly. Stir in raisins. Set aside.

3. Place carrots into the Vitamix container and secure lid.

4. Select Variable 2.

5. Switch machine to Start. Blend for a few seconds until very finely chopped. Stop machine and remove lid.

6. Add eggs, sugar and oil to the carrots in the Vitamix container and secure lid.

» **carrot raisin muffins** continues on page 198

»

create your own

If you prefer a richer carrot flavor, set chopped carrots aside in Step 3 and proceed with this recipe. Add carrots with dry ingredients in Step 10.

kitchen chemistry

power breakfast

Carrots (rich in folate and dietary fiber), raisins (packed with boron, a mineral that aids in bone density) and light olive oil (the good kind of fat) make this muffin a triple-treat.

On the weekends, bake a batch of muffins and then wrap them individually for freezing. Each weeknight, take one out to thaw on the counter. In the morning, pop it in the microwave to warm up for a few seconds and you've got a tasty muffin to get your day off to a great start—fast!

continued from page 197

carrot raisin
muffins

7. Select Variable 1.

8. Switch machine to Start and slowly increase speed to Variable 6.

9. Blend for 20 seconds until thick and creamy.

10. Pour carrot mixture into flour mixture and fold by hand to combine. Spoon the mixture into prepared muffin tin.

11. Bake for 20 to 25 minutes until golden brown. Transfer to a wire rack to cool before serving.

nutritional information

per muffin: *Calories: 273, Total Fat: 13 g, Saturated Fat: 2 g, Protein: 3 g, Fiber: 2 g, Carbohydrates: 37 g, Sodium: 291 mg, Cholesterol: 36 mg*

dutch apple *baby*

preparation: 15 minutes | **processing:** 20 seconds
bake time: 20 minutes | **yield:** 8 servings

apples:

3 large apples, cored, sliced

2 Tablespoons (30 g) butter

¼ cup (50 g) granulated sugar

½ teaspoon ground cinnamon

¼ teaspoon nutmeg

pancake:

3 large eggs

½ cup (60 g) all-purpose flour

½ cup (120 ml) milk

1 Tablespoon sour cream
or plain yogurt

½ teaspoon salt

1 teaspoon vanilla extract

Powdered sugar for garnish

1. Preheat oven to 400°F (200°C). Spray a 9–inch (23 cm) pie pan with cooking spray.

2. Sauté sliced apples in butter with sugar, cinnamon and nutmeg until slightly soft. Transfer to prepared pie pan and distribute evenly.

3. Place all Pancake ingredients into the Vitamix container in the order listed and secure lid.

4. Select Variable 1.

5. Switch machine to Start and slowly increase speed to Variable 4. Blend for 20 seconds. Pour over apples. Bake for 20 minutes.

6. Garnish with powdered sugar.

nutritional information

per serving: Calories: 157, Total Fat: 5 g, Saturated Fat: 3 g, Protein: 4 g,
Fiber: 2 g, Carbohydrates: 25 g, Sodium: 200 mg, Cholesterol: 90 mg

potato cheddar
breakfast bake

preparation: 10 minutes | ***processing:*** 20-25 seconds
bake time: 1 hour 20 minutes | ***yield:*** 10 servings

1 ¼ pounds (568 g)
Russet potatoes, cubed

8 large eggs

2 cups (480 ml) milk

½ teaspoon salt

8 ounces (227 g) cheddar
cheese, in large cubes

¼ cup (40 g) chopped
green pepper

¼ cup (40 g) chopped onion

1 ½ cups (210 g) diced ham

1. Preheat oven to 350°F (180°C). Spray a 9-inch x 9-inch
    (23 cm x 23 cm) baking pan with cooking spray.

2. Hash potatoes using the wet chop method (see sidebar).
    Drain, reserve.

3. Place eggs, milk, salt and cheese into the Vitamix container
    in the order listed and secure lid.

4. Select Variable 1.

5. Switch machine to Start and slowly increase speed to
    Variable 5. Blend for 10 seconds. Reduce speed to Variable 1
    and remove the lid plug. Add peppers, onion, potatoes and
    ham through the lid plug opening. Blend for 10 to 15 seconds.

6. Pour into prepared pan. Bake covered for 40 to 45 minutes.
    Uncover and bake another 30 to 35 minutes until firm
    and lightly browned.

nutritional information

per serving: *Calories: 238, Total Fat: 12 g, Saturated Fat: 6 g, Protein: 7 g,
Fiber: 1 g, Carbohydrates: 16 g, Sodium: 556 mg, Cholesterol: 204 mg*

kitchen chemistry

what is wet chopping?

Adding H_2O to the equation
really helps when you're
chopping large quantities
of dense or heavy foods in
the Vitamix blender. The
weight of cubed potatoes, for
example, won't allow the food
to rotate down to the blades
properly. If water is added
to the container, everything
circulates much easier.

Follow this method for wet
chopping the potatoes in the
Potato Cheddar Breakfast
Bake recipe:

Fill the Vitamix container
with quartered potatoes
to the 4 cup (960 ml) level.
Add water to the 6 cup
(1.4 L) level and secure lid.
Select Variable 5 and pulse
4 to 5 times until chopped.
Drain well. Spread potatoes
out on cookie sheet and
press with paper towels to
absorb any excess liquid.

oatmeal cranberry
pancakes

preparation: 5 minutes | ***processing:*** 20 seconds | ***yield:*** 3 cups (600 ml) or 10 pancakes

1 ½ cups (360 ml) milk

1 large egg

1 cup (120 g) whole wheat flour

2 teaspoons baking powder

½ teaspoon baking soda

½ teaspoon salt

¼ cup (40 g) flax seed meal

¾ cup (115 g) uncooked rolled oats

¼ cup (30 g) dried cranberries

2 Tablespoons (20 g) unsalted sunflower seeds

1. Place milk, egg, flour, baking powder, baking soda, salt and flax seed meal into the Vitamix container in the order listed and secure lid.

2. Select Variable 1.

3. Switch machine to Start and slowly increase speed to Variable 8.

4. Blend for 10 seconds. Stop machine and remove lid. Add oats, cranberries and sunflower seeds into the Vitamix container and secure lid.

5. Select Variable 1.

6. Switch machine to Start and blend for 10 seconds, using the tamper if necessary to press the ingredients into the blades.

7. Let batter sit for 5 to 10 minutes before cooking to yield best texture and flavor.

nutritional information

per pancake: *Calories: 121, Total Fat: 3 g, Saturated Fat: 1 g, Protein: 6 g, Fiber: 3 g, Carbohydrates: 19 g, Sodium: 293 mg, Cholesterol: 24 mg*

corned beef **hash**

preparation: 10 minutes | **processing:** pulsing
cook time: 20 minutes | **yield:** 5 servings

ingredient IQ

Egg substitutes work in many recipes, but not in this one; be sure to use real, whole eggs so they cook properly in the hash "wells."

1 ¼ pounds (568 g) small red potatoes, halved

½ small onion, halved, about ¼ cup (45 g)

1 small green bell pepper, seeded, cut in eighths, about 1 cup (145 g)

½ pound (227 g) deli corned beef (cut ½-inch (1.3 cm) thick), cut in 1 ½-inch (4 cm) chunks

2 Tablespoons (30 ml) vegetable oil

¼ teaspoon black pepper

¼ cup (60 ml) water

5 large eggs, if desired

1. Place potatoes, onion and bell pepper into the Vitamix container. Add water to just cover vegetables and secure lid.

2. Select Variable 3.

3. Pulse 6 times. Pour into colander; drain well.

4. Add corned beef to the Vitamix container and secure lid.

5. Select Variable 5. Pulse 2 times.

6. Heat oil in 12-inch (30 cm) heavy nonstick skillet over medium heat. Add potato mixture and corned beef. Stir in black pepper.

7. Cook 8 to 10 minutes, turning mixture over 2 or 3 times, until brown and crisp. Add ¼ cup (60 ml) water. If desired, make 5 depressions in surface of hash. Drop an egg into each depression. Cover; turn heat to Low. Cook 8 to 10 minutes or until potatoes are tender and eggs are cooked to desired doneness.

nutritional information

per serving (with egg): *Calories: 228, Total Fat: 9 g, Saturated Fat: 3 g, Protein: 16 g, Fiber: 2 g, Carbohydrates: 20 g, Sodium: 393 mg, Cholesterol: 239 mg*

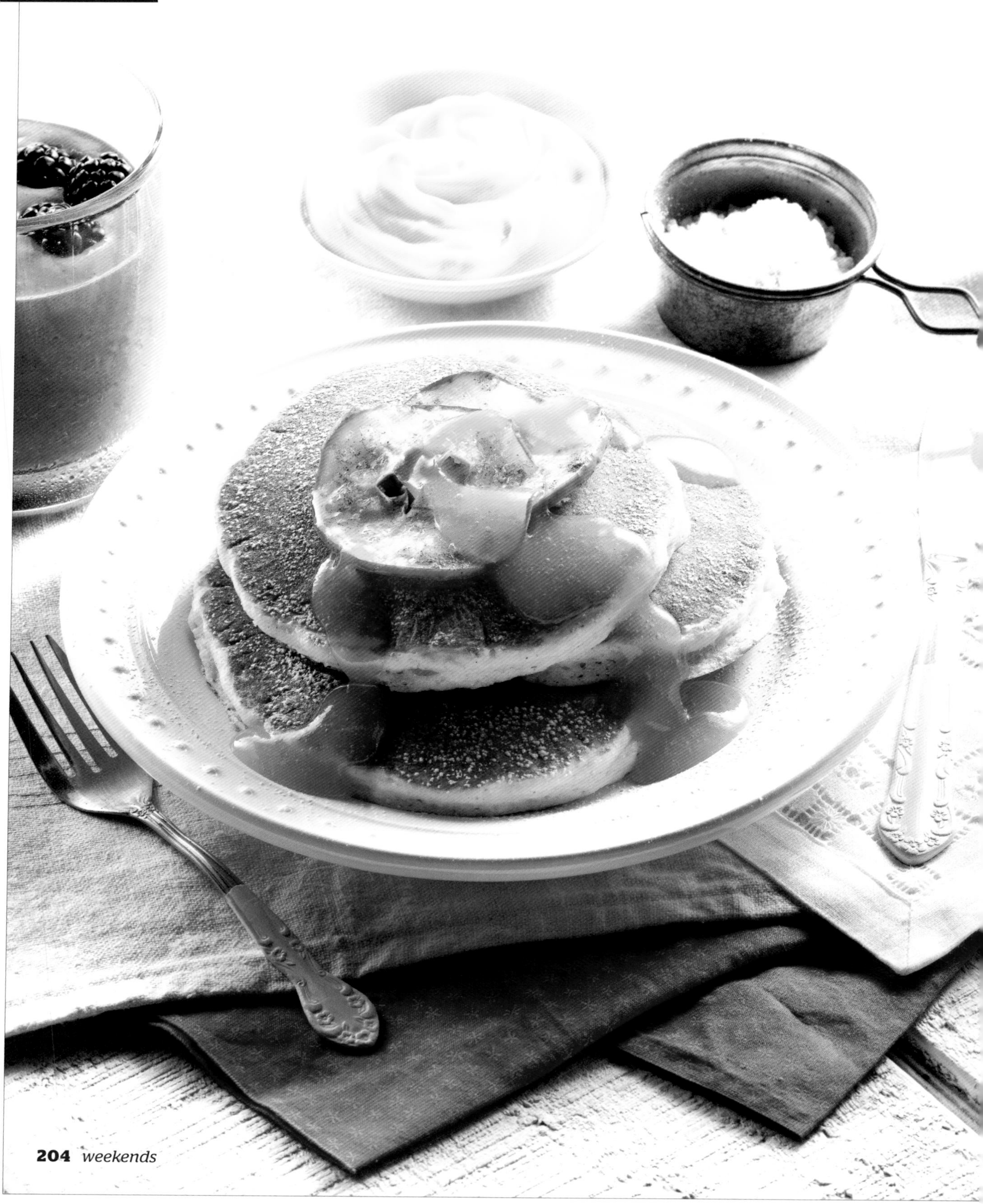

apple *pancakes*

preparation: 10 minutes | ***processing:*** 20 seconds
yield: 26 pancakes, about 6 ½ cups (1.5 L) batter

on the menu

These Apple Pancakes pair perfectly with Fresh Fruit Syrup (page 53). For a perfect weekend breakfast, serve with Honey Butter (page 48) and Powdered Sugar (page 325).

2 cups (240 g) whole wheat flour

2 Tablespoons (30 g) baking powder

1 teaspoon salt

6 Tablespoons (76 g) sugar

½ teaspoon nutmeg

1 teaspoon baking soda

2 cups (480 ml) milk

2 large eggs

1 Tablespoon butter

½ teaspoon vanilla extract

1 medium apple, seeded, quartered

1. Combine flour, baking powder, salt, sugar, nutmeg and baking soda in a medium-sized mixing bowl by hand. Set aside.

2. Place milk, eggs, butter, vanilla extract and apple into the Vitamix container in the order listed and secure lid.

3. Select Variable 1.

4. Switch machine to Start and slowly increase speed to Variable 3.

5. Blend for 20 seconds.

6. Pour wet mixture into dry mixture and mix by hand until combined.

7. Let batter sit for 5 to 10 minutes before cooking to yield best texture and flavor.

nutritional information

per serving (2 pancakes): *Calories: 133, Total Fat: 2 g, Saturated Fat: 1 g, Protein: 5 g, Fiber: 3 g, Carbohydrates: 25 g, Sodium: 515 mg, Cholesterol: 38 mg*

orange date *muffins*

preparation: 10 minutes | ***processing:*** 20 seconds + pulsing | ***bake time:*** 16–20 minutes | ***yield:*** 12 muffins

1 ½ cups (188 g) all-purpose flour

⅓ cup (40 g) whole wheat flour

1 Tablespoon baking powder

1 teaspoon pumpkin pie spice
or cinnamon

¼ teaspoon coarse salt

1 orange, peeled, halved, seeded

⅓ cup (73 g) firmly packed
light brown sugar

¼ cup (60 ml) canola oil

1 large egg

¾ cup (113g) whole pitted dates

¾ cup (180 ml) skim milk

1. Preheat oven to 375°F (190°C). Spray 12-cup muffin tin with cooking spray or line
   cups with paper liners.

2. Combine flours, baking powder, pumpkin pie spice and salt in a medium-sized mixing bowl. Set aside.

3. Place orange, brown sugar, oil and egg into the Vitamix container in the order listed and secure lid.

4. Select Variable 1.

5. Switch machine to Start and slowly increase speed to Variable 4. Blend for 15 seconds until
   smooth. Stop machine and remove lid. Add dates to the Vitamix container and secure lid.

6. Select Variable 3.

7. Pulse 10 to 12 times until dates are chopped. Remove lid. Add milk and dry ingredients
   to the Vitamix container and secure lid.

8. Switch machine to Start and blend 5 seconds until smooth. Fill muffin cups ¾ full.
   Bake 16 to 20 minutes or until golden brown.

nutritional information

per muffin: *Calories: 174, Total Fat: 5 g, Saturated Fat: 1 g, Protein: 3 g,*
Fiber: 2 g, Carbohydrates: 30 g, Sodium: 165 mg, Cholesterol: 18 mg

artichoke, red pepper
and **parmesan frittata**

preparation: 10 minutes | **processing:** 10 seconds | **cook time:** 10–15 minutes | **yield:** 5 servings

2 Tablespoons (30 ml) olive oil

¼ cup (60 ml) milk

6 large eggs

1 garlic clove, roasted, peeled

¼ teaspoon salt

¼ teaspoon red pepper flakes

¼ teaspoon freshly cracked black pepper

7.5-ounce (213 g) jar grilled marinated artichoke hearts, drained

½ cup (65 g) marinated roasted red pepper, drained

⅓ cup (33 g) freshly grated Parmesan cheese

1. Heat an 8–inch (20 cm) skillet over medium heat. Add olive oil.

2. Meanwhile, place milk, eggs, garlic, salt, red pepper flakes and pepper into the Vitamix container in the order listed and secure lid.

3. Select Variable 1. Switch machine to Start and slowly increase speed to Variable 2. Blend for 5 seconds or until smooth. Stop machine and remove lid. Add artichoke hearts and roasted red peppers and secure lid.

4. Select Variable 1. Switch machine to Start and slowly increase speed to Variable 2. Blend for 5 seconds; small chunks will remain.

5. Pour into skillet. Cook over medium heat until edges are lightly browned (8 to 10 minutes). Sprinkle top with Parmesan cheese.

6. Place skillet under broiler set on high. Broil for 1 to 2 minutes or until top is lightly browned and no longer wet.

nutritional information

per serving: *Calories: 210, Total Fat: 15 g, Saturated Fat: 4 g, Protein: 12 g, Fiber: 2 g, Carbohydrates: 8 g, Sodium: 522 mg, Cholesterol: 264 mg*

onion cheese *frittata*

preparation: 15 minutes | ***processing:*** 15 seconds
bake time: 20–25 minutes | ***yield:*** 8 servings

¼ cup (40 g) chopped onion

1 cup (115 g) diced squash

¼ cup (40 g) diced red
bell pepper

¼ cup (40 g) diced green
bell pepper

2 Tablespoons (30 ml) olive oil

6 large eggs

½ cup (50 g) grated
Parmesan cheese

½ teaspoon dried oregano

⅛ teaspoon nutmeg

½ teaspoon salt

¼ teaspoon black pepper

½ cup (65 g) cubed
cheddar cheese

1. Preheat oven to 350°F (180°C). Spray a 9–inch (23 cm)
   pie pan with cooking spray.

2. Sauté onion, squash and peppers in olive oil until soft.
   Place in bottom of prepared pie pan.

3. Place eggs, Parmesan, oregano, nutmeg, salt and pepper
   into the Vitamix container in the order listed and secure lid.

4. Select Variable 1.

5. Switch machine to Start and slowly increase speed to Variable 2.
   Blend for 10 seconds. Remove lid plug. Add cheddar cheese
   through the lid plug opening and blend an additional 5 seconds.

6. Pour mixture over vegetables. Bake 20 to 25 minutes or until set.

nutritional information

per serving: *Calories: 133, Total Fat: 10 g, Saturated Fat: 4 g, Protein: 9 g,*
Fiber: 1 g, Carbohydrates: 3 g, Sodium: 354 mg, Cholesterol: 175 mg

build a meal

not-so-basic brunch

The perfect brunch spread
combines savory and sweet,
and hearty and light. Start
with an Onion and Cheese
Frittata. To balance the rich
egg dish, offer a side salad
of fresh arugula, drizzled in
tangy Balsamic Fig Dressing
(page 100). Toss on some
chopped figs and shaved
Parmesan for added flavor.

To round out the meal,
bake assorted mini muffins,
like Glorious Morning
Muffins (page 37) and
Lemon Ginger Muffins
(page 35), and make sure to
have plenty of Honey Butter
(page 48) on hand. Finally,
nothing completes a brunch
like a fresh and light cocktail;
serve a Pineapple Coconut
Curacao (page 335).

swedish pancakes with
blueberry syrup

preparation: 10 minutes | **processing:** 2 ½ minutes | **cook time:** 2–4 minutes | **yield:** 12 servings

2 cups (480 ml) milk

1 ½ cups (188 g) all-purpose flour

4 large eggs

⅓ cup (67 g) sugar

3 Tablespoons (45 g)
butter, melted

¼ teaspoon coarse salt

1 package (12 ounces) frozen
blueberries, completely thawed

¾ cup (150 g) sugar

1 teaspoon lemon juice

3 cups (500 g) sliced strawberries

1. Place milk, flour, eggs, sugar, butter and salt into the Vitamix container in order listed and secure lid.

2. Select Variable 1.

3. Switch machine to Start and slowly increase speed to Variable 3. Blend for 10 seconds.
   Let stand at room temperature 20 minutes.

4. Heat a 9–inch (23 cm) nonstick skillet over medium-high heat until a drop of water sizzles.
   Add about ⅓ cup (80 ml) batter and swirl to cover bottom of pan. Cook 1 to 2 minutes or until
   golden brown on bottom and top is dry. Turn and cook the second side. Repeat with remaining
   batter. Serve with blueberry syrup and strawberries.

5. For syrup, place blueberries, sugar and lemon juice into the Vitamix container and secure lid.

6. Select Variable 1.

7. Switch machine to Start and slowly increase speed to Variable 10. Blend for 2 ½ minutes
   until smooth and thick or steam escapes from the vented lid plug.

nutritional information

per serving (with syrup and strawberries): *Calories: 215, Total Fat: 5 g, Saturated Fat: 3 g,
Protein: 6 g, Fiber: 2 g, Carbohydrates: 38 g, Sodium: 104 mg, Cholesterol: 82 mg*

cinnamon spice
puff pancake

preparation: 5 minutes | ***processing:*** 5 seconds | ***bake time:*** 20 minutes | ***yield:*** 4 servings

pancake:

3 Tablespoons (45 g) butter

¾ cup (180 ml) milk

2 large eggs

¾ teaspoon vanilla extract

⅔ cup (94 g) all-purpose flour

¾ teaspoon ground cinnamon

½ teaspoon salt

¼ teaspoon ground cardamom

optional toppings:

Real maple syrup

Mixed fruits

Fresh lemon juice

Powdered sugar

1. Preheat oven to 400°F (200°C). Place butter in 9-inch (23 cm) glass pie plate; heat in oven until butter is melted (4 to 5 minutes). Remove from oven.

2. Place remaining pancake ingredients into the Vitamix container in the order listed and secure lid.

3. Select Variable 1.

4. Switch machine to Start and slowly increase speed to Variable 3.

5. Blend for 5 seconds, just until blended. Pour mixture into pie plate.

6. Bake 20 minutes or until pancake rises (puffs) along edges and is golden brown.

7. Serve with desired toppings.

nutritional information

per serving (without topping): *Calories: 201, Total Fat: 11 g, Saturated Fat: 6 g, Protein: 7 g, Fiber: 1 g, Carbohydrates: 18 g, Sodium: 408 mg, Cholesterol: 133 mg*

strawberry
agua fresca

preparation: 5 minutes | **processing:** 1 minute
yield: 4 cups (960 ml)

1 cup (150 g) fresh strawberries

4 cups (620 g) cubed, seeded watermelon

¼ cup (60 ml) lemon juice

2 cups (480 ml) ice cubes

1. Place all ingredients into the Vitamix container in the order listed and secure lid.

2. Select Smoothie program.

3. Switch machine to Start and allow machine to complete programmed cycle.

nutritional information

per 1 cup (240 ml) serving: Calories: 57, Total Fat: 0 g, Saturated Fat: 0 g, Protein: 1 g, Fiber: 2 g, Carbohydrates: 18 g, Sodium: 6 mg, Cholesterol: 0 mg

family time

fresh and sweet kid-friendly treat

It's a hot summer day and your kids are craving something cold. Homemade frozen pops made from fresh juice blends are a healthy alternative to the store-bought brands, which may contain high fructose corn syrup and artificial ingredients.

Start by mixing up one recipe each of Strawberry Agua Fresca and Lime and Mint Agua Fresca (page 219). Pour into ice cube trays, cover with tin foil and insert a wooden craft stick through the foil into each juice-filled compartment. (Hint: for super fancy ones, use actual frozen pop molds.) Place in the freezer, and you're good to go.

carrot orange *apple juice* 💧

preparation: 5 minutes | ***processing:*** 1 minute | ***yield:*** 3 cups (720 ml)

½ cup (120 ml) cold water

1 orange, peeled, halved, seeded

½ apple, seeded

½-inch-thick (1.3 cm) slice pineapple, core included

1 medium carrot, halved

1 cup (240 ml) ice cubes

1. Place all ingredients into the Vitamix container in the order listed and secure lid.

2. Select Smoothie program.

3. Switch machine to Start and allow machine to complete programmed cycle.

4. Serve immediately.

nutritional information

per 1 cup (240 ml) serving: *Calories: 55, Total Fat: 0 g, Saturated Fat: 0 g, Protein: 1 g, Fiber: 3 g, Carbohydrates: 14 g, Sodium: 16 mg, Cholesterol: 0 mg*

lemonade *blush*

preparation: 10 minutes | ***processing:*** 20 seconds | ***yield:*** 6 cups (1.4 L)

¼–½ cup (60–120 ml) agave syrup

1 teaspoon chopped fresh rosemary

½ cup (120 ml) lemon juice

6 cups (930 g) cubed, seeded watermelon

2–4 cups (480–960 ml) ice cubes

1. Place agave, rosemary, lemon juice and watermelon into the Vitamix container in the order listed and secure lid.

2. Select Variable 1.

3. Switch machine to Start and slowly increase speed to Variable 5.

4. Blend for 20 seconds. Serve over ice cubes.

nutritional information

per 1 cup (240 ml) serving: *Calories: 99, Total Fat: 0 g, Saturated Fat: 0 g, Protein: 1 g, Fiber: 1 g, Carbohydrates: 30 g, Sodium: 5 mg, Cholesterol: 0 mg*

ginger peach
pineapple juice 💧

preparation: 5 minutes | ***processing:*** 1 minute | ***yield:*** 6 cups (1.4 L)

2 cups (480 ml) unsweetened pineapple juice

2 cups (480 ml) orange juice

1 cup (190 g) frozen unsweetened peach slices

1 teaspoon peeled, chopped ginger

1. Place all ingredients into the Vitamix container in the order listed and secure lid.

2. Select Smoothie program.

3. Switch machine to Start and allow machine to complete programmed cycle.

4. Serve immediately.

nutritional information

per 1 cup (240 ml) serving: *Calories: 93, Total Fat: 0 g, Saturated Fat: 0 g, Protein: 0 g, Fiber: 0 g, Carbohydrates: 23 g, Sodium: 2 mg, Cholesterol: 0 mg*

apple juice 💧

preparation: 5 minutes | ***processing:*** 1 minute
yield: 1 ½ cups (360 ml) strained

1 ¼ pounds (570 g), about 4 medium
to large apples, cored, quartered

¼ cup (60 ml) cool water

2 double layers of cheesecloth

1. Place apples and water into the Vitamix container
   in the order listed and secure lid.

2. Select Smoothie program.

3. Switch machine to Start and allow machine
   to complete programmed cycle.

4. Transfer purée to a bowl lined with cheesecloth
   and twist until juice is extracted.

nutritional information

per 1 cup (240 ml) serving: *Calories: 196, Total Fat: 1 g,
Saturated Fat: 0 g, Protein: 1g, Fiber: 9 g, Carbohydrates: 52 g,
Sodium: 5 mg, Cholesterol: 0 mg*

healthy choices

ABCs of vitamin rich fruits

Vitamins are essential
for good health. Here's
where those vitamins are
found in your favorite fruits:

A: cantaloupes, grapefruits

B1: grapes, grapefruits,
mangos, oranges, pineapples

B2: bananas, grapes,
mangos, pomegranates

B3: mangos, nectarines,
peaches

B6: bananas, dates, grapes,
mangos, pineapples

C: oranges, grapefruits,
kiwis, mangos, pineapples,
strawberries

E: blueberries, cranberries,
guavas, mangos, nectarines,
peaches, raspberries

K: blueberries, grapes,
pears, plums, raspberries

lime *and* mint agua fresca

preparation: 5 minutes | **processing:** 1 minute | **yield:** 2 ¾ cups (660 ml)

1 Tablespoon agave nectar

¼ cup (60 ml) fresh lime juice

7-ounce (200 g) cucumber, peeled, cut into 1-inch (2.5 cm) pieces

1 Tablespoon chopped fresh spearmint

1 teaspoon lime zest

2 ½ cups (600 ml) ice cubes

1. Place all ingredients into the Vitamix container in the order listed and secure lid.

2. Select Smoothie program.

3. Switch machine to Start and allow machine to complete programmed cycle.

4. Serve immediately.

5. Garnish with mint sprigs.

nutritional information

per 1 cup (240 ml) serving: *Calories: 37, Total Fat: 0 g, Saturated Fat: 0 g, Protein: 1 g, Fiber: 1 g, Carbohydrates: 10 g, Sodium: 3 mg, Cholesterol: 0 mg*

brazilian *lemonade*

preparation: 5 minutes | **processing:** 20 seconds
yield: 4 ¾ cups (1.1 L)

create your own

This Brazilian favorite is actually made with limes. Add another taste of Rio with a shot of Cachaça (fermented sugar cane) and crushed ice for an adults-only version.

3 limes, peeled, halved

⅓ cup (67 g) sugar

3 Tablespoons (45 ml)
sweetened condensed milk

1. Place all ingredients into the Vitamix container in the order listed, add 4 cups (960 ml) of water and secure lid.

2. Select Variable 1.

3. Switch machine to Start and slowly increase speed to Variable 10.

4. Blend for 20 seconds.

5. Strain into a pitcher and then, with the strainer still resting above the pitcher, slowly pour 1 cup (240 ml) water through the strainer to extract residual sugar and juice.

nutritional information

per 1 cup (240 ml) serving: *Calories: 109, Total Fat: 1 g, Saturated Fat: 1 g, Protein: 1 g, Fiber: 1 g, Carbohydrates: 26 g, Sodium: 15 mg, Cholesterol: 3 mg*

create your own

If you prefer a touch of rich sweetness in rice milk, add ½ teaspoon vanilla extract with the other ingredients; pure vanilla extract provides the best flavor.

rice milk

preparation: 45 minutes | ***processing:*** 2 ½ – 3 minutes
yield: 2 ½ cups (600 ml)

2 cups (480 ml) water

½ cup (100 g) cooked brown rice, cooled

½ Tablespoon brown sugar or
other sweetener, to taste

1. Place all ingredients into the Vitamix container in the order listed and secure lid.

2. Select Variable 1.

3. Switch machine to Start and slowly increase speed to Variable 10.

4. Blend for 2 ½ to 3 minutes or until desired consistency is reached. Store in refrigerator. Shake well before using.

nutritional information

per 1 cup (240 ml) serving: *Calories: 54, Total Fat: 0 g, Saturated Fat: 0 g, Protein: 1 g, Fiber: 1 g, Carbohydrates: 12 g, Sodium: 9 mg, Cholesterol: 0 mg*

soy milk

preparation: 8 hours | **processing:** 1 minute
yield: 4 ½ cups (1.0 L)

1 cup (200 g) dried soy beans

1 Tablespoon sugar

3 ½ cups (840 ml) water

1. Clean dried soy beans and soak in water for 4 to 8 hours.
   Steam for about 15 minutes.

2. Drain soy beans and let cool. Measure 1 ½ cups (258 g) cooked beans.

3. Place cooked beans, sugar and water into the Vitamix container
   in the order listed and secure lid.

4. Select Purée program.

5. Switch machine to Start and allow machine to complete
   programmed cycle.

6. To obtain commercial-style soy milk, strain the milk through a
   nut milk bag or pass through a fine-mesh sieve.

create your own

For a refreshing burst of crisp, gingery flavor, add a 1-inch (2.5 cm) cube of ginger root with the other ingredients in Step 3 before blending.

nutritional information

per 1 cup (240 ml) serving: *Calories: 179, Total Fat: 8 g, Saturated Fat: 1 g,
Protein: 15 g, Fiber: 3 g, Carbohydrates: 15 g, Sodium: 8 mg, Cholesterol: 0 mg*

almond milk

preparation: 3 minutes | **processing:** 2 minutes
yield: 3 ½ cups (840 ml)

3 cups (720 ml) water

1 cup (140 g) raw almonds

sugar or sweetener, to taste (optional)

1. Place all ingredients into the Vitamix container in the order listed and secure lid.

2. Select Variable 1.

3. Switch machine to Start and slowly increase speed to Variable 10.

4. Blend for 2 minutes or until desired consistency is reached.

nutritional information

per 1 cup (240 ml) serving (without sweetener): *Calories: 235, Total Fat: 20 g, Saturated Fat: 2 g, Protein: 9 g, Fiber: 5 g, Carbohydrates: 9 g, Sodium: 9 mg, Cholesterol: 0 mg*

kitchen chemistry

enjoy smooth, creamy nut milks

Because nut milks—such as almond or cashew milks—are made from uncooked nuts, they are often strained to remove any solids that may have not been fully incorporated when blended. Straining is easily done by placing a fine-mesh sieve over a large bowl.

For even smoother milk, line the strainer with a layer of cheesecloth. (If you make nut milks often, you might want to look into purchasing a reusable nut milk bag.) Slowly pour the milk into the sieve, allowing it to filter through at its own pace. You can also speed things up a bit by gently stirring the milk with a spatula or the back of a spoon to encourage it to pass through the sieve more quickly. Freshly made nut milks will last two to three days in the refrigerator.

dips & spreads

appetizer mains

chutneys & relishes

AFTER WORKING HARD in your kitchen all week, your Vitamix Professional Series is ready to help you entertain easily on weekends. Get the scoop on *Dips & Spreads* (page 229), whip up some *Appetizer Mains* (page 251) and check out the *Chutneys & Relishes* (page 267). Along with these fast and delicious recipes, we've included entertaining and presentation tips to enhance any occasion.

weekends

appetizers

DIPS & SPREADS / APPETIZER MAINS / CHUTNEYS & RELISHES

pineapple, pepper *and* pecan cheese spread

preparation: 10 minutes
processing: 30 seconds + pulsing
yield: 2 ¼ cups (540 g)

11 ounces (312 g)
cream cheese, softened

⅛ teaspoon cayenne pepper

3 green onions, cut in
1–inch (2.5 cm) pieces
(white and pale green only)

½ green bell pepper,
cut in 4 pieces

½ cup (83 g) fresh
pineapple cubes

½ cup (50 g) pecan halves

1. Place cheese, cayenne pepper and green onions
   into the Vitamix container and secure lid.

2. Select Variable 1.

3. Switch machine to Start and blend for 20 seconds.
   Stop machine and remove lid.

4. Add bell pepper to the Vitamix container and secure lid.

5. Select Variable 2.

6. Pulse 5 times. Stop machine and use rubber spatula
   to loosen ingredients under blades.

7. Add pineapple to the Vitamix container and secure lid.

» **pineapple, pepper and pecan cheese spread**
continues on page 230

for two or twenty

going beyond the bowl

Make your presentations
just as appetizing as your
dips by getting creative.
A scooped-out pineapple
half is a fun way to present
fruit dips such as the
Pineapple, Pepper and
Pecan Cheese Spread.

To make Roasted Red Pepper
Hummus (page 244) stand
out on the buffet table,
place a single pita round
in the center of a large,
round serving platter. Pile
hummus on top of the pita,
and sprinkle with chopped
parsley. Surround the
hummus with a ring of olives,
roasted red peppers and
roasted garlic.

continued from page 229

pineapple, pepper *and* pecan cheese spread

8. Select Variable 3.

9. Pulse 3 times, scraping sides of the container with a rubber spatula once if necessary.

10. Add nuts to the Vitamix container and secure lid.

11. Select Variable 2.

12. Pulse 2 or 3 times.

13. Remove lid and scrape sides of the container with a spatula. Loosen any ingredients caught under the blades and secure lid.

14. Select Variable 1.

15. Switch machine to Start and blend 10 seconds.

16. Scrape into serving bowl or covered storage container. If desired, refrigerate several hours to blend flavors. May be stored in refrigerator up to a week. Serve with crackers or fresh vegetable crudités.

nutritional information

per 2 tablespoon (30 g) serving: *Calories: 86, Total Fat: 8 g, Saturated Fat: 4 g, Protein: 2 g, Fiber: 1 g, Carbohydrates: 1 g, Sodium: 2 mg, Cholesterol: 19 mg*

cucumber *and* **mint dip**

preparation: 10 minutes | ***processing:*** 15 seconds | ***yield:*** 2 ½ cups (600 g)

2 cups (480 g) plain
Greek-style yogurt

1 scallion, cut into 4 pieces,
about 1 Tablespoon

1 teaspoon sugar

1 garlic clove, peeled, chopped
into 4 pieces, about ½ teaspoon

½ teaspoon Kosher salt

¼ teaspoon freshly cracked
black pepper

1 cup (133 g) chopped
English cucumber

⅓ cup (7 g) coarsely
chopped fresh mint

1. Place yogurt, scallion, sugar, garlic, salt and pepper into the Vitamix container in the order listed and secure lid.

2. Select Variable 1.

3. Switch machine to Start and slowly increase speed to Variable 5.

4. Blend for 10 seconds or until smooth.

5. Reduce speed to Variable 4 and remove lid plug.

6. Add cucumber and mint through the lid plug opening.

7. Blend an additional 5 seconds. Serve immediately.

nutritional information

per ¼ cup (60 g) serving: *Calories: 34, Total Fat: 2 g, Saturated Fat: 1 g, Protein: 2 g, Fiber: 0 g, Carbohydrates: 3 g, Sodium: 119 mg, Cholesterol: 6 mg*

kitchen prep

The blended mixture may appear thin at first, but will thicken as the ingredients set. For the best consistency, make it at least an hour before serving.

lemon **gremolata dip**

preparation: 10 minutes | **processing:** 20–25 seconds
yield: 2 ½ cups (600 g)

1 cup (240 g) sour cream

1 cup (240 g) plain
Greek-style yogurt

1 cup (60 g) fresh parsley,
washed, dried, stems removed

¼ cup (24 g) lemon peel

¼ lemon, peeled, seeded

1 teaspoon agave

2 garlic cloves, peeled

½ teaspoon ground coriander

¼ teaspoon salt

⅛ teaspoon freshly
cracked black pepper

1. Place all ingredients into the Vitamix container
   in the order listed and secure lid.

2. Select Variable 1.

3. Switch machine to Start and slowly increase speed to Variable 10.

4. Blend for 20 to 25 seconds or until smooth.

5. Refrigerate leftovers.

nutritional information

per ¼ cup (60 g) serving: Calories: 70, Total Fat: 5 g, Saturated Fat: 3 g,
Protein: 2 g, Fiber: 1 g, Carbohydrates: 4 g, Sodium: 81 mg, Cholesterol: 19 mg

apple raisin *spread* ❄

preparation: 10 minutes | **processing:** 45 seconds
cook time: 30–45 minutes | **yield:** 3 cups (720 g)

on the menu

Serve this savory, spicy spread spooned over grilled pork or grilled chicken, or spread it on crostini for an intriguing appetizer.

1 ¼ lbs (568 g) Granny Smith apples, (3 medium) rough chop

¼ cup (100 g) brown sugar

½ cup (80 g) chopped onion

½ cup (70 g) golden raisins

1 ounce (28 g) walnuts or 14 halves

1 garlic clove, peeled

2 Tablespoons (30 ml) apple cider vinegar

¼-inch (.6 cm) lemon slice with peel

1 Tablespoon chopped fresh ginger root

¼ ounce fresh hot chili peppers

¼ teaspoon nutmeg

¼ teaspoon ground cloves

1. Combine all ingredients in a sauce pot and simmer until reduced and slightly thickened. Cool 10 minutes.

2. Place into the Vitamix container and secure lid.

3. Select Frozen Dessert program.

4. Switch machine to Start and allow machine to complete programmed cycle, using the tamper to press ingredients into the blades.

5. Refrigerate and store covered until needed.

nutritional information

per 2 tablespoon (30 g) serving: *Calories: 42, Total Fat: 1 g, Saturated Fat: 0 g, Protein: 0 g, Fiber: 1 g, Carbohydrates: 9 g, Sodium: 2 mg, Cholesterol: 0 mg*

california *salsa*

preparation: 5 minutes | ***processing:*** pulsing | ***yield:*** 2 ¼ cups (540 g)

½ medium onion, peeled,
about ⅓ cup (47 g) chopped

1 jalapeño pepper, seeds and
membranes removed

¼ cup (5 g) fresh cilantro leaves

½ lemon or lime, juiced

½ teaspoon salt

6 ripe Roma tomatoes,
quartered (24 quarters)

1. Place onion, jalapeño, cilantro, lime, salt and six of the tomato
   quarters into the Vitamix container in the order listed and secure lid.

2. Select Variable 5. Pulse 2 times.

3. Add the remaining tomato quarters through the lid plug opening.
   Pulse 5 times or until desired consistency is reached.

4. Serve with tortilla chips.

nutritional information

per ¼ cup (60 g) serving: *Calories: 11, Total Fat: 0 g, Saturated Fat: 0 g,*
Protein: 0 g, Fiber: 1 g, Carbohydrates: 3 g, Sodium: 142 mg, Cholesterol: 0 mg

pepper dip

preparation: 10 minutes | **processing:** 25 seconds | **yield:** 3 cups (720 g)

8-ounce (227 g) package
cream cheese, cut into 8 pieces

1 cup (150 g) coarsely chopped
bell pepper (any color)

1 cup (113 g) hot pepper
cheese cubes

½ cup (100 g) roasted red pepper,
drained and patted dry

1 scallion, cut into 4 pieces

¼ fresh jalapeño pepper, seeded,
about 1 Tablespoon chopped

1 Tablespoon half and half

½ teaspoon salt

⅛ teaspoon freshly cracked
black pepper

1. Place all ingredients into the Vitamix container
   in the order listed and secure lid.

2. Select Variable 1.

3. Switch machine to Start and slowly increase speed to Variable 5.

4. Blend for 25 seconds or until smooth. Use tamper if necessary.

5. If a thinner dip is desired, add 1 additional Tablespoon half and half.

6. Refrigerate leftovers.

nutritional information

per ¼ cup (60 g) serving: Calories: 118, Total Fat: 10 g, Saturated Fat: 6 g,
Protein: 4 g, Fiber: 0 g, Carbohydrates: 3 g, Sodium: 302 mg, Cholesterol: 30 mg

lime *garlic dip*

preparation: 10 minutes | **processing:** 20–25 seconds | **yield:** 2 ½ cups (600 g)

1 cup (240 g) sour cream

1 cup (240 g) plain
Greek-style yogurt

1 cup (60 g) fresh parsley leaves,
washed, dried

¼ cup (24 g) lime peel

1 Tablespoon Worcestershire sauce

2 garlic cloves, peeled

½ teaspoon ground cumin

½ teaspoon salt

¼ teaspoon chili powder

¼ teaspoon onion powder

¼ teaspoon paprika

⅛ teaspoon freshly cracked
black pepper

3 dashes of cayenne pepper,
or to taste

1. Place all ingredients into the Vitamix container
   in the order listed and secure lid.

2. Select Variable 1.

3. Switch machine to Start and slowly increase speed to Variable 10.

4. Blend for 20 to 25 seconds or until smooth.

5. Refrigerate leftovers.

nutritional information

per ¼ cup (60 g) serving: Calories: 70, Total Fat: 5 g, Saturated Fat: 3 g,
Protein: 2 g, Fiber: 1 g, Carbohydrates: 3 g, Sodium: 158 mg, Cholesterol: 19 mg

guacamole

preparation: 5 minutes | **processing:** pulsing
yield: 2 ½ cups (600 g)

freshen up

If you like spicy dips, nothing adds zip to guacamole like half of a seeded fresh jalapeño. Add to the Vitamix container in Step 1.

2 ripe avocados, peeled, pitted, halved

1 Roma tomato, quartered

½ cup (10 g) fresh cilantro leaves

¼ cup (40 g) chopped red onion

2 Tablespoons (30 ml) lemon juice

½ teaspoon Kosher salt

1. Place all ingredients into the Vitamix container in the order listed and secure lid.

2. Select Variable 4.

3. Pulse 5 to 6 times or until ingredients are mixed, using the tamper to push the ingredients into the blades while processing.

4. Do not over blend. Leave chunky. Serve with tortilla chips.

nutritional information

per 2 tablespoon (30 g) serving: Calories: 34, Total Fat: 3 g, Saturated Fat: 0 g, Protein: 0 g, Fiber: 1 g, Carbohydrates: 2 g, Sodium: 50 mg, Cholesterol: 0 mg

onion jam

preparation: 10 minutes | **processing:** pulsing
cook time: 15 – 20 minutes | **yield:** 2 ⅔ cups (640 g)

4 large sweet onions, peeled, quartered, divided use	½ cup (120 ml) honey
	⅓ cup (67 g) sugar
2 Tablespoons (30 ml) vegetable oil	½ cup (83 g) golden raisins
1 Tablespoon butter	½ teaspoon salt
⅓ cup (80 ml) balsamic vinegar	¼ teaspoon ground black pepper

1. Place half of the onions into the Vitamix container, add water to the 8 cup level and secure lid.

2. Select Variable 3.

3. Pulse 5 times. Drain.

4. Spread out on cookie sheet and press with paper towels to remove excess moisture. Repeat with remaining onions.

5. Heat oil and butter in a 12-inch (30 cm) nonstick skillet over medium heat. Add onions and cook 8 to 10 minutes or until onions start turning translucent, stirring occasionally. Add all remaining ingredients. Cook until simmering. Cook 5 to 8 minutes or until moisture is absorbed and mixture is thickened. Any liquid should be syrupy.

6. Spoon into containers and store covered in refrigerator.

nutritional information

per 2 tablespoon (30 g) serving: *Calories: 84, Total Fat: 2 g, Saturated Fat: 1 g, Protein: 1 g, Fiber: 1 g, Carbohydrates: 17 g, Sodium: 66 mg, Cholesterol: 1 mg*

gifts from your kitchen

jam is always welcome

Homemade jams and spreads are ideal little treasures for friends or family. Spoon the jam or spread into small decorative jam jars, seal and finish with a pretty ribbon. Attach the recipe and suggestions for use.

For a more elaborate gift, place a jar of Onion Jam in a basket along with a cloth napkin, small spreading knife, round of Brie cheese and box of artisan crackers. Include a card with storage instructions (refrigerate the jam and cheese until using) as well as suggestions for serving. (Spoon the jam over the cheese and bake at 350°F (180°C) for 15 to 20 minutes or until the cheese is softened. Spread over the crackers or toasted thin slices of French bread.)

spinach and
feta hummus ❄

preparation: 10 minutes | ***processing:*** 45 seconds | ***yield:*** 3 cups (720 g)

15–ounce (426 g) can
chickpeas, not drained

2 Tablespoons (18 g)
sesame seeds

¼ cup + 2 Tablespoons
(90 ml) olive oil

1 cup (40 g) fresh spinach
leaves, packed

1 garlic clove, roasted, peeled

3 Tablespoons (45 ml) lemon juice

1 ½ ounces (43 g) crumbled
feta cheese

¼ teaspoon crushed
red pepper flakes

¼ teaspoon salt

1. Place all ingredients into the Vitamix container
   in the order listed and secure lid.

2. Select Frozen Dessert program.

3. Switch machine to Start and allow machine
   to complete programmed cycle.

4. Refrigerate leftovers.

nutritional information

per ¼ cup (60 g) serving: *Calories: 110, Total Fat: 9 g, Saturated Fat: 2 g,
Protein: 3 g, Fiber: 1 g, Carbohydrates: 5 g, Sodium: 186 mg, Cholesterol: 3 mg*

hummus

preparation: 5 minutes | **processing:** 1 minute
yield: 2 ½ cups (600 g)

2 15–ounce (426 g) cans chickpeas (garbanzos), one drained, one with liquid

¼ cup (35 g) raw sesame seeds

1 Tablespoon olive oil

¼ cup (60 ml) lemon juice

¼ cup (60 ml) water

1 garlic clove, peeled

1 teaspoon cumin

½ teaspoon salt

1. Place all ingredients into the Vitamix container in the order listed and secure lid.

2. Select Purée program.

3. Switch machine to Start and allow machine to complete programmed cycle.

nutritional information

per ¼ cup (60 g) serving: *Calories: 121, Total Fat: 4 g, Saturated Fat: 0 g, Protein: 5 g, Fiber: 4 g, Carbohydrates: 16 g, Sodium: 143 mg, Cholesterol: 0 mg*

---

bright idea

Hummus is the new "basic black dress" of the kitchen. Dress it up on a cracker with olive slices and parsley, or use as a healthy substitution for mayo in a sandwich.

roasted red
pepper hummus Ⓩ

preparation: 10 minutes | ***processing:*** 1 minute | ***yield:*** 3 ½ cups (840 g)

6 ounces (170 g) roasted
red peppers

½ cup (120 ml) water

2 Tablespoons (30 ml) olive oil

½ cup (120 g) tahini paste

2 ½ Tablespoons (38 ml)
lemon juice

2 garlic cloves, peeled

1 teaspoon hot sauce

3 cups (720 g) canned garbanzo
beans, drained

1 teaspoon cumin powder

1 teaspoon salt

½ teaspoon black pepper

1. Place all ingredients into the Vitamix container
   in the order listed and secure lid.

2. Select Purée program.

3. Switch machine to Start and allow machine to complete
   programmed cycle. Add water if necessary to keep mixture
   flowing freely through blades.

nutritional information

per ¼ cup (60 g) serving: *Calories: 136, Total Fat: 7 g, Saturated Fat: 1 g,*
Protein: 5 g, Fiber: 3 g, Carbohydrates: 13 g, Sodium: 454 mg, Cholesterol: 0 mg

caponata *(eggplant spread)*

preparation: 10 minutes | **processing:** pulsing
cook time: 15 minutes | **yield:** 2 cups (480 g)

¾ pound (340 g) eggplant

1 lemon, halved, seeded, divided use

2 teaspoons salt, divided use

½ red onion, peeled, quartered

½ celery stalk, cut in 1–inch
(2.5 cm) pieces

2 garlic cloves, peeled

6 Tablespoons (90 ml) extra
virgin olive oil, divided use

¼ teaspoon black pepper

1 large Roma tomato, halved

2 Tablespoons (8 g) fresh
oregano leaves

2 Tablespoons (17 g) drained capers

2 Tablespoons (30 ml)
red wine vinegar

2 Tablespoons (30 ml) honey

1. Cut eggplant in quarters lengthwise, then crosswise in thirds.
   Place half the chunks into the Vitamix container and secure lid.

2. Select Variable 2.

3. Pulse 4 times.

4. Scrape into a colander set over a bowl or in a sink; squeeze a lemon half over
   the chopped eggplant and sprinkle with 1 teaspoon salt. Repeat with
   remaining eggplant, lemon and salt. Let stand while proceeding.
   (No need to rinse container.)

5. Place onion, celery and garlic into the Vitamix container and secure lid.

6. Select Variable 4.

» **caponata** *continues on page 246*

continued from page 245

caponata *(eggplant spread)*

7. Pulse 2 times. Stop machine and use rubber spatula to loosen any large pieces from under the blades. Secure lid and Pulse once more.

8. Heat 2 Tablespoons (30 ml) oil in large nonstick skillet over medium heat. Scrape onion mixture into skillet; stir in pepper. Cook 3 to 4 minutes or until tender, stirring occasionally.

9. Rinse eggplant in running water; drain well and squeeze to remove as much moisture as possible. Add remaining 4 Tablespoons (60 ml) oil to skillet and scoop eggplant into skillet. Cook 5 minutes or until softened, stirring occasionally.

10. Add tomato and oregano to the Vitamix container and secure lid.

11. Select Variable 4.

12. Pulse 2 times.

13. Scrape into skillet. Add capers, red wine vinegar and honey. Cook until mixture is thick and vegetables are tender. Serve warm or at room temperature with pita chips. Store leftovers covered in refrigerator.

nutritional information

per ¼ cup (60 g) serving: *Calories: 133, Total Fat: 11 g, Saturated Fat: 2 g, Protein: 1 g, Fiber: 2 g, Carbohydrates: 10 g, Sodium: 651 mg, Cholesterol: 0 mg*

aioli

preparation: 5 minutes | ***processing:*** 1 minute | ***yield:*** 1 ¾ cups (420 g)

3 large pasteurized egg yolks

¼ cup (60 ml) lemon juice

1 teaspoon salt

⅛ teaspoon white pepper

3 garlic cloves, peeled

1 ½ cups (360 ml) light olive oil

1. Place egg yolks, lemon juice, salt, pepper and garlic into the Vitamix container in the order listed and secure lid.

2. Select Variable 1.

3. Switch machine to Start and slowly increase speed to Variable 3. Remove the lid plug.

4. While machine is running, slowly pour oil through the lid plug opening. As mixture begins to thicken, the oil may be added at a faster rate. Process should take no longer than 1 minute.

5. Refrigerate in an airtight container.

nutritional information

per 1 tablespoon (15 g) serving: *Calories: 115, Total Fat: 12 g, Saturated Fat: 2 g, Protein: 0 g, Fiber: 0 g, Carbohydrates: 0 g, Sodium: 84 mg, Cholesterol: 22 mg*

cheese fondue

preparation: 5 minutes | **processing:** 4 minutes | **yield:** 3 ¾ cups (900 ml)

¾ cup (180 ml) dry white wine

¾ cup (180 ml) water

1 ½ Tablespoons Kirsch, if desired

2 Tablespoons (16 g) cornstarch

¼ teaspoon nutmeg

1 teaspoon ground black pepper

8 ounces (227 g) cubed Gruyère cheese

8 ounces (227 g) cubed Emmental cheese

1. Place all ingredients into the Vitamix container in the order listed and secure lid.

2. Select Variable 1.

3. Switch machine to Start and slowly increase speed to Variable 8.

4. Blend for 4 minutes until mixture is smooth and warm.

5. Pour mixture into fondue pot.

nutritional information

per 2 tablespoon (30 ml) serving: *Calories: 66, Total Fat: 5 g, Saturated Fat: 3 g, Protein: 4 g, Fiber: 0 g, Carbohydrates: 1 g, Sodium: 40 mg, Cholesterol: 15 mg*

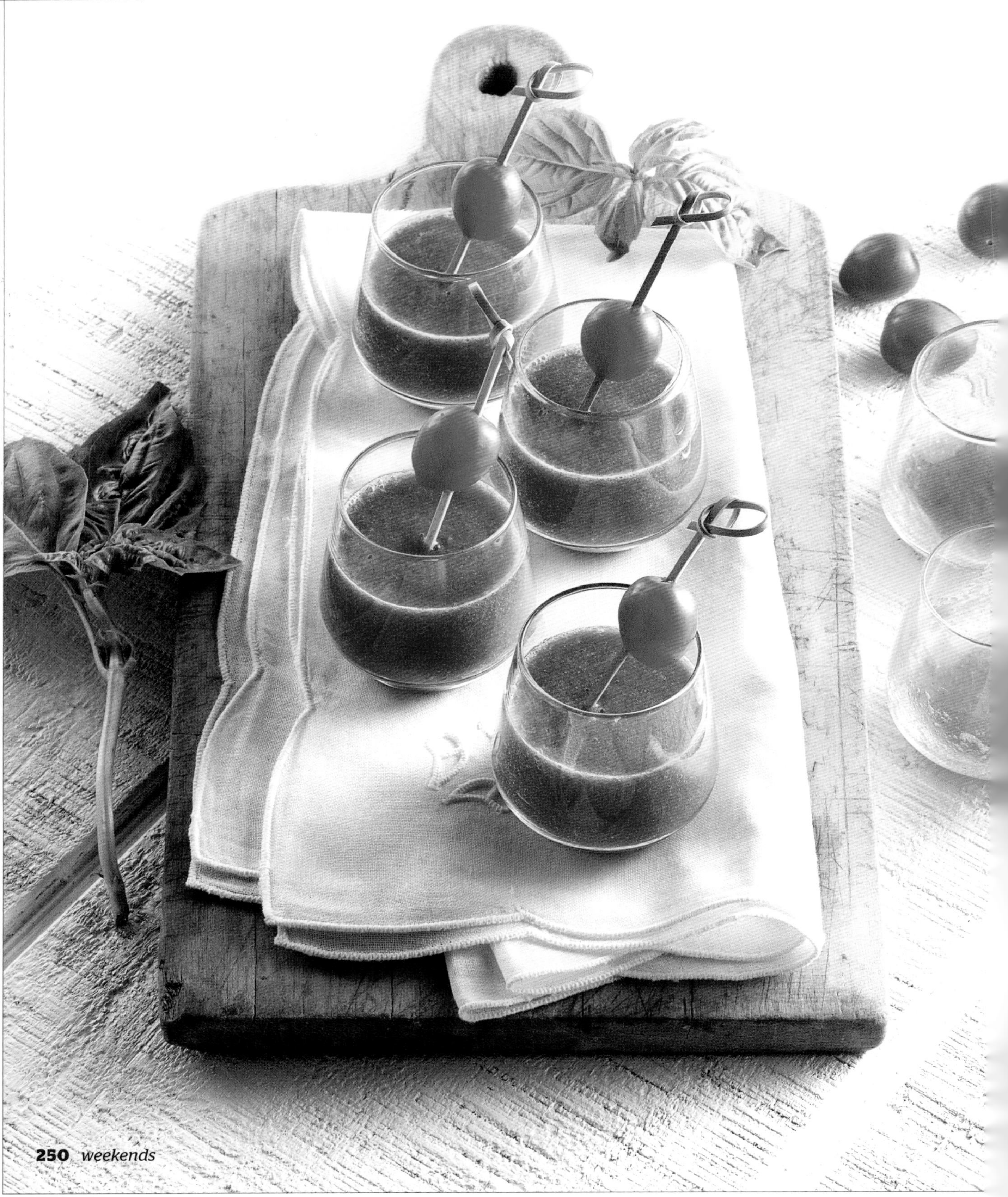

strawberry-tomato
soup shooters

preparation: 10 minutes | **processing:** 13 seconds
yield: 15 shooters

1 cup (240 ml) diced canned
tomatoes including liquid

2 Tablespoons (30 g)
tomato paste

½ pound (227 g) fresh
strawberries, hulled

2 Tablespoons (3 g) fresh
basil leaves, firmly packed

¾-inch (2 cm) wedge
of sweet onion, peeled

1 small garlic clove, peeled

1 Tablespoon packed
brown sugar

1 Tablespoon white
balsamic vinegar

¼ teaspoon kosher salt

¾ cup (180 ml) chilled
white wine

15 2-ounce (60 ml) glasses

Small basil leaves or wedges
of small strawberries for
garnish, if desired

1. Place tomatoes, tomato paste, strawberries, basil, onion, garlic, sugar, vinegar and salt into the Vitamix container and secure lid.

2. Select Variable 1.

3. Switch machine to Start and slowly increase speed to Variable 5. Blend for 10 seconds until smooth. Turn machine off and remove lid. Add wine to the Vitamix container and secure lid.

4. Select Variable 2.

5. Switch machine to Start and blend for 3 seconds. Pour about 3 Tablespoons (45 ml) of soup into each glass.

nutritional information

per serving: *Calories: 26, Total Fat: 0 g, Saturated Fat: 0 g, Protein: 0 g, Fiber: 0 g, Carbohydrates: 4 g, Sodium: 71 mg, Cholesterol: 0 mg*

for two or twenty

create strawberry garnishes

A strawberry fan or strawberry flower will add flair to the presentation of any strawberry recipe.

strawberry fan: Cut whole strawberries in ⅛-inch slices, stopping ¼-inch from the stem so that the base of the berry is still intact. Then carefully fan out slices.

strawberry flower: Set whole strawberry stem side down and make four shallow slices into the berry near the bottom, circling the berry, as if releasing four "petals." Repeat once higher on berry, slicing so that the petals on upper row are offset from first row. Take care not to slice all the way through. Gently press petals outward until they resemble a flower.

ingredient IQ

The cream cheese will blend more easily if it is very soft. Microwave on Low power for 30 to 40 seconds. Microwaves vary; make sure it doesn't melt!

potted *cheese*

preparation: 10 minutes | **processing:** 2 minutes + pulsing
yield: 2 cups (480 g)

10-ounce (284 g) block cold extra sharp Cheddar cheese, cut in 1 ½-inch x 1-inch (4 cm x 2.5 cm) pieces

8-ounce (227 g) package cream cheese, softened

1-inch (2.5 cm) wedge of a medium onion, peeled

4 ounces (113 g) crumbled blue cheese

3 Tablespoons (45 ml) brandy

2 teaspoons Worcestershire sauce

1. Place Cheddar cheese into the Vitamix container and secure lid.

2. Select Variable 3.

3. Pulse 5 times until chopped. Stop machine. Use a small rubber spatula to loosen cheddar cheese from under blades.

4. Add cream cheese, onion, blue cheese, brandy and Worcestershire sauce to the cheese in the Vitamix container and secure lid.

5. Select Variable 1.

6. Switch machine to Start and slowly increase speed to Variable 3.

7. Blend for 2 minutes, using the tamper to push the ingredients into the blades.

8. Spoon into container and refrigerate, covered, for several hours to blend flavors. Serve as a spread for cocktail bread, crackers or apple slices.

nutritional information

per 2 tablespoon (30 g) serving: *Calories: 157, Total Fat: 13 g, Saturated Fat: 8 g, Protein: 6 g, Fiber: 0 g. Carbohydrates: 1 g, Sodium: 262 mg, Cholesterol: 40 mg*

pineapple and **ham kabobs**

preparation: 20 minutes | ***processing:*** 5 seconds+pulsing
bake time: 15 minutes | ***yield:*** 12 servings

¼ pound (113 g) chunk of baked ham, cut in 1 ½-inch (4 cm) cubes

1-inch (2.5 cm) wedge of sweet onion, peeled

½ pound (227 g) lean (93%) ground turkey

1 teaspoon dry ground mustard

1 teaspoon Worcestershire sauce

¼ teaspoon ground black pepper

24 1-inch (2.5 cm) cubes fresh pineapple

1 small green bell pepper cut in 1-inch (2.5 cm) pieces

24 6-inch (15 cm) wooden skewers

1. Preheat oven to 375°F (190°C). Spray 1 large or 2 small cookie sheets with cooking spray.

2. Place ham and onion into the Vitamix container and secure lid.

3. Select Variable 4.

4. Pulse 3 times for 1 second each time. Use rubber spatula to loosen ham from under blades. Add turkey, mustard, Worcestershire sauce and black pepper to the Vitamix container and secure lid.

5. Select Variable 2.

6. Switch machine to Start and blend for 5 seconds or until mixed.

7. Form 24 1-inch (2.5 cm) balls, using level Tablespoon or small cookie scoop sprayed with cooking spray. For easier shaping, dampen hands with water.

8. Spear pineapple chunks with skewers, pushing to about half way onto skewers. Add ham ball and bell pepper piece to each skewer. Place about ½-inch (1.3 cm) apart on cookie sheets. Bake 10 minutes; turn over. Bake an additional 5 minutes or until ham is browned and thoroughly cooked, and meat thermometer inserted in center of ham ball reaches 165°F (74°C).

nutritional information

per serving (2 kabobs): *Calories: 48, Total Fat: 2 g, Saturated Fat: 0 g, Protein: 5 g, Fiber: 0 g, Carbohydrates: 3 g, Sodium: 144 mg, Cholesterol: 15 mg*

crab cakes *with* sweet chilli
dipping sauce

preparation: 15 minutes | **processing:** 30 seconds + pulsing | **cook time:** 8 minutes
cooling time: 30 minutes – 2 hours | **yield:** 4 servings

crab cakes:

5–6 slices of bread, torn into large pieces

1 red pepper, quartered, seeded

2 spring onions, halved

3 cilantro sprigs

14 ounces (400 g) white crabmeat, divided use

3 Tablespoons (45 g) mayonnaise

1 large egg white

zest of 1 lime

1 Tablespoon lime juice

pinch cayenne pepper

dash of hot sauce

salt and freshly ground black pepper

3 Tablespoons (45 ml) olive oil

dipping sauce:

2 tomatoes, quartered

4 ounces (110 g) superfine sugar

6 Tablespoons (90 ml) rice wine vinegar

2 red chilies, seeded

2 garlic cloves, peeled

1 Tablespoon lime juice

1 Tablespoon Thai fish sauce

1. To make the crab cakes, secure lid on the Vitamix machine and select Variable 2.

2. Switch machine to Start, remove lid plug and drop bread pieces through the lid plug opening into the container, using the tamper to push it into the blades.

3. Blend 5 seconds or until it has formed breadcrumbs. Transfer to a bowl and set aside.

» **crab cakes with sweet chilli dipping sauce**
continues on page 256

continued from page 254

crab cakes *with* **sweet chilli** *dipping sauce*

4. Place the red pepper, spring onions and cilantro into the Vitamix container and secure lid.

5. Select Variable 3.

6. Pulse 2 to 3 times until finely chopped. Use the tamper to push the vegetables into the blades if necessary. Remove the lid and add 4 ounces (113 g) crabmeat, mayonnaise, egg white, lime zest, lime juice, cayenne pepper, hot sauce, salt and pepper to the Vitamix container.

7. Continue to Pulse a few times until the mixture forms a coarse paste. Do not over process.

8. Transfer to a bowl and mix in remaining 10 ounces (284 g) crabmeat. Stir gently to combine. Add enough of the breadcrumbs to form a stiff mixture. Put the remaining breadcrumbs on a plate. Wash the Vitamix machine.

9. Shape the crab mixture into 8 patties of equal size. Coat in the breadcrumbs, pressing the crumbs onto each side.

10. Transfer to a clean plate, cover with cling film and chill at least 30 minutes up to 2 hours.

11. Place all sauce ingredients into the Vitamix container and secure lid.

12. Select Variable 1.

13. Switch machine to Start and slowly increase speed to Variable 8. Blend for 25 seconds. Pour the sauce into a bowl and set aside.

14. Heat the olive oil in a frying pan over a medium–high heat, add half of the crab cakes and fry for 2 minutes on each side until crisp and golden. Transfer to a plate and keep warm while you cook the remaining cakes. Serve warm with the dipping sauce.

nutritional information

per serving (2 crab cakes and 2 tablespoons sauce): *Calories: 524, Total Fat: 22 g, Saturated Fat: 2 g, Protein: 28 g, Fiber: 4 g Carbohydrates: 67 g, Sodium: 1254 mg, Cholesterol: 74 mg*

shrimp **pâté**

preparation: 10 minutes | **processing:** 26 seconds + pulsing | **yield:** 2 cups (480 g)

¼ cup (60 g) butter, softened

8-ounce (227 g) package
cream cheese, softened

¼ cup (60 g) pickled
onions, well-drained

2 Tablespoons (30 ml) sherry

1 thin slice lemon

8 ounces (227 g) cooked peeled,
deveined, tail off small shrimp
(thaw and drain well if frozen)

¼ cup (15 g) fresh parsley sprigs

1. Place butter, cream cheese, onions, sherry and lemon into the Vitamix container and secure lid.

2. Select Variable 1.

3. Switch machine to Start and slowly increase speed to Variable 3. Blend 20 seconds or until smooth. Stop machine and remove lid. Add shrimp to the Vitamix container and secure lid.

4. Select Variable 1.

5. Switch machine to Start and slowly increase speed to Variable 3. Blend 6 seconds or until finely chopped. Stop machine and remove lid. Add parsley to the Vitamix container and secure lid.

6. Select Variable 3.

7. Pulse 3 times.

8. Spoon into container. Cover and refrigerate 4 hours or overnight to blend flavors. Serve with crackers, crostini or bagel chips.

nutritional information

per 2 tablespoon (30 g) serving: *Calories: 93, Total Fat: 8 g, Saturated Fat: 5 g, Protein: 4 g, Fiber: 0 g, Carbohydrates: 1 g, Sodium: 119 mg, Cholesterol: 45 mg*

prosciutto, fig *and*
parmesan canapés

preparation: 20 minutes | **processing:** 5 seconds + pulsing | **cook time:** 15–20 minutes
cooling time: 1 hour | **yield:** 24 appetizers

1 orange, peeled, plus 1–inch x 2–inch
(2.5 x 5 cm) strip of the zest

¼ lemon, peeled, plus 1–inch x 1–inch
(2.5 cm x 2.5 cm) strip of the zest

2 thin slices ginger

1 cup (240 ml) dry red wine

8–ounce (227 g) package Calimyrna
dried figs, stems removed

¼ cup (60 ml) honey

2 Tablespoons (25 g) sugar

2 Tablespoons (30 ml) white balsamic vinegar

24 slices crostini or toasted whole
grain cocktail bread

8 slices prosciutto, cut crosswise in thirds

2 cups (72 g) baby lettuce, arugula or spinach

2 ounces (56 g) Parmesan cheese, shaved

1. Place orange and zest, lemon and zest, ginger and wine into the Vitamix container and secure lid.

2. Select Variable 1.

3. Switch machine to Start and slowly increase speed to Variable 5.

4. Blend 5 seconds or until almost smooth. Stop machine and remove lid.

5. Add figs to the Vitamix container and secure lid.

6. Select Variable 4.

7. Pulse 5 to 6 times to coarsely chop.

8. Pour fig mixture into medium-sized saucepan and add honey, sugar and vinegar. Cook over medium-low heat, stirring occasionally, 15 to 20 minutes or until figs are soft and most of liquid is absorbed. Spoon into container. Cover and refrigerate 1 hour until cool.

9. Spread fig mixture on crostini. Top with prosciutto (pleating to fit), some of the lettuce and a few cheese shavings.

nutritional information

per canapé: *Calories: 114, Total Fat: 1 g, Saturated Fat: 0 g, Protein: 4 g, Fiber: 2 g, Carbohydrates: 20 g, Sodium: 267 mg, Cholesterol: 5 mg*

herbology

make any dish look polished

Growing your own herb garden makes it easy to grab a sprig for a quick garnish, especially for unexpected company. Luckily, there are many herbs that grow well indoors all year round.

Both curly and flat-leaf parsley do well in pots. Parsley plants have a long root system, so they require a taller pot (at least 10 inches deep).

Mint is very invasive, so make sure you plant it in its own pot.

Vietnamese coriander tastes similar to cilantro, but requires less sunlight.

Chives grow especially well indoors, even with limited sunlight in winter.

cheesy crisp sliders
with onion jam

preparation: 35 minutes | ***processing:*** 3 seconds + pulsing | ***cook time:*** 8 minutes | ***yield:*** 20 sliders

2 ounces (56 g) Parmesan cheese,
cut in 1-inch (2.5 cm) pieces

2 slices sandwich bread, torn into
4 pieces each

4 ounces (113 g) smoky sharp Cheddar
cheese, cut in 1-inch (2.5 cm) pieces

1 ½ pounds (680 g) extra lean
(85 to 90%) ground beef

½ teaspoon salt

¼ teaspoon black pepper

1 Tablespoon oil

2 loaves ciabatta bread,
5-inches x 12-inches (13 cm x 30 cm) each
or 20 turkey buns or white mountain rolls

1 ¾ cups (420 g) Onion Jam,
warmed (page 240)

½ cup (68 g) crumbled blue cheese

2 cups (72 g) baby lettuce, baby
spinach or arugula

1. Place Parmesan cheese into the Vitamix container and secure lid.

2. Select Variable 1.

3. Switch machine to Start and slowly increase speed to Variable 3.

4. Blend for 3 seconds. Stop machine and use rubber spatula to scrape under
   blades and around sides to loosen cheese. Add torn sandwich bread to
   the Vitamix container and secure lid.

5. Select Variable 5.

6. Pulse 3 times. Pour cheesy breadcrumbs into small bowl.

7. Place Cheddar cheese into the Vitamix container and secure lid.

on the menu

Onion Jam (page 240), a tart-sweet blend of onions, sugar, honey, raisins and balsamic vinegar, is the perfect accent for these savory sliders.

8. Select Variable 4.

9. Pulse 3 times for 1 second each time.
   Scrape into large bowl.

10. Add ground beef, salt and pepper to the bowl.
    Mix well and shape into 20 balls (1 ½–inch (4 cm) diameter).
    Roll balls in breadcrumb mixture, pressing into meat.
    Shape each into a 2–inch (5 cm) patty and place on plate,
    stacking if necessary. (Discard any remaining breadcrumbs.)

11. Heat a griddle to 350°F (180°C) or a 12–inch (30 cm) nonstick skillet
    over medium heat. Brush with oil. Add as many patties as possible.
    Cook, turning once or twice, 6 to 8 minutes or until deep golden brown
    and meat thermometer registers 165°F (74°C). If using a griddle, turn to
    low and keep patties warm. If using a skillet, heat oven to 250°F (120°C).
    Place cooked patties on baking sheet and keep warm in warm oven.

12. Split ciabatta bread in half horizontally. Cut in half lengthwise and then
    crosswise in fifths to make 10 small squares from each loaf (or split buns).
    Spoon 1 rounded spoonful of jam on bottom of each bread piece. Top each
    with 1 teaspoon blue cheese, cooked patty and a couple leaves of baby
    lettuce. Add bread tops and secure with toothpick if desired. Serve warm.

nutritional information

per slider: Calories: 247, Total Fat: 10 g, Saturated Fat: 4 g, Protein: 13 g,
Fiber: 2 g, Carbohydrates: 33 g, Sodium: 417 mg, Cholesterol: 38 mg

potstickers

preparation: 20 minutes | **processing:** pulsing
cook time: 10 minutes per batch | **yield:** 144 potstickers

bright idea

Potstickers are great for quick appetizers! Make ahead and freeze in resealable bags; steaming just takes minutes. Serve with Citrus Marinade (page 144) as a dip.

1 ¼ pounds (567 g) Chinese, Napa or Savoy cabbage, cut into 1 ½–inch (4 cm) chunks, divided use

1 ½ bunches green onions, washed, halved, divided use

8 garlic cloves, peeled, divided use

½ cup (65 g) chopped ginger root, divided use

¼ cup (60 ml) soy sauce

1 Tablespoon dark sesame oil

1 teaspoon fish sauce

1 package gyoza wrappers

1 teaspoon cornstarch mixed with 1 Tablespoon cold water

1 tablespoon canola oil

1. Place half of the cabbage, green onions, garlic and ginger into the Vitamix container, float with water and secure lid.

2. Select Variable 8.

3. Pulse 5 times. Drain and repeat with the remaining ingredients. Place in large bowl. Add soy sauce, sesame oil and fish sauce to the chopped vegetables and mix by hand until evenly combined.

4. Lay gyoza wrappers flat and fill with about 1 to 1 ½ teaspoons filling. Moisten a fingertip in the cornstarch and water mixture then rub along the edge of the dumpling. Pull bottom up and pinch together excess dumpling dough. Try to squeeze as much air out of the dumpling as you can while pinching sides. It will look like a pierogi. Press firmly together with a fork until it sticks.

5. Heat a heavy nonstick skillet with tight-fitting lid over medium-high heat. Pour canola oil into skillet and swirl to coat the bottom. Sauté potstickers for 3 minutes. Add ½ cup (120 ml) warm water to the pan and immediately place the lid on the pan. If cooking them fresh, steam with the lid on for 5 minutes. If starting with frozen, steam for 8 minutes. When time is up, remove lid and cook an additional 1 to 2 minutes so the potstickers can brown.

nutritional information

per serving (four potstickers): *Calories: 107, Total Fat: 1 g, Saturated Fat: 0 g, Protein: 5 g, Fiber: 0 g, Carbohydrates: 22 g, Sodium: 346 mg, Cholesterol: 4 mg*

asparagus spears
with **romesco dip**

preparation: 10 minutes | ***processing:*** 15 seconds + pulsing | ***cook time:*** 1 minute
yield: 1 ¼ cups (300 g) sauce; 14 appetizer servings

1 pound (454 g) thin asparagus
spears, trimmed (about 28)

1 teaspoon salt

½ cup (73 g) whole blanched
almonds, toasted

2 Roma tomatoes, halved, seeded

½ red bell pepper, quartered

1-inch (2.5 cm) wedge of
medium onion, peeled

2 garlic cloves, peeled

¼ teaspoon salt

¼ cup (60 g) mayonnaise

2 Tablespoons (30 g) chili sauce

1. Bring 1-inch (2.5 cm) of water to a boil in a 12-inch (30 cm) skillet;
   add 1 teaspoon salt. Add asparagus. Cover and cook 1 minute.
   Immediately plunge spears into ice water to chill. Drain.

2. Place almonds into the Vitamix container and secure lid.

3. Select Variable 5.

4. Pulse 5 times or until finely chopped. Scrape into small bowl.

5. Add tomatoes, bell pepper, onion, garlic cloves and salt to the
   Vitamix container and secure lid.

6. Select Variable 1.

7. Switch machine to Start and slowly increase speed to Variable 3.

8. Blend for 5 seconds or until finely chopped, using tamper to push food
   into blades. Stop machine and remove lid.

9. Add almonds, mayonnaise and chili sauce to the Vitamix container and secure lid.

10. Select Variable 1.

11. Switch machine to Start and slowly increase speed to Variable 3.

12. Blend for 5 seconds. Stop machine and remove lid. Scrape down the sides of the container with a spatula and secure lid.

13. Switch machine to Start and blend 5 additional seconds.

14. Pour into bowl and serve with asparagus spears.

nutritional information

per serving: *Calories: 73, Total Fat: 6 g, Saturated Fat: 1 g, Protein: 2 g, Fiber: 2 g, Carbohydrates: 4 g, Sodium: 306 mg, Cholesterol: 1 mg*

for two or twenty

give it your best shot

Special touches are often simple—like using shot glasses for serving appetizers. Individual servings in small glassware make it easier for your guests to eat while enjoying party conversation.

Cut roasted asparagus into smaller spears and stand them up in shot glasses. Add a spoonful of Romesco dip for an intriguing appetizer.

Place two cocktail shrimp and a basil leaf in a shot glass for mini shrimp cocktails. Serve with a complementary dip such as Spicy Tomato Sauce (page 150).

A champagne sorbet can also be served in shot glasses as an appetizer; garnish with a raspberry on the rim.

dried apricot chutney

preparation: 5 minutes | **processing:** 5 seconds
cook time: 25–30 minutes | **yield:** 2 cups (480 g)

on the menu

Serve this sweet condiment as a perfect accent for grilled pork chops. It will keep for up to two weeks in the refrigerator.

6 ounces (170 g) red pepper, quartered, seeded

1-inch (2.5 cm) piece ginger root, peeled

7-ounce (200 g) bag dried apricots, about 30 apricots

½ cup (120 ml) water

½ cup (120 ml) distilled vinegar

⅓ cup (67 g) sugar

1. Place red pepper, ginger root and apricots into the Vitamix container in the order listed and secure lid.

2. Select Variable 1.

3. Switch machine to Start and slowly increase speed to Variable 3. Blend for 5 seconds, using the tamper to push the ingredients into the blade while processing.

4. Pour into 2-quart saucepan and add water, vinegar and sugar. Mix well.

5. Bring to a boil over medium-high heat, stirring occasionally. Reduce heat to medium-low and simmer 15 to 20 minutes, stirring often to prevent sticking, until thickened.

6. Pour into storage containers and cool to room temperature. Cover and chill until needed.

nutritional information

per ¼ cup (60 g) serving: *Calories: 104, Total Fat: 0 g, Saturated Fat: 0 g, Protein: 1 g, Fiber: 1 g, Carbohydrates: 24 g, Sodium: 4 mg, Cholesterol: 0 mg*

build a meal

spice things up

Chutneys are spicy condiments made of fruit, vinegar, sugar and spices; they can be smooth or chunky, mild or hot. Pairing well with roasts and curries, chutneys also make first-rate spreads and dips.

Relishes are cooked or pickled sauces made with vegetables or fruit. They can be sweet or spicy. Like chutneys, relishes are often served with meats or used to punch up sandwich flavors.

Pairing suggestions include: Dried Apricot Chutney with Feta-Stuffed Chicken Breasts (page 131), Piccalilli (page 272) spooned over Corned Beef Hash (page 202) and Corn Relish (page 273) on Black Bean Burgers (page 110) or Zucchini Burgers (page 115).

cucumber
orange relish

preparation: 10 minutes | ***processing:*** 10 seconds | ***yield:*** 2 cups (480 g)

1 orange, peeled, halved, seeded

¼ cup (2 g) fresh dill

12 ounces (340 g) English cucumber,
cut into 2–inch (5 cm) pieces

4 teaspoons rice vinegar

½ teaspoon sugar

¼ teaspoon coarse salt

1. Place orange and dill into the Vitamix container and secure lid.

2. Select Variable 1.

3. Switch machine to Start and slowly increase speed to Variable 5.

4. Blend for 5 seconds.

5. Reduce speed to Variable 3 and remove the lid plug.

6. Add cucumber through lid plug opening, one piece at a time,
until coarsely chopped.

7. Place in a medium-sized bowl and add vinegar, sugar and salt. Mix well.

8. Cover and chill 2 hours or until needed. Relish should be used the same day.

nutritional information

per ¼ cup (60 g) serving: *Calories: 13, Total Fat: 0 g, Saturated Fat: 0 g,
Protein: 0 g, Fiber: 1 g, Carbohydrates: 3 g, Sodium: 61 mg, Cholesterol: 0 mg*

mango *chutney*

preparation: 10 minutes | ***processing:*** 8 seconds + pulsing | ***cook time:*** 1 hour | ***yield:*** 3 cups (720 g)

3 semi-ripe mangoes, seeded, unpeeled, cut into chunks, divided use

6 ounces (170 g) onion, peeled, quartered

1-inch (2.5 cm) piece ginger root, peeled

2 garlic cloves, peeled

1 cup (165 g) golden raisins

1 cup (220 g) firmly packed light brown sugar

½ cup (120 ml) distilled vinegar

1 teaspoon mustard seeds

¼ teaspoon ground allspice

6 whole cloves

1. Place ⅓ mango, onion, ginger root and garlic into the Vitamix container in order listed and secure lid.

2. Select Variable 1.

3. Switch machine to Start and blend for 8 seconds. Stop machine and remove lid. Add remaining ⅔ mangoes and secure lid.

4. Select Variable 1.

5. Pulse 8 times, until coarsely chopped, using the tamper to push the ingredients into the blade while processing.

6. Pour into 3-quart saucepan and add remaining ingredients. Mix well. Bring to a boil over medium-high heat, stirring occasionally. Reduce heat to medium and simmer 1 hour, stirring often to prevent sticking, until thickened. Remove cloves.

7. Pour into storage containers and cool to room temperature. Cover and chill until needed.

nutritional information

per ¼ cup (60 g) serving: *Calories: 155, Total Fat: 0 g, Saturated Fat: 0 g, Protein: 1 g, Fiber: 2 g, Carbohydrates: 38 g, Sodium: 10 mg, Cholesterol: 0 mg*

pineapple **cranberry relish**

preparation: 10 minutes | **processing:** pulsing
cook time: 30 – 40 minutes | **yield:** 1 ¾ cups (420 g)

3 cups (500 g) fresh pineapple chunks

2 cups (220 g) fresh cranberries

¼ cup (60 ml) honey

¼ cup (27 g) slivered almonds, toasted

1 Tablespoon freshly grated orange zest

1. Place pineapple and cranberries into the Vitamix container and secure lid.

2. Select Variable 2.

3. Pulse 8 to 10 times until coarsely chopped.

4. Pour into 2–quart saucepan and add honey. Mix well.

5. Bring to a boil over medium-high heat, stirring occasionally. Reduce heat to medium-low and simmer 15 to 20 minutes, stirring often to prevent sticking, until thickened. Remove from heat and stir in almonds and orange zest.

6. Pour into storage container and cool to room temperature. Cover and chill until needed.

nutritional information

per ¼ cup (60g) serving: *Calories: 102, Total Fat: 2 g, Saturated Fat: 0 g, Protein: 1 g, Fiber: 2 g, Carbohydrates: 22 g, Sodium: 2 mg, Cholesterol: 0 mg*

ingredient IQ

If you prefer more heat in Piccalilli, add ½ teaspoon chili powder. To go even hotter, add half of a fresh jalapeño pepper, chopped.

piccalilli

preparation: 10 minutes | **processing:** pulsing
cook time: 8 minutes | **yield:** 3 ½ cups (840 g)

1 cup (240 ml) water

8 ounces (227 g) red onion, peeled, quartered

8 ounces (227 g) zucchini, cut into chunks

1 pound (454 g) cucumber, cut into chunks

1 teaspoon coarse salt

1 cup (220 g) firmly packed light brown sugar

1 cup (240 ml) cider vinegar

1 Tablespoon pickling spice

1 teaspoon mustard seed

1. Place water, onion, zucchini and cucumber into the Vitamix container in the order listed and secure lid.

2. Select Variable 3.

3. Pulse 8 to 10 times, using the tamper to push ingredients into the blades while processing.

4. Place vegetables in a medium-sized bowl and add salt. Mix well. Divide into pint storage containers.

5. Combine brown sugar, vinegar, pickling spice and mustard seed in a saucepan. Bring to a boil. Reduce heat and simmer 2 minutes.

6. Ladle hot brine over vegetables and cool to room temperature. Cover and chill until needed.

nutritional information

per ¼ cup (118 g) serving: Calories: 79, Total Fat: 0 g, Saturated Fat: 0 g, Protein: 1 g, Fiber: 1 g, Carbohydrates: 19 g, Sodium: 145 mg, Cholesterol: 0 mg

corn relish

preparation: 10 minutes | **processing:** 5–10 seconds
cook time: 20 minutes | **yield:** 4 ½ cups (1.0 kg)

on the menu

Corn Relish will keep for up to three weeks in the refrigerator, which is very handy since it goes with so many different meat, fish and poultry dishes.

4 ears corn on the cob, husked

6 ounces (340 g) red onion, peeled, quartered

6 ounces (340 g) green pepper, seeded, quartered

6 ounces (340 g) red pepper, seeded, quartered

1 cup (240 ml) cider vinegar

½ cup (100 g) sugar

½ cup (120 ml) water

1 teaspoon celery seeds

¼ teaspoon coarse salt

1. Bring a large pot of water to a boil. Add corn on the cob and cook 3 minutes. Cool corn and remove kernels from the cob. Place in a medium-sized bowl.

2. Place onion, green pepper and red pepper into the Vitamix container in the order listed and secure lid.

3. Select Variable 2.

4. Switch machine to Start and blend 5 to 10 seconds, using the tamper to push the vegetables into the blade. Add to corn.

5. Combine vinegar, sugar, water, celery seeds and salt in a small saucepan. Heat over medium heat until mixture comes to a boil. Reduce heat to low and cook 1 minute.

6. Pour hot brine over vegetables. Cool to room temperature. Divide into pint storage containers. Cover and chill until needed.

nutritional information

per ¼ cup (81 g) serving: *Calories: 64, Total Fat: 1 g, Saturated Fat: 0 g, Protein: 1 g, Fiber: 2 g, Carbohydrates: 13 g, Sodium: 31 mg, Cholesterol: 0 mg*

send in a sub!

relish the thought

Relishes can turn everyday dishes into something truly extraordinary. Try these flavorful and colorful substitutions for traditional accompaniments:

Spoon Corn Relish atop grilled flank steak rather than steak sauce.

For a gourmet alternative, offer Cucumber Orange Relish (page 268) with hamburgers and hot dogs.

Instead of traditional cranberry sauce, try Pineapple Cranberry Relish (page 270) with your Thanksgiving turkey. Great with baked ham or baked chicken as well.

Skip tartar sauce and serve salmon, tilapia or other fish filets with a side of zesty Mango Chutney (page 269).

AS THE LAST IMPRESSION of a great meal, dessert should be a memorable finale. Your Vitamix will help you create desserts with professional flair—great tools are one of a chef's secrets. Start with *Milkshakes* (page 277) for both kids and grown-ups. You'll find entertaining recipes and tips in *Frozen Desserts* (page 291) and *Baked Desserts* (page 303). Finishing touches are addressed in *Dessert Condiments* (page 317) so you can garnish your creations like a pro.

weekends

desserts

MILKSHAKES / FROZEN DESSERTS / BAKED DESSERTS / DESSERT CONDIMENTS

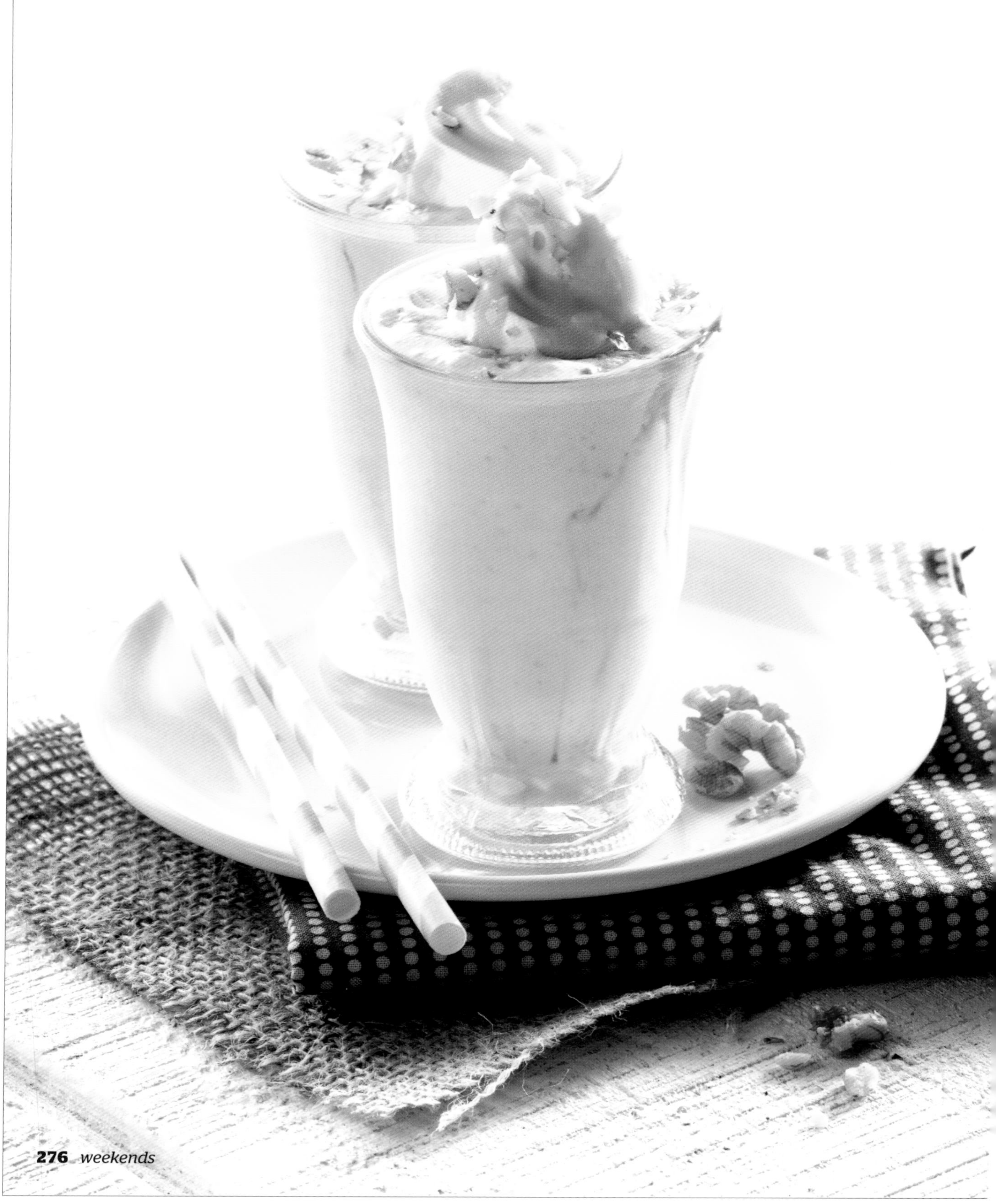

maple nut
milkshake

preparation: 5 minutes | **processing:** 15 seconds
yield: 3 cups (720 ml)

3 cups (400 g) vanilla ice cream

¼ cup + 2 Tablespoons (90 ml) milk

1 ½ teaspoons vanilla extract

3 Tablespoons (45 ml) maple syrup

¼ cup (25 g) walnuts

1. Place all ingredients into the Vitamix container in the order listed and secure lid.

2. Select Variable 1.

3. Switch machine to Start and slowly increase speed to Variable 8.

4. Blend for 15 seconds using the tamper to press the ingredients into the blades.

nutritional information

per 1 cup (240 ml) serving: *Calories: 392, Total Fat: 20 g, Saturated Fat: 10 g, Protein: 7 g, Fiber: 1 g, Carbohydrates: 48 g, Sodium: 124 mg, Cholesterol: 60 mg*

for two or twenty

milkshakes after five

A milkshake needs only a little help to become a fun frozen cocktail. Try a small amount of chocolate-, vanilla- or coffee-flavored liqueur in any of the milkshake recipes in this section.

For more spirited additions, rum will deepen the flavor of a Maple Nut Milkshake or the World's Best Malted Milkshake (page 288), bourbon livens up a Basic Vanilla Milkshake (page 278), and brandy adds a twist to the Banana Cream Pie Milkshake (page 287).

Be sure to stir in only a tablespoon or two of alcohol, as too much will overpower the flavors and prevent the drink from freezing properly.

basic vanilla
milkshake

preparation: 5 minutes | ***processing:*** 15 seconds | ***yield:*** 4 ¾ cups (1.1 L)

4 cups (520 g) vanilla ice cream

1 ¾ cups (420 ml) milk

2 ½ teaspoons vanilla extract

1. Place all ingredients into the Vitamix container in the order listed and secure lid.

2. Select Variable 1.

3. Switch machine to Start and slowly increase speed to Variable 8.

4. Blend for 15 seconds.

nutritional information

per 1 cup (240 ml) serving: *Calories: 271, Total Fat: 13 g, Saturated Fat: 8 g, Protein: 7 g, Fiber: 1 g, Carbohydrates: 31 g, Sodium: 137 mg, Cholesterol: 54 mg*

strawberry white
chocolate milkshake ❄

preparation: 5 minutes | ***processing:*** 45 seconds | ***yield:*** 4 cups (960 ml)

1 cup (240 ml) milk

2 cups (268 g) vanilla ice cream

½ cup (120 g) white chocolate chips

2 cups (300 g) frozen unsweetened strawberries

1. Place all ingredients into the Vitamix container in the order listed and secure lid.

2. Select Frozen Dessert program.

3. Switch machine to Start and allow machine to complete programmed cycle, using the tamper to press the ingredients into the blades.

nutritional information

per 1 cup (240 ml) serving: *Calories: 346, Total Fat: 18 g, Saturated Fat: 11 g, Protein: 7 g, Fiber: 2 g, Carbohydrates: 44 g, Sodium: 117 mg, Cholesterol: 43 mg*

peanut butter cup
milkshake

preparation: 5 minutes | **processing:** 30 seconds
yield: 3 cups (720 ml)

¼ cup + 2 Tablespoons (90 ml) milk

3 cups (400 g) vanilla ice cream

3 Tablespoons (45 g) peanut butter

3 Tablespoons (45 ml) chocolate syrup

1. Place all ingredients into the Vitamix container in the order listed and secure lid.

2. Select Variable 1.

3. Switch machine to Start and slowly increase speed to Variable 8.

4. Blend for 30 seconds or until desired consistency is reached.

nutritional information

per 1 cup (240 ml) serving: *Calories: 424, Total Fat: 23 g, Saturated Fat: 11 g, Protein: 10 g, Fiber: 2 g, Carbohydrates: 48 g, Sodium: 209 mg, Cholesterol: 60 mg*

---

family time

milkshakes and a movie

A good movie, plus an even better milkshake, equals a memorable stay-at-home Saturday night with the family.

Set up an assembly line of your favorite extras, all in small disposable dishes: chocolate sauce, caramel sauce, chocolate chips, fruit syrups, chopped nuts, peanut butter, bananas, strawberries, blueberries and more. Everyone selects their own ingredients to create variations on the Basic Vanilla Milkshake (page 278). Make up fun names for your personalized concoctions.

Stocking up on inexpensive soda fountain-type glasses, long ice cream parlor-style spoons, and colorful straws adds to the fun. Top the milkshake creations with whipped cream and a maraschino cherry for that special finishing touch.

looking good

Serve in classic soda fountain glasses with a swirl of chocolate sauce and sliced strawberries on top, or place a strawberry dipped in dark chocolate on each rim.

chocolate covered
strawberry milkshake

preparation: 5 minutes | **processing:** 15 seconds
yield: 3 ½ cups (840 ml)

3 cups (400 g) vanilla ice cream

¼ cup + 2 Tablespoons (90 ml) milk

1 ½ teaspoons vanilla extract

6 fresh strawberries, hulled

3 Tablespoons (45 g) chocolate milk powder

1. Place all ingredients into the Vitamix container in the order listed and secure lid.

2. Select Variable 1.

3. Switch machine to Start and slowly increase speed to Variable 8.

4. Blend for 15 seconds using the tamper to press the ingredients into the blades.

nutritional information

per 1 cup (240 ml) serving: Calories: 289, Total Fat: 13 g, Saturated Fat: 8 g, Protein: 7 g, Fiber: 1 g, Carbohydrates: 36 g, Sodium: 128 mg, Cholesterol: 52 mg

strawberry frost
milkshake ❄

preparation: 5 minutes | **processing:** 45 seconds
yield: 5 cups (1.2 L)

6-ounce (170 g) can frozen pink
lemonade concentrate

1 cup (240 ml) milk

2 cups (300 g) frozen
unsweetened strawberries

2 cups (264 g) vanilla ice cream

fresh strawberries for garnish (optional)

1. Place concentrate, milk, frozen strawberries and ice cream
   into the Vitamix container in the order listed and secure lid.

2. Select Frozen Dessert program.

3. Switch machine to Start and allow machine
   to complete programmed cycle, using the
   tamper to press the ingredients into the blades.

4. Garnish glass with strawberry slices.

nutritional information

per 1 cup (240 ml) serving: *Calories: 211, Total Fat: 6 g, Saturated
Fat: 4 g, Protein: 4 g, Fiber: 2 g, Carbohydrates: 37 g, Sodium: 71 mg,
Cholesterol: 26 mg*

build a meal

berry good brunch

A perfect three-course
menu for a spring brunch
or shower starts with
Swedish Pancakes with
Blueberry Syrup (page
210). Follow up with small
portions of a refreshing
Strawberry Grand Marnier
Sorbet (page 292). For a
third course, serve wedges
of Potato Cheddar Breakfast
Bake (page 200) and
mini muffins made with
the Cranberry Nut Bread
recipe (page 183). When
it's time for dessert, bring
out a tray of Strawberry
Frost Milkshakes. Garnish
the rim of each glass with
a strawberry rolled in
Powdered Sugar (page 325).

chocolate *banana malt*

preparation: 5 minutes | ***processing:*** 30 seconds | ***yield:*** 4 ½ cups (1.0 L)

1 cup (133 g) vanilla ice cream

1 ½ cups (360 ml) low fat milk

⅓ cup (100 g) malted milk powder

¼ cup (60 ml) chocolate syrup

½ banana, peeled, frozen

1 cup (240 ml) ice cubes

1. Place all ingredients into the Vitamix container in the order listed and secure lid.

2. Select Variable 1.

3. Switch machine to Start and slowly increase speed to Variable 8.

4. Blend for 30 seconds or until desired consistency is reached.

nutritional information

per 1 cup (240 ml) serving: *Calories: 259, Total Fat: 6 g, Saturated Fat: 4 g, Protein: 8 g, Fiber: 1 g, Carbohydrates: 43 g, Sodium: 179 mg, Cholesterol: 24 mg*

banana cream pie
milkshake

preparation: 5 minutes | **processing:** 15 seconds
yield: 4 ½ cups (1.0 L)

¼ cup + 2 Tablespoons (90 ml) heavy cream

3 cups (400 g) vanilla ice cream

1 banana, peeled, cut into large chunks

¼ cup + 2 Tablespoons (36 g) graham cracker crumbs

1. Place all ingredients into the Vitamix container in the order listed and secure lid.

2. Select Variable 1.

3. Switch machine to Start and slowly increase speed to Variable 8.

4. Blend for 15 seconds or until desired consistency is reached.

nutritional information

per 1 cup (240 ml) serving: *Calories: 299, Total Fat: 18 g, Saturated Fat: 11 g, Protein: 4 g, Fiber: 1 g, Carbohydrates: 33 g, Sodium: 120 mg, Cholesterol: 66 mg*

ingredient IQ

For graham cracker crumbs, place 24 graham cracker squares into the Vitamix container, select Variable 1, switch machine to Start and slowly increase to Variable 5, blending for 15 to 20 seconds.

send in a sub!

skinny shakes

You can enjoy your favorite shakes with fewer calories if you do a bit of experimenting; see how low you can go! Substitute low-fat frozen yogurt for the ice cream, and skim milk for the heavy cream in the recipe. Adjust the amounts just a bit to get the consistency you like the best.

Reduce calories and fat even further by trying nonfat frozen yogurt instead of ice cream; using nonfat frozen yogurt could save as much as 300 calories and 35g of fat. Adding a sliced banana may replace some of the creaminess without adding fat back into your shake.

world's best
malted milkshake

preparation: 5 minutes | ***processing:*** 30 seconds | ***yield:*** 3 ¼ cups (780 ml)

¼ cup (60 ml) cold milk

¼ cup (60 ml) chocolate syrup

3 cups (400 g) vanilla ice cream

¼ cup (66 g) malted milk powder

1. Place all ingredients into the Vitamix container in the order listed and secure lid.

2. Select Variable 1.

3. Switch machine to Start and slowly increase speed to Variable 8.

4. Blend for 30 seconds using the tamper to press the ingredients into the blades.

nutritional information

per 1 cup (240 ml) serving: *Calories: 426, Total Fat: 16 g, Saturated Fat: 10 g, Protein: 9 g, Fiber: 1 g, Carbohydrates: 63 g, Sodium: 228 mg, Cholesterol: 61 mg*

pink grapefruit granita

preparation: 3–4 hours | **processing:** pulsing
yield: 3 cups (720 ml)

2 ½ cups (600 ml) fresh pink grapefruit juice

1 cup (240 ml) water

⅓ cup (67 g) sugar

1. Combine juice, water and sugar in a bowl and whisk until sugar has dissolved. Pour liquid into a baking pan and freeze until hard, 3 to 4 hours.

2. With a fork, break granita into large chunks. Transfer chunks to the Vitamix container and secure lid.

3. Select Variable 2.

4. Pulse 6 to 8 times using the tamper to press the ingredients into the blades.

5. Serve immediately.

nutritional information

per ½ cup (120 ml) serving: *Calories: 83, Total Fat: 0 g, Saturated Fat: 0 g, Protein: 1 g, Fiber: 0 g, Carbohydrates: 21 g, Sodium: 3 mg, Cholesterol: 0 mg*

change it up

frozen versatility

A simple and refreshing grapefruit juice granita is often served in fine restaurants as an intermezzo to clear the palate between courses. Be creative and dream up your own granita for any occasion or time of year. If it's a liquid and it will freeze, you can make a granita out of it! Just change out the grapefruit juice in this recipe for the beverage of your choice. Champagne mixed with pink lemonade makes a lovely granita for bridal showers. For a summertime dessert, serve a coffee granita or try other juices such as pomegranate, mango or passion fruit. For fall menus, surprise guests with a refreshing apple juice granita.

strawberry
grand marnier sorbet ❄

preparation: 5 minutes | ***processing:*** 45 seconds | ***yield:*** 3 cups (720 ml)

¼ cup (60 ml) orange juice

2 ounces (60 ml) Grand Marnier

⅓ cup (50 g) frozen pineapple chunks

1 pound (454 g) frozen unsweetened strawberries

1. Place all ingredients into the Vitamix container in the order listed and secure lid.

2. Select Frozen Dessert program.

3. Switch machine to Start and allow machine to complete programmed cycle, using the tamper to press the ingredients into the blades.

4. Serve immediately.

nutritional information

per ½ cup (120 ml) serving: *Calories: 71, Total Fat: 0 g, Saturated Fat: 0 g, Protein: 0 g, Fiber: 1 g, Carbohydrates: 15 g, Sodium: 2 mg, Cholesterol: 0 mg*

orange sorbet ❄

preparation: 5 minutes | **processing:** 45 seconds
yield: 3 cups (720 ml)

2 oranges, peeled, halved, seeded

2 Tablespoons (25 g) sugar

4 cups (960 ml) ice cubes

1. Place all ingredients into the Vitamix container in the order listed and secure lid.

2. Select Frozen Dessert program.

3. Switch machine to Start and allow machine to complete programmed cycle, using the tamper to press the ingredients into the blades.

4. Serve immediately.

nutritional information

per ½ cup (120 ml) serving: *Calories: 37, Total Fat: 0 g, Saturated Fat: 0 g, Protein: 0 g, Fiber: 1 g, Carbohydrates: 9 g, Sodium: 0 mg, Cholesterol: 0 mg*

looking good

» Serve each scoop of Orange Sorbet in a hollowed-out orange half and top with orange zest, a drizzle of honey or a sprinkling of grated dark chocolate.

ingredient IQ

 Soy milk is a mixture of ground soy beans and water, with nutrition profiles similar to cow's milk. Purchase unsweetened, unflavored soy milk for this recipe.

peach soy *sherbet* ❄

preparation: 5 minutes | **processing:** 45 seconds
yield: 3 ½ cups (840 ml)

1 cup (240 ml) soy milk

¼–½ cup (50–100 g) sugar

½ teaspoon vanilla extract

1 pound (454 g) frozen unsweetened peach slices

1. Place all ingredients into the Vitamix container in the order listed and secure lid.

2. Select Frozen Dessert program.

3. Switch machine to Start and allow machine to complete programmed cycle, using the tamper to press the ingredients into the blades.

4. Serve immediately.

nutritional information

per ½ cup (120 ml) serving: *Calories: 118, Total Fat: 1 g, Saturated Fat: 0 g, Protein: 2 g, Fiber: 1 g, Carbohydrates: 27 g, Sodium: 22 mg, Cholesterol: 0 mg*

strawberry
yogurt freeze ❄

preparation: 5 minutes | **processing:** 45 seconds
yield: 5 cups (1.2 L)

1 ½ cups (360 g) vanilla yogurt

1 ½ pounds (680 g) frozen
unsweetened strawberries

1. Place all ingredients into the Vitamix container
   in the order listed and secure lid.

2. Select Frozen Dessert program.

3. Switch machine to Start and allow machine
   to complete programmed cycle, using the
   tamper to press the ingredients into the blades.

4. Serve immediately.

nutritional information

*per ½ cup (120 ml) serving: Calories: 60, Total Fat: 0 g,
Saturated Fat: 0 g, Protein: 1 g, Fiber: 2 g, Carbohydrates: 13 g,
Sodium: 24 mg, Cholesterol: 2 mg*

for two or twenty

hot summer cool down

When the heat is on, it's
time to turn off the oven.
Making frozen treats is fun
and easy, giving you plenty
of time to relax with a few
friends on the patio, break
the ice with a new neighbor,
or just cool off after working
in the yard.

Mix up a quick Strawberry
Yogurt Freeze or an Orange
Sorbet (page 293) as a
reward for mowing the
lawn. If you're planning a
summer evening gathering,
the complex flavors of Berry
Sorbet with Mixed Spices
(page 300) are perfect
for an elegant dessert.
After dark, add drama
with a single pink or white
birthday-size candle and
a mint leaf placed on
each serving.

looking good

 To make this dessert extra special, garnish with Whipped Cream (page 324), chopped maraschino cherries, chopped walnuts and a cinnamon stick.

frozen **bananas foster** ❄

preparation: 5 minutes | **processing:** 45 seconds
yield: 4 ½ cups (1.0 L)

⅔ cup (160 g) vanilla yogurt

5 large frozen bananas, peeled, halved

2 teaspoons rum extract (optional)

2 Tablespoons (30 ml) caramel sauce

1 Tablespoon honey

1 teaspoon cinnamon

½ cup (50 g) pecans

1. Place all ingredients into the Vitamix container in the order listed and secure lid.

2. Select Frozen Dessert program.

3. Switch machine to Start and allow machine to complete programmed cycle, using the tamper to press the ingredients into the blades.

4. Serve immediately.

nutritional information

per ½ cup (120 ml) serving: *Calories: 150, Total Fat: 5 g, Saturated Fat: 1 g, Protein: 2 g, Fiber: 3 g, Carbohydrates: 27 g, Sodium: 28 mg, Cholesterol: 1 mg*

pineapple
strawberry sorbet ❄

preparation: 5 minutes + overnight soaking | **processing:** 45 seconds
yield: 6 cups (1.4 L)

1 cup (240 ml) orange juice or soy milk

1 cup (160 g) dried pineapple,
unsweetened, unsulphured

1 cup (150 g) fresh organic strawberries
(or defrosted frozen strawberries)

2 ½ pounds (568 g) frozen
unsweetened strawberries

1. Soak dried pineapple in orange juice (or soy milk)
   overnight in refrigerator. Do not drain.

2. Place all ingredients into the Vitamix container
   in the order listed and secure lid.

3. Select Frozen Dessert program.

4. Switch machine to Start and allow machine
   to complete programmed cycle, using the
   tamper to press the ingredients into the blades.

5. Serve immediately.

nutritional information

per ½ cup (120 ml) serving: *Calories: 80, Total Fat: 0 g, Saturated Fat: 0 g,
Protein: 1 g, Fiber: 3 g, Carbohydrates: 21 g, Sodium: 7 mg, Cholesterol: 0 mg*

berry sorbet with _mixed spices_ ❄

**preparation:** 20 minutes | _**processing:**_ 1 minute 5 seconds | _**yield:**_ 4 ¼ cups (1.0 L)

½ ounce (14 g) fresh ginger, peeled

½ cup (120 ml) cold water

½ cup (100 g) granulated sugar

1 cup (150 g) frozen unsweetened strawberries

1 cup (140 g) frozen unsweetened blueberries

1 cup (140 g) frozen unsweetened blackberries

1 cup (140 g) frozen unsweetened red raspberries

2 cups (300 g) frozen pitted Bing cherries

½ cup (13 g) fresh mint leaves

⅛ teaspoon ground cloves

⅛ teaspoon ground allspice

¼ teaspoon ground nutmeg

½ teaspoon ground cinnamon

1 teaspoon vanilla extract

1. Partially thaw frozen berries for 20 minutes; set aside.

2. Place ginger, water and sugar into the Vitamix container and secure lid.

3. Select Variable 1.

4. Switch machine to Start and slowly increase speed to Variable 8. Blend for 20 seconds until ginger is finely chopped. Stop machine and remove lid. Add berries, mint, cloves, allspice, nutmeg, cinnamon and vanilla to the container with ginger mixture and secure lid.

5. Select Frozen Dessert program.

6. Switch machine to Start and allow machine to complete programmed cycle, using the tamper to press the ingredients into the blades.

7. Serve immediately.

nutritional information

**per ½ cup (120 ml) serving:** _Calories: 107, Total Fat: 1 g, Saturated Fat: 0 g, Protein: 1 g, Fiber: 3 g, Carbohydrates: 26 g, Sodium: 2 mg, Cholesterol: 0 mg_

almond cookies

preparation: 5 minutes | ***processing:*** 40 – 60 seconds
bake time: 12 – 15 minutes | ***yield:*** 24 cookies

¾ cup (94 g)
all-purpose flour

¾ cup (90 g)
whole wheat flour

¼ teaspoon salt

¼ teaspoon baking soda

½ cup (120 g)
butter, softened

1 large egg

½ cup (100 g) sugar

1 Tablespoon milk

½ teaspoon
almond extract

½ cup (50 g)
slivered almonds

1. Preheat oven to 350°F (180°C).

2. Combine flours, salt and baking soda in a
   medium-sized mixing bowl. Set aside.

3. Place butter, egg, sugar and milk into the Vitamix
   container in the order listed and secure lid.

4. Select Variable 1.

5. Switch machine to Start and slowly increase
   speed to Variable 3.

6. Blend for 10 to 15 seconds until ingredients are
   creamed and remove the lid plug.

7. Add almond extract and almonds through
   the lid plug opening.

» ***almond cookies*** continues on page 304

change it up

fancy finishes

It's easy to dress up these buttery Almond Cookies for a special occasion. Press a roasted almond into the center of each cookie after removing from the oven, or place cookies on a wire rack over sheets of waxed paper and drizzle with melted milk chocolate or white chocolate. Let set before serving.

You may also make almond crescents: before baking, gently shape each dough ball on the cookie sheet into a crescent shape. After baking, let cookies cool completely. Dust the almond crescents with Powdered Sugar (page 325), or dip each crescent halfway into melted milk chocolate or dark chocolate and let set on sheets of waxed paper.

continued from page 303

almond cookies

8. Blend an additional 10 to 15 seconds or until well mixed. If necessary, use the tamper to press the ingredients into the blades. Stop machine and remove lid.

9. Add half of the flour mixture to the Vitamix container and secure lid.

10. Select Variable 1.

11. Switch machine to Start and slowly increase speed to Variable 5.

12. Blend for 10 to 15 seconds using the tamper to press the ingredients into the blades.

13. Stop machine and remove lid. Add remaining half of flour mixture to the container and secure lid.

14. Select Variable 1.

15. Switch machine to Start and slowly increase speed to Variable 5.

16. Blend for 10 to 15 seconds until completely blended.

17. Portion dough by teaspoons, roll gently and place 1 inch (2.5 cm) apart on parchment-lined cookie sheet.

18. Bake 12 to 15 minutes or until golden brown.

nutritional information

per cookie: *Calories: 91, Total Fat: 5 g, Saturated Fat: 3 g, Protein: 2 g, Fiber: 1 g, Carbohydrates: 10 g, Sodium: 67 mg, Cholesterol: 19 mg*

eggnog *cheesecake* 💧

preparation: 15 minutes | **processing:** 1 minute
bake time: 55–65 minutes | **yield:** 16 servings

1 cup (100 g) graham
cracker crumbs

2 Tablespoons (25 g) sugar

3 Tablespoons (45 g)
butter, melted

1 ½ pounds (682 g)
reduced fat cream cheese
(or 3 8–ounce packages)

1 cup (200 g) sugar

3 Tablespoons (25 g)
all-purpose flour

¾ cup (180 ml) eggnog,
light or regular

2 large eggs

2 Tablespoons (30 ml) rum

¼ teaspoon nutmeg

1. Preheat oven to 350°F (180°C).

2. Combine graham cracker crumbs, sugar and melted butter
   in a bowl and press into the bottom of a 9–inch (23 cm) spring
   form pan. Bake for 10 to 15 minutes until light gold. Cool.

3. Place cream cheese, sugar, flour, eggnog, eggs, rum and
   nutmeg into the Vitamix container and secure lid.

4. Select Smoothie program.

5. Switch machine to Start and allow machine
   to complete programmed cycle.

6. Pour mixture into pre-baked crust and bake an additional
   45 to 50 minutes, or until cake is barely firm to the touch.
   Remove from oven and loosen cake rim. Cool cake completely.
   Cover and refrigerate until completely chilled before serving.

nutritional information

per serving: *Calories: 231, Total Fat: 12 g, Saturated Fat: 7 g, Protein: 6 g,
Fiber: 0 g, Carbohydrates: 25 g, Sodium: 189 mg, Cholesterol: 62 mg*

surprise visitors

instant festivity

An Eggnog Cheesecake is
a quick and delightful holiday
treat to keep on hand for
drop-in guests. If you have
a cheesecake waiting in the
freezer, individual slices can
be ready in minutes.

Make the cheesecake before
the holiday rush begins.
After the baked cheesecake
has been chilled, use a knife
dipped in hot water to cut
the cheesecake into slices.
Wrap each slice in waxed
paper, place slices back
together and freeze whole
cheesecake on a baking
sheet just until firm. Wrap
cheesecake in waxed paper
and aluminum foil and freeze
for up to 2 months.

To serve, microwave one
slice at a time on the Defrost
setting for about 40 seconds.
Garnish with cranberries
and a mint leaf, dust with
cinnamon or sprinkle with
crushed peppermint candies.

looking good

Garnish these luscious lemon desserts with Whipped Cream (page 324), slices of candied lemon and mint leaves, or dust lightly with Powdered Sugar (page 325).

lemon cupcakes
with lemon curd

preparation: 15 minutes | **processing:** 20 seconds
bake time: 25–30 minutes | **yield:** 4 servings

½ cup (120 g) unsalted butter, room temperature

⅔ cup (130 g) granulated sugar

3 large eggs

¼ cup (60 ml) milk

1 teaspoon vanilla extract

zest of one large lemon

1 ½ cups (190 g) all-purpose flour

1 ½ teaspoons baking powder

¼ teaspoon salt

1. Preheat oven to 350°F (180°C). Grease 4 6-ounce ramekins with butter.

2. Cut butter into pieces, place into the Vitamix container with sugar and eggs and secure lid.

3. Select Variable 1.

4. Switch machine to Start and slowly increase speed to Variable 4. Blend for 10 seconds.

5. Decrease speed to Variable 1 and remove the lid plug. Add milk, vanilla and lemon zest through the lid plug opening. Replace lid plug and slowly increase speed to Variable 4. Blend for 10 seconds.

6. In a separate bowl, whisk together the flour, baking powder and salt. Pour liquid mixture into dry and mix by hand until combined.

7. Spoon into prepared ramekins. Bake for 25 to 30 minutes.

8. Serve with Lemon Curd.

» **lemon cupcakes with lemon curd** *continues on page 308*

continued from page 306

lemon curd ♨

preparation: 5 minutes | *processing:* 6 minutes 15 seconds | *yield:* 3 ½ cups (840 g)

5 large eggs

½ cup (120 ml) fresh lemon juice

zest of 3 lemons

1 ½ cups (300 g) granulated sugar

⅛ teaspoon salt

½ cup (120 g) unsalted butter, room temperature, cut into small pieces

1. Place eggs, lemon juice, lemon zest, sugar and salt into the Vitamix container and secure lid.

2. Select Hot Soup program.

3. Switch machine to Start and allow machine to complete programmed cycle.

4. Select Variable 1.

5. Switch machine to Start and slowly increase speed to Variable 3. Remove the lid plug. Add butter through the lid plug opening and replace lid plug.

6. Blend an additional 30 seconds.

nutritional information

per serving (1 cupcake and 2 tablespoons (29 g) lemon curd): Calories: 632, Total Fat: 30 g, Saturated Fat: 28 g, Protein: 11 g, Fiber: 1 g, Carbohydrates: 80 g, Sodium: 392 mg, Cholesterol: 269 mg

carrot bread with
cream cheese icing

preparation: 15 minutes | **processing:** 20 seconds + pulsing
bake time: 55–60 minutes | **yield:** 1 loaf (16 slices)

2 cups (250 g) all-purpose flour

⅔ cup (147 g) packed brown sugar

2 teaspoons baking powder

1 teaspoon ground cinnamon

½ teaspoon ground nutmeg

¼ teaspoon baking soda

¼ teaspoon salt

20 baby carrots

2 large eggs

⅔ cup (160 ml) milk

⅓ cup (80 ml) canola oil

cream cheese icing:

2 Tablespoons (30 g) cream
cheese, softened

¾ cup (90 g) powdered sugar

1–2 Tablespoons milk

1. Preheat oven to 350°F (180°C). Spray an 8 ½–inch x 4 ½–inch (22 cm x 11 cm) loaf pan with cooking spray.

2. In a large-sized mixing bowl, combine flour, sugar, baking powder, cinnamon, nutmeg, baking soda and salt. Set aside.

3. Place carrots into the Vitamix container and secure lid.

4. Select Variable 5.

5. Pulse 7 times. Scrape down sides of container with a spatula. Measure 2 cups (220 g) and stir into dry ingredients.

» **carrot bread with cream cheese icing** continues on page 310

continued from page 309

carrot bread with
cream cheese icing

6. Place eggs, milk, and oil into the Vitamix container in the order listed and secure lid.

7. Select Variable 1.

8. Switch machine to Start and slowly increase speed to Variable 4.

9. Blend for 20 seconds.

10. Pour liquid mixture into dry and mix by hand just until moistened.

11. Pour into prepared loaf pan. Bake for 55 to 60 minutes or until a knife inserted into middle comes out clean.

12. Cool in pan 20 minutes. Remove and cool completely on a wire rack. Glaze with Cream Cheese Icing.

13. To prepare icing, whisk together cream cheese, sugar and 1 Tablespoon of milk until smooth. Add the additional milk if necessary to obtain a glaze-like consistency.

nutritional information

per iced slice: *Calories: 175, Total Fat: 6 g, Saturated Fat: 1 g, Protein: 3 g, Fiber: 1 g, Carbohydrates: 28 g, Sodium: 141 mg, Cholesterol: 30 mg*

greek walnut *spice cake*

preparation: 15 minutes | **processing:** 30 seconds | **bake time:** 35–45 minutes
cook time: 10 minutes | **yield:** 12 servings

1 cup (100 g) chopped walnuts

1 ½ cups (180 g) whole wheat flour

½ cup (75 g) barley flour

2 teaspoons baking powder

1 teaspoon ground cinnamon

¾ teaspoon ground cloves

½ teaspoon baking soda

¼ teaspoon ground nutmeg

¼ teaspoon salt

2 teaspoons freshly grated
orange zest

2 large eggs

¾ cup (165 g) packed brown sugar

⅔ cup (160 g) Greek yogurt

½ cup (120 ml) orange juice

¼ cup (60 ml) extra virgin olive oil

syrup:

⅓ cup (80 ml) orange juice

¼ cup (55 g) packed brown sugar

1 small strip orange zest

2 cloves

1. Preheat oven to 350°F (180°C). Spray an 8-inch x 8-inch (20 cm x 20 cm) baking pan with cooking spray and dust with flour, shaking out the rest.

2. Spread walnuts on a baking sheet and toast, stirring once halfway, about 7 minutes. Transfer to a plate to cool. Reduce oven temperature to 325°F (160°C).

3. Place flours, baking powder, cinnamon, cloves, baking soda, nutmeg and salt into the Vitamix container and secure lid.

4. Select Variable 1.

» **greek walnut spice cake** continues on page 312

continued from page 311

greek walnut *spice cake*

5. Switch machine to Start and slowly increase speed to Variable 2.

6. Blend for 10 seconds and pour into a large-sized mixing bowl. Stir in orange zest.

7. Place eggs, brown sugar, yogurt, orange juice and oil into the Vitamix container and secure lid.

8. Select Variable 1.

9. Switch machine to Start and slowly increase speed to Variable 5.

10. Blend for 20 seconds.

11. Pour into dry ingredients and stir by hand to combine. Fold in walnuts. Spread batter into prepared pan.

12. Bake for 35 to 45 minutes or until a knife inserted into the center comes out mostly clean. Transfer to a wire rack and pierce the top all over with a toothpick.

13. To prepare Syrup, combine orange juice, brown sugar, orange zest strip and cloves in a heavy saucepan. Bring to a boil over medium-high heat, stirring a few times. Maintain a simmer and cook until thickened, about 4 to 5 minutes. Remove zest and cloves. Cool.

14. Brush the syrup over the cake 3 or 4 times, allowing it to seep in each time.

nutritional information

per serving: *Calories: 279, Total Fat: 13 g, Saturated Fat: 2 g, Protein: 6 g, Fiber: 3 g, Carbohydrates: 38 g, Sodium: 150 mg, Cholesterol: 38 mg*

low fat **pumpkin pie**

preparation: 5 minutes | **processing:** 10–15 seconds | **bake time:** 1 hour | **yield:** 16 slices

1 cup (240 ml) egg substitute

3 ½ cups (850 g) canned pumpkin

1 ½ cups (300 g) granulated sugar

1 teaspoon salt

2 teaspoons ground cinnamon

1 teaspoon ground ginger

½ teaspoon ground cloves

3 cups (720 ml) evaporated nonfat milk

2 unbaked 9-inch (23 cm) deep-dish pie shells

whipped topping (optional)

1. Preheat oven to 350˚F (180˚C).

2. Place all ingredients into the Vitamix container in the order listed and secure lid.

3. Select Variable 1.

4. Switch machine to Start and slowly increase speed to Variable 3.

5. Blend for 10 to 15 seconds or until desired consistency is reached.

6. Pour into 2 unbaked 9-inch (23 cm) deep-dish pie shells.

7. Bake for about 1 hour. Filling will be soft, but firms up as it sets and cools.

8. Top with whipped topping. Chill and serve.

nutritional information

per slice (without whipped topping): *Calories: 220, Total Fat: 6 g, Saturated Fat: 1 g, Protein: 6 g, Fiber: 2 g, Carbohydrates: 36 g, Sodium: 331 mg, Cholesterol: 2 mg*

chocolate sour cream cupcakes

preparation: 20 minutes | **processing:** 20 seconds
bake time: 20–25 minutes | **yield:** 18 cupcakes

bright idea

For maximum chocolate indulgence, frost these rich cupcakes with deliciously smooth Killer Fudge Frosting (page 318), easily made with your Vitamix.

4 ounces (113 g) unsweetened chocolate, chopped

1 cup (240 ml) hot, strong brewed coffee

2 cups (250 g) all-purpose flour

¾ teaspoon baking soda

½ teaspoon salt

2 cups (400 g) sugar

½ cup (120 ml) canola oil

2 large eggs

½ cup (120 g) sour cream

1. Preheat oven to 375°F (190°C). Line muffin pan with cupcake papers.

2. In a sauce pan, melt the chocolate in the hot coffee over low heat.

3. Combine flour, baking soda and salt in a medium-sized mixing bowl and set aside.

4. Place sugar, oil, eggs and sour cream into the Vitamix container and secure lid.

5. Select Variable 1.

6. Switch machine to Start and slowly increase speed to Variable 5. Blend for 20 seconds.

7. Pour into dry mixture and stir by hand until combined.

8. Fill muffin cups ⅔ full. Bake 20 to 25 minutes.

nutritional information

per serving (1 cupcake and 2 tablespoons (30 g) frosting): *Calories: 350, Total Fat: 16 g, Saturated Fat: 6 g, Protein: 5 g, Fiber: 2 g, Carbohydrates: 52 g, Sodium: 143 mg, Cholesterol: 32 mg*

vanilla
custard sauce

preparation: 10 minutes
processing: 5 minutes 45 seconds
yield: 4 ½ cups (1.0 L)

6 egg yolks

1 ½ cups (360 ml) half and half

¼ cup (30 g) all-purpose flour

½ cup (100 g) sugar

⅛ teaspoon salt

1 Tablespoon vanilla extract

1 Tablespoon butter

1. Place all ingredients into the Vitamix container in the order listed and secure lid.

2. Select Hot Soup program.

3. Switch machine to Start and allow machine to complete programmed cycle.

nutritional information

per ¼ cup (60 ml) serving: *Calories: 83, Total Fat: 5 g, Saturated Fat: 3 g, Protein: 2 g, Fiber: 0 g, Carbohydrates: 8 g, Sodium: 33 mg, Cholesterol: 82 mg*

for two or twenty

razzle and dazzle

You can turn an ordinary dessert into an extraordinary work of culinary art simply by adding a drizzle, a swirl or a swoosh of colorful syrup or sauce.

Drizzle Fresh Fruit Syrup (page 53) over the Whipped Cream (page 324) garnish of any dessert just before serving. Swirl Mixed Berry Purée (page 320) or chocolate sauce on white plates before adding a piece of cake or pie; swirl Vanilla Custard Sauce on dark plates for contrast. Place a slice of Eggnog Cheesecake (page 305) in a pool of Mixed Berry Purée and use a toothpick to draw patterns in the sauce around the slice of cheesecake.

*killer **fudge frosting***

preparation: 10 minutes | ***processing:*** 40 seconds | ***yield:*** 1 ¾ cups (420 g)

4 ounces (113 g) unsweetened chocolate, chopped

¾ cup (180 ml) evaporated milk

1 cup (200 g) sugar

1. Melt the chocolate in the microwave on medium power. Stir. Cool slightly.

2. Place the evaporated milk and sugar into the Vitamix container and secure lid.

3. Select Variable 1.

4. Switch machine to Start and slowly increase speed to Variable 5.
    Blend for 5 seconds. Stop machine and remove the lid.

5. Add the chocolate to the Vitamix container and secure lid.

6. Select Variable 1.

7. Switch machine to Start and slowly increase speed to Variable 10.
    Blend for 35 seconds until the frosting is thick and shiny.

8. Spoon into a bowl and cover, allowing to sit at room temperature for 30 minutes.

nutritional information

per 2 tablespoon (30 g) serving: *Calories: 113, Total Fat: 5 g, Saturated Fat: 3 g, Protein: 2 g, Fiber: 1 g, Carbohydrates: 18 g, Sodium: 15 mg, Cholesterol: 4 mg*

spiced chocolate bisque

preparation: 15 minutes | **processing:** 5 minutes 45 seconds
yield: 6 cups (1.4 L)

2 cups (480 ml) heavy cream

1 cup (240 ml) milk

½ cup (100 g) sugar

1 vanilla bean, split

1 stick of cinnamon

zest of 1 orange

1 Tablespoon fresh ginger

1 teaspoon cocoa powder

¾ teaspoon instant
coffee powder

6 large egg yolks

5 ounces (140 g)
dark chocolate, chopped

looking good

Serve in shot glasses, topped with Whipped Cream (page 324) and grated chocolate. Arrange on a silver salver with sliced oranges or fresh berries.

1. Place all ingredients into the Vitamix container in the order listed and secure lid.

2. Select Hot Soup program.

3. Switch machine to Start and allow machine to complete programmed cycle.

nutritional information

per ½ cup (120 ml) serving: Calories: 266, Total Fat: 21 g, Saturated Fat: 12 g, Protein: 3 g, Fiber: 1 g, Carbohydrates: 19 g, Sodium: 31 mg, Cholesterol: 158 mg

mixed berry *purée*

preparation: 5 minutes | **processing:** 5 minutes 45 seconds
yield: 3 ½ cups (840 ml)

½ cup (120 ml) water

1 Tablespoon fresh lemon juice

1 ½ cups (210 g) frozen unsweetened
raspberries, partially thawed

1 ½ cups (150 g) frozen unsweetened
strawberries, partially thawed

1 cup (155 g) frozen unsweetened
blueberries, partially thawed

¾ cup (150 g) sugar

1. Place all ingredients into the Vitamix container
   in the order listed and secure lid.

2. Select Hot Soup program.

3. Switch machine to Start and allow machine
   to complete programmed cycle.

nutritional information

per ¼ cup (60 ml) serving: *Calories: 61, Total Fat: 0 g, Saturated Fat: 0 g,
Protein: 0 g, Fiber: 2 g, Carbohydrates: 15 g, Sodium: 1 mg, Cholesterol: 0 mg*

on the menu

For an easy dessert,
mix 3 cups ricotta with
1 ½ tablespoons sugar.
Spoon into parfait glasses,
drizzle with Mixed Berry
Purée and add fresh
berries, if desired.

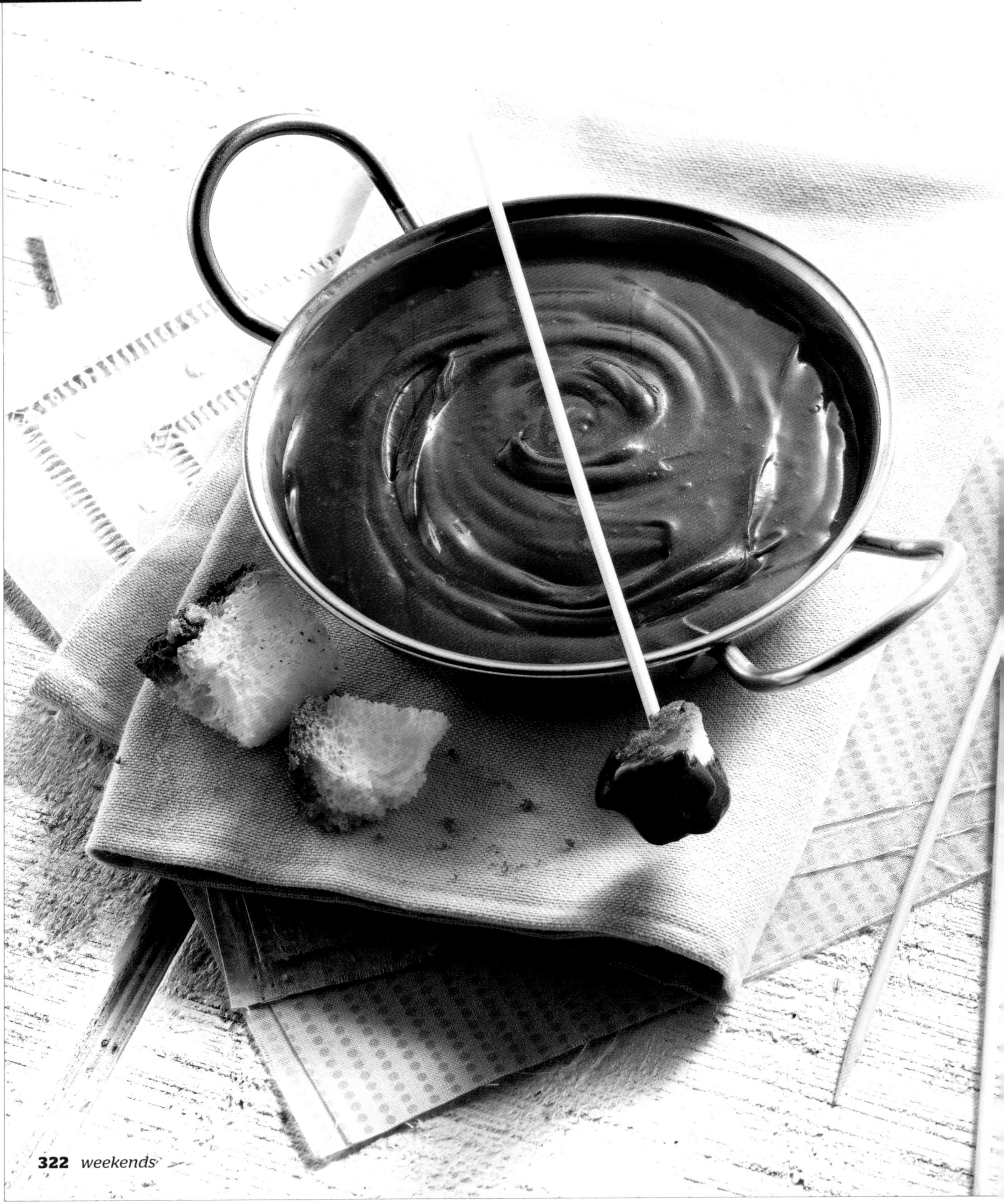

chocolate marshmallow
fondue ♨

preparation: 15 minutes | **processing:** 6 minutes 5 seconds
yield: 3 cups (720 ml)

½ cup (120 ml) water

1 cup (240 ml) heavy whipping cream

3 Tablespoons (22 g) powdered sugar

12 ounces (340 g) semi-sweet baking chocolate, chopped

2 ½ cups (600 g) mini marshmallows

1. Place water, cream, sugar and chocolate into the Vitamix container in the order listed and secure lid.

2. Select Hot Soup program.

3. Switch machine to Start and allow machine to complete programmed cycle.

4. Add marshmallows to the Vitamix container and secure lid.

5. Select Variable 1.

6. Switch machine to Start and slowly increase speed to Variable 10. Blend for 20 seconds. Pour mixture into fondue pot.

nutritional information

per ¼ cup (60 ml) serving: *Calories: 249, Total Fat: 15 g, Saturated Fat: 10 g, Protein: 3 g, Fiber: 2 g, Carbohydrates: 29 g, Sodium: 16 mg, Cholesterol: 27 mg*

for two or twenty

fantastic fondue

It's easy to throw together a quick dessert that will gather everyone around the kitchen island. Prepare your fondue and set up bowls with some delicious dippers:

- Graham crackers or animal crackers

- Shortbread or biscotti

- Pound cake or angel food cake cubes

- Strawberries, orange wedges, dried figs

- Grilled bananas or grilled pineapple

- Pretzels

- Belgian waffle pieces

whipped cream ⓩ

preparation: 3 minutes | ***processing:*** 1 minute | ***yield:*** 2 cups (480 ml)

2 cups (480 ml) heavy whipping cream

1. Place cream into the Vitamix container and secure lid.

2. Select Purée program.

3. Switch machine to Start and allow machine to complete programmed cycle.

4. Cream will become firm and whipped.

nutritional information

per ¼ cup (60 ml) serving: *Calories: 205, Total Fat: 22 g, Saturated Fat: 14 g, Protein: 1 g, Fiber: 0 g, Carbohydrates: 2 g, Sodium: 23 mg, Cholesterol: 82 mg*

powdered sugar

preparation: 5 minutes | ***processing:*** 40 seconds | ***yield:*** 2 cups (240 g)

1 ½ cups (300 g) granulated sugar

1 Tablespoon cornstarch

1. Place sugar into the Vitamix container and secure lid.

2. Select Variable 1.

3. Switch machine to Start and slowly increase speed to Variable 10.
   Blend for 30 seconds.

4. Reduce speed to Variable 3 and remove the lid plug. Add in cornstarch
   through the lid plug opening and replace lid plug.

5. Slowly increase speed to Variable 10.

6. Blend an additional 10 seconds.

nutritional information

per 2 tablespoon (19 g) serving: *Calories: 75, Total Fat: 0 g, Saturated Fat: 0 g,
Protein: 0 g, Fiber: 0 g, Carbohydrates: 19 g, Sodium: 0 mg, Cholesterol: 0 mg*

dark chocolate mousse

preparation: 10 minutes | **processing:** 20–25 seconds | **yield:** 3 cups (720 g)

5 ounces (142 g) bittersweet chocolate,
finely chopped

2 Tablespoons (30 g) unsalted butter, diced

2 Tablespoons (30 ml) hot coffee

1 ½ cups (360 ml) heavy cream

2 Tablespoons (16 g) powdered sugar

1. Combine chocolate, butter and coffee in the top of a double boiler over hot, but not simmering water, stirring frequently until smooth. Remove from the heat and let cool.

2. When chocolate mixture is cool, place cream and sugar into the Vitamix container and secure lid.

3. Select Variable 1.

4. Switch machine to Start and slowly increase speed to Variable 8.

5. Blend for 20 to 25 seconds or until firmly whipped.

6. Scrape mixture into bowl atop cooled chocolate; fold in cream just until incorporated and serve immediately.

nutritional information

per ½ cup (95 g) serving: *Calories: 367, Total Fat: 36 g, Saturated Fat: 21 g, Protein: 3 g, Fiber: 2 g, Carbohydrates: 16 g, Sodium: 24 mg, Cholesterol: 92 mg*

cocktails

FOR CASUAL GATHERINGS or festive celebrations, your Vitamix is the life of the party. Mix drinks like a skilled bartender with the help of these fun, adventurous recipes. Try a frosty Piña Colada (page 346) or a Whole Fruit Margarita (page 344). This section features a collection of intriguing cocktails made with whiskey, rum, gin, tequila or liqueurs. Stock up on ice and get creative!

weekends

cocktails

cider and whiskey cocktail

preparation: 5 minutes | **processing:** 15 seconds
yield: 1 ½ cups (360 ml)

½ cup (120 ml) fresh apple cider

3 ~~2~~ ounces (~~60 ml~~) bourbon whiskey

2 Tablespoon real maple syrup

¼ small lemon, peeled, seeded

1 cup (240 ml) ice cubes

1. Place all ingredients into the Vitamix container in the order listed and secure lid.

2. Select Variable 1.

3. Switch machine to Start and slowly increase speed to Variable 5.

4. Blend for 15 seconds or until desired consistency is reached.

nutritional information

per 1 cup (240 ml) serving: *Calories: 165, Total Fat: 0 g, Saturated Fat: 0 g, Protein: 0 g, Fiber: 0 g, Carbohydrates: 20 g, Sodium: 10 mg, Cholesterol: 0 mg*

ingredient IQ

For best results, use fresh apple cider from the refrigerated section of the supermarket and real, pure maple syrup (made without high fructose corn syrup).

send in a sub!

play *with* flavors

Flavored rums and vodkas are quite popular and new ones are arriving on the market almost every day. Create your own zingy cocktails by substituting a flavorful infusion for "plain" rum or vodka.

Rums are available in lemon, lime, cherry, orange, raspberry, peach, coconut varieties and more. Vodkas really push the flavor envelope with pomegranate, mango, watermelon, chocolate, whipped cream and bubble gum!

Try a coconut-flavored rum to intensify the taste of a Piña Colada (page 346), a lime-flavored rum to accent a Cranberry Lime Sparkle (page 336) or a pineapple-flavored rum in a Pineapple Coconut Curacao (page 335).

benedictine and
lemon squeeze

preparation: 5 minutes | ***processing:*** 20 seconds | ***yield:*** 2 ½ cups (600 ml)

2 ounces (60 ml) gin

2 ounces (60 ml) water

1 ½ ounces (45 ml) Benedictine liqueur

2 Tablespoons (25 g) sugar

1 ½ small lemons, peeled, seeded

2 cups (480 ml) ice cubes

1. Place all ingredients into the Vitamix container in the order listed and secure lid.

2. Select Variable 1.

3. Switch machine to Start and slowly increase speed to Variable 6.

4. Blend for 20 seconds or until desired consistency is reached.

nutritional information

per 1 cup (240 ml) serving: *Calories: 145, Total Fat: 0 g, Saturated Fat: 0 g, Protein: 0 g, Fiber: 1 g, Carbohydrates: 19 g, Sodium: 2 mg, Cholesterol: 0 mg*

raspberry
coconut silver

preparation: 5 minutes | **processing:** 30 seconds | **yield:** 2 cups (480 ml)

2 ounces (60 ml) light rum *(used Bacardi Raspberry)*

2 ounces (60 ml) cream of coconut

1 ½ ounces (45 ml) orange liqueur

1 cup (123 g) fresh raspberries, cleaned, dried *(Used frozen)*

1 cup (240 ml) ice cubes *(with frozen berries use only scant ½ C)*

1. Place all ingredients into the Vitamix container in the order listed and secure lid.

2. Select Variable 1.

3. Switch machine to Start and slowly increase speed to Variable 8.

4. Blend for 30 seconds or until desired consistency is reached.

nutritional information

per 1 cup (240 ml) serving: *Calories: 246, Total Fat: 5 g, Saturated Fat: 4 g, Protein: 1 g, Fiber: 0 g, Carbohydrates: 31 g, Sodium: 11 mg, Cholesterol: 0 mg*

pomarita *cocktail*

preparation: 5 minutes | **processing:** 1 minute
yield: 3 cups (720 ml)

kitchen prep

The tequila, pomegranate, triple sec and lime flavors will intensify if drink is made ahead of time and chilled in freezer just until ice crystals begin to appear.

½ cup (120 ml) tequila

1 cup (240 ml) 100% pomegranate juice

¼ cup (60 ml) triple sec

½ lime, peeled

2 Tablespoons (25 g) sugar

2 cups (480 ml) ice cubes

1 fresh lime, thinly sliced

1. Place all ingredients except lime slices into the Vitamix container in the order listed and secure lid.

2. Select Smoothie program.

3. Switch machine to Start and allow machine to complete programmed cycle.

4. Serve in a chilled cocktail glass and garnish each serving with one or two thin slices of fresh lime.

nutritional information

per 1 cup (240 ml) serving: *Calories: 247, Total Fat: 0 g, Saturated Fat: 0 g, Protein: 1 g, Fiber: 0 g, Carbohydrates: 28 g, Sodium: 11 mg, Cholesterol: 0 mg*

pineapple
coconut curacao

preparation: 5 minutes | **processing:** 30 seconds
yield: 2 ¾ cups (660 ml)

2 ounces (60 ml) cream of coconut

2 ounces (60 ml) light rum

1 ½ ounces (45 ml) orange Curacao

1 cup (165 g) fresh pineapple chunks

2 cups (480 ml) ice cubes

1. Place all ingredients into the Vitamix container in the order listed and secure lid.

2. Select Variable 1.

3. Switch machine to Start and slowly increase speed to Variable 5.

4. Blend for 30 seconds or until desired consistency is reached.

5. Garnish with a pineapple spear or an orange slice.

nutritional information

per 1 cup (240 ml) serving: *Calories: 189, Total Fat: 3 g, Saturated Fat: 3 g, Protein: 1 g, Fiber: 1 g, Carbohydrates: 23 g, Sodium: 9 mg, Cholesterol: 0 mg*

planning ahead

raising *the* bar

The classic cocktail is making a comeback. If that leaves you rather shaken (or at least mildly stirred), here's what you'll need to begin building a bar:

You'll need highball, lowball, martini, wine and beer glasses, plus champagne flutes.

Basic soft drinks (cola and lemon/lime soda) are needed for mixers, plus tonic, ginger ale and various juices (orange, cranberry, tomato, etc.). Always have water and a non-alcohol beverage option for guests to enjoy.

Standard garnishes include lime wedges (for gin and tonics, gimlets and margaritas), maraschino cherries, lemon peel twists or orange wedges (for Old Fashioneds) and olives (for martinis).

looking good

To create sugar-rimmed glasses, moisten rims with a lime wedge and then dip the rims in a shallow dish of white or colored sugar.

cranberry lime
sparkle

preparation: 5 minutes | ***processing:*** 15–20 seconds
yield: 3 cups (720 ml)

½ cup (120 ml) 100% cranberry juice

4 ounces (120 ml) light rum

2 ounces (60 ml) vodka

2 Tablespoons (25 g) sugar

¼ small lime, peeled, seeded

¼ cup (25 g) fresh cranberries

2 cups (480 ml) ice cubes

1. Place all ingredients into the Vitamix container in the order listed and secure lid.

2. Select Variable 1.

3. Switch machine to Start and slowly increase speed to Variable 10.

4. Blend for 15 to 20 seconds or until desired consistency is reached.

5. Pour into a sugar-rimmed glass and serve immediately.

nutritional information

per 1 cup (240 ml) serving: *Calories: 193, Total Fat: 0 g, Saturated Fat: 0 g, Protein: 0 g, Fiber: 1 g, Carbohydrates: 14 g, Sodium: 3 mg, Cholesterol: 0 mg*

citrus tequila
squeeze ⬤

preparation: 5 minutes | **processing:** 1 minute | **yield:** 2 ¼ cups (540 ml)

2 ounces (60 ml) fresh
orange juice

2 ounces (60 ml) tequila

1 ½ ounces (45 ml)
orange Curacao

1 Tablespoon fresh lime juice

2 Tablespoons (25 g) sugar

1 cup (100 g) fresh cranberries

1 cup (240 ml) ice cubes

1. Place all ingredients into the Vitamix container
   in the order listed and secure lid.

2. Select Smoothie program.

3. Switch machine to Start and allow machine
   to complete programmed cycle.

4. Pour into a salt-rimmed glass and serve immediately.

nutritional information

per 1 cup (240 ml) serving: Calories: 200, Total Fat: 0 g, Saturated Fat: 0 g,
Protein: 0 g, Fiber: 2 g, Carbohydrates: 26 g, Sodium: 2 mg, Cholesterol: 0 mg

strawberry *daiquiri* ⬤

preparation: 5 minutes | ***processing:*** 1 minute | ***yield:*** 3 cups (720 ml)

4 ounces (120 ml) light rum

2 ounces (60 ml) triple sec

2 Tablespoons (30 ml)
fresh lime juice

1 cup (150 g) frozen strawberries,
softened for 10 minutes

2–4 Tablespoons (16–32 g)
powdered sugar

2 cups (480 ml) ice cubes

1. Place all ingredients into the Vitamix container
   in the order listed and secure lid.

2. Select Smoothie program.

3. Switch machine to Start and allow machine
   to complete programmed cycle.

nutritional information

per 1 cup (240 ml) serving: *Calories: 182, Total Fat: 0 g, Saturated Fat: 0 g,*
Protein: 0 g, Fiber: 1 g, Carbohydrates: 18 g, Sodium: 1 mg, Cholesterol: 0 mg

blueberry maple
whiskey cocktail

preparation: 5 minutes | **processing:** 20 seconds
yield: 3 ¾ cups (900 ml)

2 ½ ounces (75 ml) white wine

4 ounces (120 ml) whiskey

¾ cup (180 ml) real maple syrup

½ cup (78 g) frozen unsweetened blueberries

2 cups (480 ml) ice cubes

1. Place all ingredients into the Vitamix container in the order listed and secure lid.

2. Select Variable 1.

3. Switch machine to Start and slowly increase speed to Variable 8.

4. Blend for 20 seconds or until desired consistency is reached.

nutritional information

per 1 cup (240 ml) serving: *Calories: 152, Total Fat: 0 g, Saturated Fat: 0 g, Protein: 0 g, Fiber: 1 g, Carbohydrates: 17 g, Sodium: 3 mg, Cholesterol: 0 mg*

frozen blue
vodka lemonade

preparation: 5 minutes | *processing:* 20 seconds
yield: 2 cups (480 ml)

⅓ cup (80 ml) Blue Vodka

⅓ cup (80 ml) cold water

1 ½ medium lemons, peeled, seeded, halved

3 Tablespoons (38 g) sugar

1 cup (240 ml) ice cubes

garnish:

Lemon slices

1. Place all ingredients except garnish into the Vitamix container in the order listed and secure lid.

2. Select Variable 1.

3. Switch machine to Start and slowly increase speed to Variable 5.

4. Blend for 20 seconds or until desired consistency is reached.

5. Garnish with a lemon slice and serve immediately.

nutritional information

per 1 cup (240 ml) serving: Calories: 183, Total Fat: 0 g, Saturated Fat: 0 g, Protein: 0 g, Fiber: 1 g, Carbohydrates: 23 g, Sodium: 3 mg, Cholesterol: 0 mg

for two or twenty

signature cocktails

For an easy, but stand-out party, offer a signature, seasonal cocktail.

new year's eve: Serve a tray of Pomarita Cocktails (page 334) for a simple yet festive toast.

cinco de mayo: Pair Whole Fruit Margaritas (page 344), with chips, Guacamole (page 239), and California Salsa (page 234), for an instant fiesta.

4th of july: Start the fireworks with Frozen Blue Vodka Lemonade. Garnish with fresh berries.

halloween: Try a spooky Cider and Whiskey Cocktail (page 331), or mix up a batch of maple-kissed cider (without the whiskey).

christmas: 'Tis the season for a Cranberry Lime Sparkle (page 336). Add a fresh cranberry garnish.

tootsie roll *marvel*

preparation: 5 minutes | ***processing:*** 15–20 seconds
yield: 2 cups (480 ml)

¼ cup (60 ml) Grand Marnier

¼ cup (60 ml) Kahlua

2 Tablespoons (30 ml) orange juice

2 cups (267 g) chocolate ice cream

garnishes:

Chocolate covered coffee beans

Chocolate shavings

Tootsie Roll candy pieces

1. Place all ingredients except optional garnishes into the Vitamix container in the order listed and secure lid.

2. Select Variable 1.

3. Switch machine to Start and slowly increase speed to Variable 3.

4. Blend for 15 to 20 seconds, just until blended.

5. Garnish and serve immediately.

nutritional information

per 1 cup (240 ml) serving: *Calories: 504, Total Fat: 16 g, Saturated Fat: 10 g, Protein: 6 g, Fiber: 2 g, Carbohydrates: 63 g, Sodium: 74 mg, Cholesterol: 40 mg*

ingredient IQ

For an extra-thick, creamy treat, use the highest-fat chocolate ice cream you can find. Finally, an excellent reason to skip the light ice cream.

whole fruit margarita

preparation: 5 minutes | **processing:** 1 minute
yield: 6 cups (1.4 L)

¼ cup (60 ml) water

6 ounces (180 ml) tequila

2 ounces (60 ml) Grand Marnier or triple sec

1 medium orange, peeled, seeded, halved

1 lime, peeled

1 lemon, peeled, seeded, halved

6 Tablespoons (75 g) sugar

6 cups (1.4 L) ice cubes

1. Place all ingredients into the Vitamix container in the order listed and secure lid.

2. Select Purée program.

3. Switch machine to Start and allow machine to complete programmed cycle.

4. Pour into salt-rimmed margarita glasses.

nutritional information

per 1 cup (240 ml) serving: *Calories: 173, Total Fat: 0 g, Saturated Fat: 0 g, Protein: 0 g, Fiber: 1 g, Carbohydrates: 20 g, Sodium: 1 mg, Cholesterol: 0 mg*

piña colada 🌢

preparation: 5 minutes | ***processing:*** 1 minute | ***yield:*** 3 ½ cups (840 ml)

4 ½ ounces (68 ml) light rum

4 ½ Tablespoons (68 ml)
cream of coconut

½ cup (120 ml) coconut milk

2 Tablespoons (9 g)
shredded coconut

¾ cup (100 g) fresh pineapple
chunks, core included

3 cups (720 ml) ice cubes

1. Place all ingredients into the Vitamix container
   in the order listed and secure lid.

2. Select Smoothie program.

3. Switch machine to Start and allow machine
   to complete programmed cycle.

nutritional information

per 1 cup (240 ml) serving: *Calories: 257, Total Fat: 12 g, Saturated Fat: 11 g,
Protein: 1 g, Fiber: 1 g, Carbohydrates: 18 g, Sodium: 14 mg, Cholesterol: 0 mg*

frozen abuelita drink ✐

preparation: 5 minutes | ***processing:*** 1 minute | ***yield:*** 3 cups (720 ml)

4 ounces (120 ml) Patron XO Cafe

2 ounces (60 ml) Sauza Hornitos

½ ounce Patron Citronge

3 ounces (90 ml) half and half

2 ounces (60 ml) chocolate syrup

1 teaspoon ancho chili powder

½ teaspoon chipotle chili powder

½ teaspoon ground cinnamon

7 cups (1.7 L) ice cubes

1. Place all ingredients into the Vitamix container in the order listed and secure lid.

2. Select Purée program.

3. Switch machine to Start and allow machine to complete programmed cycle, using the tamper to press the ingredients into the blades.

nutritional information

per 1 cup (240 ml) serving: *Calories: 266, Total Fat: 3 g, Saturated Fat: 2 g, Protein: 1 g, Fiber: 0 g, Carbohydrates: 15 g, Sodium: 24 mg, Cholesterol: 10 mg*

peach prodigy

preparation: 5 minutes | **processing:** 1 minute
yield: 3 cups (720 ml)

1 ½ ounces (45 ml) peach schnapps

1 ounce (30 ml) triple sec

1 ounce (30 ml) tequila

1 Tablespoon fresh lime juice

1 cup (187 g) frozen unsweetened peach slices

2 cups (267 g) French vanilla ice cream

optional garnishes:

Peach slices

Lime curls

1. Place all ingredients except garnishes into the Vitamix container in the order listed and secure lid.

2. Select Smoothie program.

3. Switch machine to Start and allow machine to complete programmed cycle.

4. Garnish with fresh peach slices or lime curls if desired.

nutritional information

per 1 cup (240 ml) serving: *Calories: 382, Total Fat: 13 g, Saturated Fat: 8 g, Protein: 5 g, Fiber: 2 g, Carbohydrates: 42 g, Sodium: 59 mg, Cholesterol: 80 mg*

---

create your own

Orange Curacao can be used in place of the Triple Sec. Fresh sliced peaches may be substituted for the frozen peaches; just shorten the blending time.

---

change it up

grown-up smoothies

Repurpose your favorite smoothie for your next cocktail party or put it on the menu for a festive Sunday brunch. The sky's the limit on your own smoothie-with-alcohol creations, but here's a few suggestions:

Add an ounce of vodka per serving to a Summer Blush Smoothie (page 14), or a Lemonade Blush (page 215).

Add an ounce of rum per serving to spice up a Fruit Combo Smoothie (page 19), or a Lime and Mint Agua Fresca (page 219).

Add an ounce of tequila per serving to turn a Key Lime Kiwi Smoothie (page 22) into a frosty margarita-style drink.

index